D0140023

OXFORD PSYCHOLOGY SERIES

EDITORS:
Donald E. Broadbent
James L. McGaugh
M. Kosslyn
Nicholas J. Mackintosh
Endel Tulving
Lawrence Weiskrantz

OXFORD PSYCHOLOGY SERIES

Working Memory

ALAN BADDELEY

MRC Applied Psychology Unit
Cambridge

OXFORD PSYCHOLOGY SERIES NO. 11

CLARENDON PRESS · OXFORD

Oxford University Press, Walton Street, Oxford OX2 6DP
Oxford New York Toronto
Delhi Bombay Calcutta Madras Karachi
Petaling Jaya Singapore Hong Kong Tokyo
Nairobi Dar es Salaam Cape Town
Melbourne Auckland
and associated companies in
Berlin Ibadan

Oxford is a trade mark of Oxford University Press

Published in the United States
by Oxford University Press, New York

First published 1986
First published in paperback 1987
Reprinted 1989, 1991

British Library Cataloguing in Publication Data
Baddeley, Alan D.
Working memory.—(Oxford psychology
series; no. 11)
1. Memory
I. Title
153.1'2 BF371
ISBN 0–19–852116–2
ISBN 0–19–852133–2 Pbk

Library of Congress Cataloging in Publication Data
Baddeley, Alan D., 1934–
Working memory.
(Oxford psychology series; no. 11)
Bibliography: p.
Includes index.
1. Short-term memory. I. Title. II. Series.
BF378.S54B33 1986 153.1'2 86–846
ISBN 0–19–852116–2
ISBN 0–19–852133–2 Pbk

Printed in Great Britain by
J. W. Arrowsmith Ltd, Bristol

To my parents
Donald and Nellie Baddeley

Preface

Although the preface is normally the first part of a book, it tends I suspect usually to be written last. If so, this preface is an exception since it is the first part of the book to be written—if indeed the book ever emerges. The purpose of a preface is often to explain why a book was written and what it aims to achieve. The logical time to write such a preface is thus before one starts to write the book, when one is debating whether or not a book should be written. Having just emerged from a debate with myself on the matter, the easiest way to start seems to be with the preface.

I plan to describe a body of research on a topic which I consider to be of importance. I shall regrettably confine much of the book primarily to a description of work by myself and co-workers; a more extensive investigation of the literature would certainly be desirable, but is unfortunately in my own case, because of substantial time constraints, simply not practicable. Is what is practicable, however, worth doing? Indeed, why am I trying to write this book? The bulk of what it contains is already published or about to be published. Then why attempt the difficult and demanding job of writing a book rather than spend the time catching up with a backlog of writing scientific papers? I would still prefer to produce a book for the following reasons.

First, a book on a single topic forces one to think long and hard about that topic for a sustained period of time. I have worked intermittently on the topic of working memory for the last decade, but during all this time theoretical elaboration of the concept has had to go hand in hand with the many other professional activities that I, like everyone else become involved in. This is my first opportunity to think consistently and intensively about the topic for a period of weeks with no administrative distractions, and no major demands from other psychological research topics. Attempting to write a monograph seems a fruitful way of trying to pull together and integrate the more piecemeal efforts that have recently been possible. It seems likely that it will lead to better theoretical development over the next few years.

It might, however, be argued that that does not require the publication of a book. This introduces the second reason; as a scientist I believe that I am taking part in a communal enterprise, and that anything I produce is only useful if it is communicated. While most of the experimental work to be described here has been published, it has led to a continuous development and change in the underlying conceptual structure. If the concepts produced are to be of value, then it is important to try to express them in a clear and accessible way. At present they are not expressed in this way since they are typically tied to empirical papers which describe a particular subset of the working memory system. This is true, even with a limited subcomponent of the system; the reader attempting to understand for example the articulatory loop would probably have some difficulty in gaining a coherent view, since empirical results have caused the model to develop and change quite substantially from its first presentation (Baddeley and Hitch 1974) to more recent versions (e.g. Salame and Baddeley 1982).

Finally, there is a third rather more quixotic reason. In the past few years, it has become fashionable in cognitive psychology to bemoan a lack of progress. We tend to castigate ourselves about our methods as in Newell's (1973) claim 'You can't play 20 questions with nature and win'. We complain about our preoccupation with the boring and the trivial; 'If X is an important or interesting aspect of human memory, then X has not been studied by psychologists' (Neisser 1978). My own view is that, in a somewhat rambling and unspectacular way, we are making genuine progress, and while I do not wish to defend all that has appeared under the name of cognitive psychology during the last decade, I feel that I am prepared to defend what I myself have been up to. And so what follows is a somewhat tentative demonstration of willingness to stand up and be counted. Tentative, because to do so seems very un-British and possibly even boastful, and tentative also because any theoretical claim is always much easier to criticize than to defend.

In what follows, however, I wish to claim that one can make genuine cumulative progress in understanding even relatively complex aspects of human cognition, and that experimental psychology need not be confined to trivial or laboratory-bound tasks. I do not, of course, wish to claim that my own particular way of doing cognitive psychology is the only way, or indeed the best. I am, however, prepared to offer it as one of many possible examples of the way in which cognitive psychology has made real if unspectacular progress during the 1970s.

How should such a book be structured? An obvious logical approach would be to describe the model and then demonstrate its application across a range of tasks and situations. Such an approach might be appropriate for certain types of model where the data to be explained are clear cut, and where the model itself is precise and clearly formulated. For better or worse, the working memory model is not of this type. It is rather, a broad framework within which it has proved fruitful to pose a range of questions about the role of temporary storage in information processing. Certain components of the model have become increasingly clearly specified, while others have remained loose and general. Consequently, while one could give an account of a wide range of phenomena in terms of the working memory model, that is not its primary purpose. Its purpose has rather been to allow one to ask fruitful questions, a process which then forces the model itself to develop in order to encompass the new findings.

A second possibility might be a chronological account. While this would have the advantage of showing the way in which the model developed as a result of its interaction with data, a strictly chronological approach would be too rambling and unstructured. For the purpose of exposition, therefore, I shall begin by discussing the earlier concept of short-term memory and the development from this, first of the modal model, and subsequently of the Levels of Processing approach. I shall then describe the evolution of the concept of a general working memory (WMG), before going on to discuss a more specific model of working memory (WMS) that evolved, with particular emphasis on the two slave systems that have been investigated, the Articulatory Loop and the Visuo-Spatial Scratchpad or Sketchpad. The final third of the book will concern the application of the concept of working memory outside the laboratory, concentrating particularly on the study of reading, and on the application of the concepts of working memory to developmental and to neuropsychological problems.

There is one part of a preface that can only be written after the completion of a book, the part that acknowledges the help the author has received in producing the book. In the present instance, much of that help will be obvious, since virtually all the research I have carried out on working memory has been collaborative. Rather less obvious is the help given by colleagues who have read part or all of the manuscript, and offered their valuable comments. While I have responded to many of these, there is a recurrent type of helpful and constructive comment to which I have not responded adequately. These are typically suggestions that I might usefully elaborate and extend my discussion of some pheno-menon or theoretical interpretation. A related issue crops up when my views on some topic of at least peripheral relevance to the discussion are clearly not entirely up-to-date. Examples include reference to the modality effect in memory, to evidence from performance on the Stroop test, and to my discussion of the distinction between pre- and post-lexical phonology in lexical access. In my work on visual memory, a better conceptualization of current models of visual processing would certainly be helpful, while my consideration of working memory in children would also benefit from a deeper and more extensive knowledge of the general developmental literature.

In all these cases, I am sure that the present book would have been improved had I been able to respond adequately to these suggestions. I have not done so at more than a superficial level for two reasons. The first of these is simple lack of available writing time; to have attempted to tackle these various potential limitations would have required at least a further year, by which time other highly relevant material on working memory would have emerged which in turn would require further consideration. The second reason is that I believe that it is a characteristic of the concept of working memory that it impinges on a very wide range of other topics. This is a strength since it means that it can potentially help unify disparate fields, and of course it makes it a particularly interesting area within which to work. The penalty of such a position is however that it becomes quite impracticable to become expert in more than a fraction of these areas of application. To do so would require a knowledge of the literature, not only of the traditional topics of human memory, but also of visual processing, speech perception and production, attention and the attentional control of action, as well as a familiarity with the various areas of potential application including reading, dyslexia, developmental psychology, and a range of topics within neuropsychology. Although I touch on all these topics and more besides, I have to accept that in many cases my approach is that of an interested outsider providing suggestions and proposals that may prove to be helpful, rather than an expert or specialist. The fact that I have not always been able to incorporate the suggestions made by my friends does not mean of course that I am any less grateful for them.

The development of the concept of working memory was a joint venture between Graham Hitch and myself; his contribution will be obvious throughout the book, not only through our collaborative work, but also through his more recent work on recency and on the development of working memory. I am grateful to him for many valuable discussions over the years, and more recently for his role in setting up and organising the informal working memory discussion group that has proved so useful and enjoyable.

I am indebted to far more individuals than it would be sensible to list here, but I would particularly like to thank Conrad, Donald Broadbent and Harold Dale; without their stimulation I would probably not have become interested in STM. I am also grateful to a wide range of colleagues with whom I have worked, including Marge Eldridge, Audrey Hull, Vivian Lewis, Bob Logie, Pierre Salame, Denise Scott, and Neil Thomson. I am grateful to Elizabeth Warrington for first interesting me in neuropsychology, and to Neil Brooks, Sergio Della Sala, Hans Spinnler, Giuseppe Vallar, and Barbara Wilson, all of whom have encouraged my attempts to apply the simplicities of the concept of working memory to the complex problems experienced by brain-damaged patients. Finally I would like to thank the many people who have taken time to discuss the often unclear concepts of the working memory model and its potential applications. I am particularly grateful to Bill Phillips and Tim Shallice for their discussion on many topics, and to Sebastian

Halliday and Charles Hulme for discussions on the development of working memory.

I am grateful to friends and colleagues who have allowed me to reproduce data that is as yet unpublished. I am also grateful for permission to publish Figs. 8.4(a) and 8.4(b) which are taken from the article by Daneman and Carpenter (1983): copyright (1983) by the American Psychological Association, reprinted by permission of the publisher and author. I am grateful to Michael Watkins and the *Journal of Verbal Learning and Verbal Behaviour* for permission to reproduce Fig. 7.3, and to Tim Shallice and the Royal Society for permission to reproduce Fig. 10.1.

Much of the first draft of this book was written during a three-month visit to Bolt, Beranek & Newman in Cambridge, Massachusetts. I am very grateful to Ray Nickerson, and to the staff of the Psychology section at B, B & N for providing a stimulating, friendly and hospitable environment. I am also grateful to Bill Estes who kindly arranged a parallel attachment to Harvard, and whose research group provided another valuable source of stimulation.

This book was dictated rather than written, and I am very grateful to Michelle Starmer of B, B & N for transcribing my strange English accent often recorded against rather unpredictable background noise. I am particularly grateful to Julie Darling who has transcribed my subsequent ramblings and has turned the whole into text, with her customary good humour and efficiency. I am grateful to the Medical Research Council, who supported this programme of work from its inception through to the present; and finally I would like to thank my wife Hilary and my three sons, Roland, Gavin, and Bart for cheerfully tolerating those weekends and holidays that were devoted to *Working memory*.

Cambridge   A. B.

Contents

Part I

Precursors

1 Short-term memory

The idea that memory might not be a single monolithic system but might have two or more components has been current for many years. William James for example used the term *primary memory* to refer to the specious present, those percepts and ideas that are simultaneously present in the mind, even though they may have happened a few seconds before, and are hence no longer physically present. Some of the empirical techniques for studying short-term memory are also far from modern. The memory span technique was devised by a London schoolmaster, Jacobs in the 1890s. The short-term forgetting task usually associated with Peterson and Peterson (1959) had previously been used by Pillsbury and Sylvester (1940), while Scripture (1905) included in his text entitled *The new psychology* a description of a short-term motor memory task almost identical to that subsequently reinvented by Adams and Dijkstra (1966).

The intensive study of short-term memory as a specific topic, however, did not achieve popularity until the late 1950s. The possibility of a distinction between long- and short-term memory was raised by Hebb (1949), who suggested that there might be two neurophysiologically separate storage systems within the brain, one involving temporarily reverberating circuits, and hence electrically based, while the other represented a permanent change based on a growth of links between nerve cells, forming what Hebb termed 'cell assemblies'. While the neurophysiological and biochemical approach to long- and short-term memory continued to develop (see for example McGaugh and Gold 1974), the most active area of research on this topic has been based on the results of cognitive rather than physiological psychologists.

Short-term forgetting: decay or interference?

The case for trace decay

The mid-1950s saw a number of British studies, mainly carried out in Cambridge, which seemed to point to the need to separate long- and short-term memory. Brown (1958) showed that very small amounts of material, well within the memory span, were rapidly forgotten if rehearsal was prevented. Since the rehearsal-preventing task involved processing material that was very different from the items being remembered, an interference theory interpretation seemed unlikely, and Brown instead suggested that short-term retention depends upon memory traces that will spontaneously decay unless refreshed by active rehearsal. Conrad (1960*a*) conducted a study in which telephonists were required to enter a prefix before dialling a telephone number; the results showed that even a very brief delay causes marked forgetting, a result that was interpreted in terms of trace decay.

In a series of studies primarily concerned with selective attention, Broadbent (1957) presented two sequences of three spoken digits to the subject simultaneously, with one sequence being fed into each ear. Subjects were then told which ear to recall first. Performance on sequences presented to this ear were uniformly good, whereas the second triplet to be recalled showed marked forgetting, a result that was consistent with the assumption that the delay in recall had allowed the memory trace to decay. Broadbent (1958) reviewed the available evidence on short-term memory, concluding that short-term forgetting appeared to reflect trace decay, and long-term forgetting the effect of interference, and hence that they must be based on separate systems.

Broadbent (1958) produced the first major information processing model of short-term memory. This comprised two subcomponents, the S system and the P system. The S system was assumed to be capable of briefly storing sensory information from many sources in parallel. It was assumed to feed information into the later P system which had a limited capacity for processing information. He suggested that it was this limitation in capacity that led to the inability of subjects to attend to many sources of information at the same time. Hence, when sequences of digits were presented to both ears simultaneously, the P system could attend to and process the stimuli reaching the attended ear, but only at the expense of allowing the unattended items to languish in the S system until after the attended items had been recalled.

Broadbent's assumption that short-term forgetting reflected trace decay and long-term forgetting reflected interference was subsequently challenged. Melton (1963) argued strongly that STM shows interference effects, while others have claimed that LTM may reflect trace decay (Baddeley 1976). However, although arguments based on the nature of forgetting have become much less prominent, Broadbent's model itself, through its direct descendants, has continued to be influential. Atkinson and Shiffrin (1968) acknowledged their debt to Broadbent, and as will become apparent from the chapters that follow, current views of working memory have much in common with Broadbent's original formulation.

In the United States, interest in short-term memory was stimulated by George Miller's classic paper *The magic number seven* (Miller 1956). Miller, influenced like Broadbent by information theory, drew attention to the similarity between the limitations on capacity for making absolute sensory judgements, and the limited memory span. In both cases Miller points out, subjects can handle about seven plus or minus two alternatives or chunks of information, suggesting that this may well represent a general limitation on human information processing.

At an empirical level, however, by far the most influential US study of this period was Peterson and Peterson's (1959) demonstration that a sequence of three consonants, well within the subject's memory span, will show precipitous forgetting over a 20 second period, provided the subject is prevented from rehearsing by an interpolated counting task. Like Brown, the Petersons argued that since the digits involved in counting were very different from the letters to be remembered, a classic interference interpretation seemed implausible. They also opted for a trace decay interpretation.

The interference theory counter-attack

In 1963, Arthur Melton, a distinguished proponent of the interference theory approach to forgetting took up the challenge and argued in an influential paper for a unitary theory of memory, with all forgetting stemming from interference. His argument rested on two main points, first the demonstration across a range of STM tasks that they were influenced by variables that were also known to influence long-term memory, and secondly that the Peterson short-term forgetting task was better explained in terms of interference than trace decay.

He began by showing that both the Peterson task and the classic digit span procedure could be shown to reflect long-term learning if the same sequences were repeatedly presented. Empirically, there is no doubt that he was right on this point. Its theoretical relevance, however, depends on the assumption that short-term memory as a label for a type of experimental task is synonymous with the hypothetical store that is assumed to play a part in performance on such tasks. There is no doubt that it is useful to use a term such as STM to refer to a whole class of memory tasks in which the amount of material to be remembered is relatively small, and the delay between the presentation and test is of the order of seconds rather than minutes. It is implausible, however, to assume that tasks fulfilling this requirement all depend exclusively on the operation of a single processor or system, with other more long-term factors playing no part in performance.

To take a concrete instance. If I were to carry out a memory span task and present you with the sequence *January, February, March, April, May, June, July, August, September, October, November, December* and then instruct you to recall, I would not be unduly suprised if you were to recall all 12 items correctly. I would not, however, wish to conclude from that that you had a memory span of 12 words, since if I were to present them again in scrambled order, you would almost certainly not be able to repeat that sequence. In the first case, I would be observing the effect of considerable past long-term learning on your performance in an STM task. Your performance in this, as in any other STM task, would be a combination of information from several sources, only one of which is the hypothetical short-term store.

In short, Melton's demonstration that some STM tasks show LTM type phenomena is readily explicable. It does, however, point out the danger of using the same term as both a theoretically neutral description of a type of task and as the name of a theoretically controversial system that is assumed to be partially responsible for that task. In order to avoid this confusion, we will adopt the terminology suggested by Atkinson and Shiffrin (1968), using the short-term memory (STM) to describe the task or situation, and short-term store (STS) to describe the underlying hypothetical memory system. In doing so, we do not, of course, wish to imply that a given phenomenon is necessarily determined by the storage characteristics of the STS, as opposed to its input or retrieval characteristics.

Melton's second objection to the view that memory comprises two separate stories carried substantially more weight. His argument was that all the phenomena of STM could be accounted for using exactly the same interference theory concepts as were applicable to LTM. That being so, it was unparsimonious to assume a separate system. The main thrust of his argument was concerned with the Peterson short-term forgetting paradigm for which he accepted the view that digits were sufficiently dissimilar to letters to rule out the possibility of an explanation in terms of retroactive interference. He pointed out however that Keppel and Underwood (1962) had just produced dramatic evidence in favour of proactive inhibition as an interpretation of short-term forgetting.

Keppel and Underwood showed that although substantial forgetting occurred with the Peterson paradigm when performance was averaged over a whole session, on the very first trial of any session, virtually no forgetting was present. By the second trial, forgetting was already beginning, and within four or five trials had reached asymptote. This pattern of results was explained by assuming that forgetting occurred because of interference from the highly similar letter sequences presented on preceding trials. The classic interference theory interpretation of PI (proactive interference) states that a subsequent item will cause the unlearning of an earlier item, but that over time the earlier item will spontaneously recover up to a point at which it is able to compete with the later item. This competition will produce interference and forgetting.

Further powerful evidence in favour of this view was produced by Wickens, Born, and Allen (1963) who modified the traditional Peterson procedure as follows. After a series of trials in which subjects were required to remember consonants, the material to be remembered was switched to numbers. Each item was tested after a constant interval of 15 seconds filled by a rehearsal-preventing task. Subjects showed the usual excellent performance on the first trial, with retention declining on subsequent tests until the material was switched from letters to numbers. At this point performance improved dramatically, so that on the first trial of the new material recall was virtually perfect once more, only to decline again on subsequent trials with the changed material. This is exactly what would be predicted on the assumption that forgetting occurs as a result of PI from earlier items; switching from one class of item to another produces a situation in which the earlier items are dissimilar, and hence unable to interfere with a current item, a phenomenon termed *Release from PI*. In a later study, Wickens (1970) showed that a similar release from PI could be produced by switching from one semantic word category to another, from groups of animals to groups of trees for example, while Loess (1968) showed that PI could be built up and released repeatedly as material is switched from category to category.

While these results seem to offer convincing evidence for an inter-ference theory interpretation of the Peterson effect, subsequent experi-ments suggested that the situation might not be so straightforward. The PI effect in STM for example appears to reach asymptote within three or four trials, whereas there is no evidence that this is the case in long-term PI. Furthermore, Peterson and Gentile (1963) showed that PI does not build up in the Peterson task if successive trials are separated by an interval of a few minutes. On a classic interference theory hypothesis, there is no reason to expect this. Furthermore, Conrad (1967) showed that the nature of the intrusion errors changes as a function of the delay between presentation and test using the Peterson procedure, being phonologically similar to the correct item after short delays (e.g. *b* for *v*, or *f* for *s*), but not after long delays. Conrad argued that interference theory would predict exactly the opposite, with prior items that were similar to the items presented on a given trial showing more unlearning than dissimilar, and hence taking longer to recover and appearing later rather than earlier. Conrad argued that his results reflected instead the fading of an acoustic or phonological trace; after short delays the relevant traces were only partially decayed, and hence contained some of the acoustic features of the original. After longer delay he suggested, such partial traces had decayed to a point at which their acoustic features were no longer discriminable. Intrusions at this point were likely to comprise mainly guesses or items from the long-term component left over from other trials.

A final source of evidence against the view that the Peterson technique demonstrates interference in the STS came from a study by Denise Scott and myself (Baddeley and Scott 1971). It was concerned with the issue of whether the very first trial did indeed show no forgetting, or whether some forgetting did occur but was obscured by performance being at ceiling. Unfortunately, since one can only test each subject once in this task, and since amount of forgetting is known to be relatively small, such studies need very large numbers of briefly available subjects. We solved this particular practical problem by parking a testing caravan in the centre of the University of Sussex campus and offering a small donation to charity for every subject who took part. We were able in a short period of time using this approach to test a total of over 900 subjects across a range of different conditions. We found that performance on this very first trial did indeed show forgetting, though the extent of forgetting was considerably less than in the standard Peterson procedure, and more importantly, appeared to reach asymptote within 5 seconds. We found no evidence for faster forgetting as a number of words in a sequence was increased, a prediction that Melton had previously made on the basis of an assumption of mutual interference among the words presented. We also failed to find any effect of word frequency on forgetting rate, as would be predicted by the extra-experimental interference hypotheses (Underwood and Postman 1960). Our results did then suggest a small but genuine STS component to the Peterson task, which is consistent with a decay rather than interference interpretation. The major source of fogetting in this task, however, appears to be confusion between the items to be remembered and the previous items.

The Peterson task, therefore, seems to comprise at least two components. One component appears to reflect spontaneous rapid forgetting over a period of about 5 seconds, but probably contributes relatively little to performance in the standard paradigm. This appears to depend primarily on a more extensive source of forgetting that stems from the problem of discriminating the relevant items, (the last ones presented), from earlier items, and in particular from the immediately prior items. The ratio of elapsed time appears to be an important variable here (Baddeley 1976, p. 129), although it is far from clear what the source of this temporal cue is, whether trace strength of some alternative form of temporal tagging. The release from PI studies show that if an additional cue is provided by ensuring that the target items come from a different category from the prior items, then the subject no longer needs to depend upon temporal discrimination, and little forgetting is observed.

The initial attraction of the Peterson paradigm was that it appeared to offer a means of directly studying the process of trace decay. It should be clear by this point that whatever one's interpretation of the Peterson effect, it certainly does not reflect the simple process of trace decay, and one might indeed question whether Peterson performance depends more than minimally on the operation of an underlying STS.

A second technique that was used in an attempt to test the trace decay hypothesis is that of the *digit probe*, developed by Waugh and Norman (1965). In this task, the subject is presented with a sequence of perhaps 15 or 20 digits or other items. The sequence is followed by a *probe* item taken from the sequence, and the subjects' task is to say which item followed the probe. Waugh and Norman presented their digits at either a slow rate, two seconds per item or a fast rate, half a second per item. They hypothesized that if trace decay were the major source of forgetting, then performance should be better with rapid presentation, since less time would elapse between presentation and test, leading to less delay and a stronger trace. On the other hand, an interference or displacement hypothesis would suggest that the crucial factor would be number of subsequent items rather than elapsed time. On this view no difference should occur between the two presentation rates, provided number of interpolated items is the same. Their results indicated that number of subsequent items rather than elapsed time was the crucial variable. Rather than adopting a classical interference interpretation however, Waugh and Norman suggested that forgetting in this paradigm stems from the displacement of items from a limited capacity short-term store.

At first sight, the Waugh and Norman result appears to rule out trace decay as a plausible hypothesis. However, closer examination suggests that rapid presentation did lead to a slightly lower level of initial performance, and that the amount of forgetting from this level was slightly less than with the slower presentation rate, suggesting that number of interpolated items is not the only determinant of forgetting. More importantly, subjects at the slower rate were not prevented from rehearsal. A subsequent study by Hockey (1973) suggests that if subjects are induced to adopt a totally passive strategy, then their performance approaches the trace decay prediction more closely, while if encouraged to rehearse, temporal delay ceases to be an important factor, and the number of items interpolated between presentation and test becomes the dominant variable. Strict control of rehearsal is always difficult to ensure (Reitman 1974), and hence it is difficult to interpret unequivocally the results of studies based on varying the rate of item presentation.

Rehearsal

A third STM technique that was investigated extensively during the 1960s was that of *free recall* in which the subjects are typically presented with a sequence of 15 to 30 unrelated words. Immediately after the last word, they are given a recall signal and attempt to recall as many words as they can in any order they wish. Performance on this task shows a very characteristic serial position curve, with recall of the initial items being reasonably good (the *primacy effect*) the middle items being recalled at a rather lower level, while the last few items are recalled extremely well (the *recency effect*). Both Postman and Phillips (1965) and Glanzer and Cunitz (1966) showed that if recall is delayed for a few seconds during which subjects are kept occupied with a rehearsal-preventing task, the recency effect is abolished, while performance on the initial and middle items is comparatively unaffected. Postman and Phillips attempted to explain the abolition of the recency effect in terms of PI from the earlier items. This is assumed to be ineffective on immediate test, but to develop after the brief delay. However, unlike the Peterson task, the PI interpretation in this context has never gained much support. More specifically, Glanzer, Gianutsos, and Dubin (1969) have shown that the crucial factor is the number of items following the end of the list, a result that would implicate RI rather than PI. However, Glanzer *et al.* (1969) further show that the degree of similarity between the list items and interfering items is not an important variable, suggesting that some form of displacement is a more plausible interpretation than a classical RI explanation.

A trace decay hypothesis fares no better than an interference interpretation insofar as the recency effect is concerned. Glanzer *et al.* (1969) showed that number of items rather than elapsed time is a crucial factor, while Baddeley and Hitch (1977) carried out a study which came to a similar conclusion. Subjects were presented with a sequence of first names, and told that their task was to classify each as male, female, or applicable to either sex. They were not told that they would need to remember the names. After the presentation of the last item, one group was immediately asked to recall the names. A second group experienced a 30 second delay during which the experimenter shuffled his papers as if looking for the next test. They were then asked to recall. On a trace decay hypothesis, the recency effect in the second group should have disappeared since other studies indicate that 30 seconds is ample time for forgetting to occur, given that subjects had no reason to rehearse. In fact the recency effect in the two groups was equivalent. It is clear then that a simple trace decay hypothesis of the recency effect is simply not adequate. We shall, however, return to the question of explaining recency in Chapter 7.

Having examined three of the most extensively used STM paradigms, it is clear that some of the earlier claims that forgetting in STM reflects trace decay is at the very best a gross oversimplification. Indeed, the evidence suggests that it is unlikely that any single explanation will prove adequate even for these three paradigms let alone for the plethora of new techniques and experimental procedures that developed in the 1960s. During the late 1960s and the early 1970s, the issue of decay or interference in short-term forgetting began to lose its popularity as other, apparently more tractable questions cropped up. However, I believe that the role of trace decay in STM still presents an important question, or rather range of questions, and will return to it from time to time in the following chapters.

One memory system or two?
The second issue that dominated theoretical discussion in STM during the 1960s was that of how many memory stores it was necessary to

assume. During the 1950s, this was not a controversial issue, largely because experimenters working on STM and those working on LTM rarely interacted. STM was primarily at this time studied in Britain, largely by a group with a strong interest in applied problems, employing theories based on a combination of trace decay and the newly developing information processing approach (see Broadbent 1958). In contrast, research on LTM was dominated by the American functionalistic tradition, strongly tied to standard verbal learning paradigms, and either relatively atheoretical or operating within a broad interference theory framework. There were, of course, exceptions; in North America, both George Miller and Paul Fitts and his group were operating within a very similar theoretical framework to that surrounding work on STM in Britain, while British work in LTM did continue, though primarily within the Bartlett tradition of using prose, or relatively realistic pictorial material rather than nonsense syllables (e.g. Belbin 1950; Kay 1955).

The controversy regarding the distinction between LTM and STM was sparked off by a combination of factors, probably most notably by Peterson and Peterson's (1959) demonstration of what appeared to be a very elegant technique for demonstrating the decay of the memory trace, followed by Melton's (1963) cogent plea that the existing tenets of interference theory were sufficient to explain all the phenomena of both long- and short-term memory, obviating the need for a theoretical distinction. Melton's paper prompted a flurry of activity concerned with collecting evidence for or against the case for a dichotomy between LTS and STS. The evidence that emerged for a separation included the following:

1. *Two component tasks.* As we saw earlier, the task of free recall can be split into two components. The recency effect leads to a high level of performance on the last few items when tested immediately, but is dissipated by a short filled delay. Performance on the rest of the list, however, is relatively resistant to delay. A series of experiments, notably by Glanzer (1972) and his colleagues, demonstrated that the recency effect is influenced by very different variables from the rest of the free recall curve. Performance on the more durable primacy and middle items can be influenced by a wide range of factors known to affect long-term learning. These include speed of presentation, word frequency, image-ability, and whether or not the subject is required to perform a secondary task simultaneously. None of these factors appear to influence the magnitude of the recency effect, which is however extremely sensitive to the effects of a brief filled delay. A number of other tasks were also shown to comprise two components. Waugh and Norman's (1965) digit probe task shows marked recency, but when followed by a filled delay, recency disappears leaving a flat recall function (Baddeley 1968a).

Another task showing two distinct components is minimal paired-associate learning. The subject is presented with a number of pairs of words; after a single presentation each pair is tested once after which the next set of different pairs is presented and tested (Murdock 1961). Peterson (1966) studied the effect on performance of following the presentation of five pairs of words with a variable delay interval during which the subject was required to count backwards to prevent rehearsal. Performance on each of the five pairs was found to be roughly equivalent with one exception. If the last pair presented is tested immediately, it leads to a very high level of recall. If instead of testing immediately, subjects are required to count backwards for a few seconds, then performance on this recency item declines markedly, while performance on earlier items actually improves. Peterson (1966) argues that this last item is held in a short-term store, with immediate recall performance excellent; he suggests that a brief delay produces forgetting due to trace decay. In the case of earlier items, such decay will already have occurred at the time of test, with the result that recall will depend entirely on LTM.

2. *Capacity.* It was suggested that whereas LTM has an enormous capacity for storage, coupled with relatively slow input and retrieval, STM is a limited capacity store with rapid input and retrieval. Arguments for this viewpoint came from two directions, theoretical and empirical.

At a theoretical level, attempts to design computers had repeatedly pointed to the desirability of separating a rapid-access limited capacity working memory from the much larger capacity passive long-term memory banks. By analogy, it was suggested that the architecture of the human computer might similarly benefit from two distinct memory systems with different characteristics and different functions.

Empirical evidence for the limited capacity of STM was abundantly available, not only from the traditional memory span task discussed by Miller (1956) but also from the more recently developed digit probe, and Peterson tasks, as well as from the recency effect in free recall which is typically limited to about three items (Craik 1971).

Evidence that input to STM is rapid and undemanding came from a study by Murdock (1965) in which subjects were required to sort cards at the same time as they heard a series of words for subsequent free recall. The difficulty of the sorting task was manipulated by varying the number of categories into which the cards had to be sorted. Murdock observed that the greater the sorting load, the poorer the performance of subjects for all except the most recent items. The recency effect was independent of concurrent load both in this and subsequent replications (e.g. Baddeley, Scott, Drynan, and Smith 1969).

Evidence for rapid retrieval from STM is provided by a study by Waugh (1970) using the digit probe task. She observed not only that more recent items are more likely to be correct, but also that correct items from the recency portion of the curve are produced more rapidly than correct items from the earlier LTM component.

3. *Differential coding.* In studying the recall of letter sequences, Conrad (1964) noted that intrusion errors tended to be phonologically similar to the correct item, hence *B* is more likely to be remembered as *V* than *F*, despite the fact that the letters are presented visually. He went on to collect a large number of intrusion errors, selecting sequences where only a single letter was wrong, so that it was clear what letter the intrusion was replacing. He was able to show that the pattern of memory intrusions was closely correlated with the listening errors that occur when subjects attempt to discriminate consonants spoken against a background of white noise. He interpreted this as evidence that STM relies on an acoustic code. Conrad and Hull (1964) subsequently showed that memory span for sequences of phonologically similar letters (e.g. *BVPCT*) was substantially worse than memory for dissimilar sequences (e.g. *KWYMR*).

While there was no doubt from Conrad's result that STM is sensitive to phonological similarity, implying that it does encode material along this dimension, this did not, of course, mean that the other coding dimensions might not be equally important. I decided to explore this question by comparing the effect on STM of phonological similarity and similarity of meaning. In one study (Baddeley 1966*a*) subjects were presented with sequences of five words that were either phonologically similar (e.g. *MAN, MAD, CAP, MAP, CAN*) or dissimilar (e.g *COW, DAY, BAR, SUP, PEN*). As one would have expected from Conrad's work, performance on the similar items was dramatically poorer than on the dissimilar (9.6 per cent vs 82.1 per cent sequences correct). I contrasted this with a further condition in which subjects recalled sequences of adjectives that were either similar in meaning (e.g. *LONG, HUGE, WIDE, TALL, BIG*) or dissimilar (e.g. *OLD, LATE, THIN, WET, FOUL*). This variable had a very small effect on performance, (64.7 per cent vs 71.0 per cent sequences correct) a difference that did reach significance on this study but failed to do so on a number of subsequent experiments.

It is clear then that STM is not equally susceptible to all dimensions of encoding. In a further study, (Baddeley 1966*b*) I studied the effects of phonological and semantic similarity on a long-term learning task. This involved presenting the subject with sequences of ten words for several trials, followed by a 20 minute filled delay and a final recall. In order to discourage the use of any type of STM strategy, each presentation of the ten word list was followed by a rehearsal-preventing task. Under these conditions, phonological similarity ceased to be an important variable, and similarity of meaning became a critical factor. These results together with a parallel set of studies carried out jointly with Harold Dale (Baddeley and Dale 1966; Dale and Baddeley 1969) seemed to suggest a clear association between memory and coding, with STM relying principally on phonological coding and LTM on semantic coding.

Evidence that this generalization might extend .beyond the simple laboratory techniques used by Dale and myself, came from a study of prose recall by Sachs (1967). She required her subjects to listen to prose passages which occasionally contained a repeated sentence that was either identical to its original presentation, or changed in either its semantic characteristics or in terms of some grammatical or surface feature. Subjects were required to judge in each case whether the sentence was identical or changed. The test sentence could occur either immediately after the critical sentence, or after one or more intervening sentences. Sachs found that subjects were able to detect changes in the surface characteristics of the prose only when the test was immediate, whereas detection of semantic changes was relatively impervious to interpolated material.

So far the evidence of coding seems to associate STM *tasks* with phonological coding, and LTM *tasks* with semantic coding. But what of the underlying storage systems? Is STS associated with phonological and LTS with semantic coding? Evidence in support of this view was presented by Kintsch and Buschke (1969) using the probe task developed by Waugh and Norman. They used sequences of words rather than digits, and observed that the recency part of the curve, typically associated with STS, was sensitive to phonological but not semantic similarity, while the earlier part of the curve was sensitive to semantic but not phonological similarity. As we shall see later, the issue of coding turns out to be considerably more complex than this, but nevertheless, by the late 1960s the pattern appeared to be reasonably straightforward, with evidence for an STS that relies primarily on phonological coding, and an LTS which although not incapable of using phonological codes (how otherwise could we ever learn a spoken language?), nevertheless, relies much more heavily on semantic coding (Baddeley 1972).

4. *Neuropsychological evidence*. Perhaps the clearest evidence for a separation between STS and LTS comes from work on brain-damaged patients. Neuropsychologists had known for many years that some patients show a combination of dense global amnesia with virtually intact memory span (e.g. Zangwill 1946). Such neuropsychological evidence, however, became much more widely known in connection with work by Milner and her colleagues on H.M., a patient who was unfortunate enough to undergo bilateral removal of the temporal lobes and hippocampus in an attempt to relieve his intractable epilepsy (Milner 1966). The operation resulted in a dense and very general amnesia which left H.M. apparently incapable of new learning. He could not learn his way around the hospital, failed to recognize people even though they had spent several hours testing him immediately beforehand, and performed abysmally poorly on standard verbal learning tasks. Despite this, his memory span was normal.

Elizabeth Warrington and I studied a range of amnesic patients with a view to establishing whether the nature of the amnesic defect could be fitted into the distinction between STS and LTS (Baddeley and Warrington 1970). Our results indicated intact performance on a range of tasks assumed to rely primarily on STS. These included memory span, the recency effect in free recall and performance on the Peterson short-term forgetting task.

This last result subsequently caused a good deal of controversy since Butters, Cermak, and their associates working in Boston typically found their amnesic Korsakoff patients to be impaired on the Peterson task (e.g. Cermak, Butters, and Moreines 1974). It now seems almost certain that this discrepancy stems from a difference in patient population, with the Boston Korsakoff cases showing rather more general intellectual impairment than the patients tested by Warrington and myself (see Baddeley 1982a; Cermak 1982 and Warrington 1982 for a more detailed discussion).

Our amnesic patients, as expected showed grossly defective LTM performance, together with one or two signs that certain aspects of LTM might be unimpaired. In the Peterson task, for example, performance after 60 seconds was relatively high in both groups, an unexpected result since we assumed that this represented the LTS component of the task. Secondly, both groups showed an equivalent amount of learning in the Hebb repeated digit series task in which unbeknown to the subject, a digit span task contains spaced repetitions of the same digit sequence. We found enhanced performance on the repeated sequences for both amnesic and control patients. It has indeed subsequently become clear that certain aspects of LTS are intact in amnesic patients (Baddeley 1982a; Cohen and Squire 1980; Jacoby and Witherspoon 1982). Overall, however, the results of this and other studies suggested clear evidence that patients could have normal STS coupled with a grossly defective LTS.

At about the same time, Shallice and Warrington (1970) reported the case of a patient K.F. with exactly the opposite pattern of defects, namely grossly defective STM coupled with unimpaired long-term learning. K.F. had suffered damage to the left parietal lobe in the general area specialized for speech perception and production. He was mildly dysphasic and somewhat dyslexic, but had no general intellectual impairment. His digit span, however, was grossly impaired, being limited to about two items with auditory presentation, but was reliably better when presentation was visual. When tested using the Peterson paradigm, he showed rapid forgetting of even a single auditory item. When tested on free recall of unrelated words, he showed normal performance on the initial and middle portion of the curve, usually assumed to depend on LTS, but a grossly impaired recency effect, which was limited to the last item. His impaired span was shown not to be due to difficulties of response production, since span was just as impaired when he was allowed to respond by pointing to the relevant digits rather than speaking them. His long-term learning ability as measured by performance on a paired-associate task for example, was quite normal, suggesting a very specific defect to an auditory-verbal STS system. Other patients with a similar specific STS deficit were later reported by Shallice and Warrington (1977), Saffran and Marin (1975), and Basso, Spinnler, Vallar, and Zanobio (1982).

The modal model

By the late 1960s, the weight of opinion was coming to accept the need to distinguish two types of memory. There was at this time almost a plethora of models; the book edited by Norman (1970) entitled *Models of human memory* had 13 contributors, all presenting a different model, and to these, one could probably add another 13 different models without difficulty. However, most STM models had a good deal in common, and approximated more or less closely to the most widely quoted model of the period, that proposed by Atkinson and Shiffrin (1968). This was essentially a development and elaboration of Broadbent's (1958) model. It contained three stages. The first of these comprised a bank of sensory buffer stores, analogous to Broadbent's S system, that were able to accept and temporarily store information from a range of different modalities. These buffers fed into the second component, a limited-capacity STS which in turn fed information into and extracted information from the third component, an LTS of much greater capacity. This probably represents the closest approximation to what Murdock (1974) has termed the *modal model*. The term 'modal' is defined by the dictionary as having two meanings, on the one hand 'approximating the mode', and hence being the most frequent, or on the other, 'having structure but no content'. While critics of the model might prefer the second definition, I assume that Murdock did in fact have the first in mind.

The central feature of the modal model is the STS. Long-term learning is assumed to depend on holding information in this temporary STS until it is transferred to LTS, the probability of learning being a direct function of the amount of time an item resides in STS. The STS is not, however, limited to this relatively passive role. It is assumed to be responsible for encoding the incoming material in a range of different ways. Atkinson and Shiffrin give the example of attempting to learn the association HRM-4, and suggest that the pair of items will be held in STS while some form of associative link is sought. A typical example might be 'homeroom' for HRM and 'fourth grade' for 4, hence suggesting that the item be encoded as the homeroom of my class during fourth grade.

The modal model also assumes STS to play an important role in retrieval. Given for example the question 'What is the capital of Australia?', the modal model would give an account of retrieval that is broadly as follows. First select a retrieval strategy (e.g. output names of Australian cities). Then select a probe, activate the relevant set of items in LTS, and transfer to STS. These candidate cities are then successively checked, using additional information to confirm whether or not they comprise the target. For example *Sydney* may be generated first as the largest Australian city but then rejected on the basis of the knowledge that the Australian capital is not the capital of any of the constituent states. The name *Canberra* might then be transferred to STS, and subsequently accepted as correct and emitted. Note the importance assigned to STS in this process, an issue that we shall return to in Chapter 3.

By the early 1970s then, superficially at least, there appeared to be a good deal of consensus about the need to assume a separate STS, and considerable agreement about its broad characteristics. However, as we shall see in the next chapter, problems were already beginning to beset the modal model, while the ever increasing number of new techniques and new models were beginning to cause growing feelings of unease as the field became more and more complex.

2 Beyond the modal model

Despite the apparent diversity of models of STM in the early 1970s, most approximated more or less closely to that put forward by Atkinson and Shiffrin (1968), which was itself a descendant of the original model proposed by Broadbent (1958). As described in Chapter 1, the Atkinson and Shiffrin model assumes three major components. The first of these is a bank of relatively peripheral sensory stores, each store capable of holding information from one sense modality. The sensory buffer stores feed information into a short-term store. This acts as a working memory that plays a crucial role in a wide range of other tasks. It is assumed to be a necessary intermediate stage in the process of transferring information to the third component, the long-term memory store. Long-term learning is assumed to occur as a result of maintaining information in the short-term store, the longer the material is maintained, the greater the probability of transfer.

The short-term store (STS) is also assumed to play an important role in selecting learning strategies and in maintaining and operating strategies for retrieval from long-term memory. While the STS was assumed to be capable of utilizing a range of control processes and strategies, the most extensively investigated by Atkinson and Shiffrin was that of rote verbal rehearsal. This emphasis fitted in well with the evidence suggesting that short-term memory appears to rely heavily on speech coding (Conrad 1964; Baddeley 1966a), in contrast to long-term memory which appears to rely more heavily on semantic coding (Baddeley 1966b; Kintsch and Buschke 1969). While the model was assumed to be a general one, most studies using the model tended to rely either on paired-associate learning or free recall, with the recency effect in free recall being regarded as a characteristic feature of the operation of the STS. By the early 1970s, however, the modal model was beginning to encounter a number of problems.

Problems of the modal model

By 1970, the modal model appeared to offer a very good account of short-term memory and its relationship to cognition. A colleague who had done distinguished work in this area commented to me about this time that 'Now we understand short-term memory, it is time to turn our attention to long-term memory'. Alas, his confidence in what had been

18

achieved began to look progressively less and less justified during the 1970s as a growing number of results emerged that did not fit at all well within the framework of the modal model. They include the following:

1. *STS and long-term learning.* A basic assumption of the Atkinson and Shiffrin (1968) model was that long-term learning was dependent upon STS, with the probability of an item being learnt increasing systematically with its time of residence in STS. A number of studies tested this assumption directly and found it wanting. In one of the more influential of these, Craik and Watkins (1973) gave their subjects a task that required them to maintain items by subvocal rehearsal in short-term memory for varying periods of time. They achieved this by presenting a long sequence of words, and instructing their subjects that their task was to remember the last word beginning with a specified letter. It might for example be the letter B and the following words: *cabbage, buffalo, grass, basin, tree, crucifix, cloud, apple, broomstick, mansion, helicopter,* RESPOND (*broomstick*). Note that the words beginning with B will have been held in store for different periods of time, *buffalo* during the presentation of one additional word, *basin* pending the processing of four, and *broomstick* during the processing of two words. The modal model would predict that if, at the end of the experiment, subjects were asked to recall unexpectedly as many of the words beginning with *B* as possible, the probability of recall would be a direct function of the amount of time held in STS, that is, of the number of interpolated words between presentation and a successful test. Craik and Watkins found almost perfect performance of the initial maintenance task coupled with a very poor level of final recall performance, and no relationship between time in STS and subsequent long-term recall. Maintaining an item in STS does not appear to result in long-term learning.

A similar conclusion can be drawn from many other studies. For example, Tulving (1966) found that requiring his subjects to read through a list of words several times before the start of a free recall experiment did not enhance the subsequent learning of the words. A similar lack of incidental learning has been demonstrated on a number of occasions under somewhat more ecologically valid conditions. Hence Morton (1967) found that subjects who had for many years used a telephone to dial letter-based telephone codes were nonetheless unable to recall accurately the location of the letters on the dial, while Nickerson and Adams (1979) tested their subjects' ability to remember the detailed appearance of a US penny, and found very poor performance. Finally, Bekerian and Baddeley (1980) studied the effect of a saturation advertising campaign which involved presenting British listeners with information about new radio wavelengths. Although subjects had typically heard the information over a thousand times, very little learning occurred.

These results and many more combined to cast grave doubts of the assumption underlying the modal model, of probabilistic but automatic transfer from STS to LTS.

2. *Neuropyschological evidence.* It may be recalled that one of the sources of evidence for a distinction between STS and LTS comes from the existence of two types of patient. The first of these, the classic amnesic patient shows grossly defective long-term learning ability but may have intact STM performance, while a second type of patient shows normal long-term learning coupled with grossly impaired STM performance, having for example an auditory digit span of only two items (Shallice and Warrington 1970; Basso *et al.* 1982).

However, if long-term learning depends crucially on STS, should not patients with defective STS also show impaired learning? Indeed, if the limited capacity STS plays as crucial a role in general cognition as is suggested by Atkinson and Shiffrin (1971), such patients should have a very general impairment in intellectual capacity. This does not appear to be the case. One such patient, J.B. studied by Shallice and Warrington lives a very active and successful life working as a personal secretary, while a second such patient, P.V. appears to have no difficulty in running her own shop, as well as living a normal life and looking after two children (Basso *et al.* 1982). Except in the case of carefully designed sentences that place a heavy demand on STS, she appears to have no difficulty in speech comprehension or production (Vallar and Baddeley 1984*a, b*).

If memory span is a good index of the capacity of STS, then it appears that STS does not play the important role in information processing suggested by Atkinson and Shiffrin (1971).

3. *Recency effects.* The modal model assumes both the recency effect in free recall and memory span to be manifestations of the same limited capacity STS. Difficulties with this view emerged from a number of directions. First, evidence began to accumulate that recency effects could be relatively long-term and resistant to disruption by tasks such as backward counting that would normally be expected to displace items from the STS. Tzeng (1973) carried out an immediate and delayed recall task which included a rather unusual condition. Subjects were presented with a list of unrelated words, but interspersed between each item was a period of backward counting to minimize rehearsal. Under these conditions, the recency effect survived a delay filled with backward counting that was enough to obliterate all recency under normal presentation conditions. Other examples of long-term recency were also observed extending up to a matter of weeks in one study where Baddeley and Hitch (1977) required rugby football players to attempt to recall rugby games they had played. It is of course arguable that such long-term recency effects are different in kind from those studied under more conventional conditions, but until one can specify the two types of recency independent of durability, such an explanation must remain circular. At best then,

the modal model can offer only a partial explanation of recency, one of the phenomena it was specifically devised to explain.

An even greater difficulty is raised by experiments carried out by Hitch and myself which will be described in greater detail later (Baddeley and Hitch 1977; see also pp. 41–3). We combined the digit span and free recall tasks by requiring our subjects to remember sequences of six un-related digits at the same time as they were attempting to learn a free recall list of unrelated words. Although we observed a general tendency for the concurrent digit span to impair long-term learning, the recency effect was just as great when subjects were remembering six concurrent digits as when they were free to concentrate on the free recall task. Six digits approached the span of our subjects, and hence ought to have pro-vided a load that would occupy most of the limited STS capacity. On any standard modal model, this would be expected to reduce the magnitude of the recency effect quite dramatically, yet no impairment was observed.

4. *Coding and the modal model.* A simple version of the modal model might hold that the STS operates entirely on phonological codes, and LTS on semantic. However, although some studies did fit neatly into this (e.g. Kintsch and Buschke 1969) such a position is obviously oversimpli-fied. In the case of long-term memory, there is clearly a need to assume a wide range of coding dimensions including of course phonological speech-coding since without such long-term coding one could never learn to speak or indeed to comprehend spoken language.

It remained possible however to argue for an absence of semantic coding in STS (Baddeley 1972), but not unfortunately to predict in detail where and when a given type of encoding would occur. The minimal paired-associate learning task for example, although assumed to depend primarily on LTS typically showed evidence of phonological rather than semantic coding (Baddeley 1970a). This appeared to be due to the diffi-culty of generating appropriate semantic codes under standard single presentation conditions, since when stimuli and responses were made semantically compatible, clear evidence of semantic coding occurred (Baddeley and Levy 1971). Such results do not of course challenge the modal model directly; they do however suggest that there is a good deal more to the role of coding than some of the earlier models might suggest.

A more direct challenge to earlier formulations came once again from the study of recency in free recall. Craik (1968a) and Shallice (1975) had both observed that phonemic intrusion errors in free recall tended to come from the last few items in the list, suggesting that the recency effect might rely heavily on phonological coding, just as does performance in the standard memory span paradigm. Glanzer, Kopenaal, and Nelson (1972) tested this by systematically varying the nature of the material intervening between presentation of a list and free recall. They argue that if the recency effect depends on phonological coding, then interposing phonologically similar items between presentation and recall should be particularly disruptive of the recency effect. They found no evidence for a particular susceptibility to either phonological or indeed semantic similarity. Amount forgotten seems to be a simple function of the number but not the nature of the interpolated items.

Fate of the modal model

There is no doubt that a modified modal model could have handled some at least of the evidence just described. However, in contrast to the almost feverish activity in the area of STM during the late 1960s, the 1970s saw an almost equally pronounced flight from the study of STM. Atkinson moved into a series of senior administrative posts that allowed him little time for developing and elaborating the model, while Shiffrin became more interested in attention and in the mathematical modelling of long-term memory. Long-term, and particularly semantic memory, seemed to offer exciting new problems, while the techniques of artificial intelligence appeared to provided powerful ways of tackling these. Investigators such as Kintsch, Norman, and Bower forsook the increasingly complex and cluttered field of STM in favour of the possibly grander prospect of studying the way in which the mind represents knowledge. Many others followed suit, with the result that the modal model was not so much destroyed as left to decay gradually until in the 1980s the last rites were read in papers such as that by Crowder (1982*a*) entitled 'The demise of short-term memory'.

Levels of Processing

Although the modal model faded away largely through neglect, there was one major precipitating factor, namely the development of what appeared to be a very promising alternative framework, that of *Levels of Processing*. The modal model was essentially structural in nature; it did have functional aspects such as control processes and encoding activities, but these were conceptually subsidiary to the underlying structural distinctions. Craik and Lockhart reversed this emphasis by de-emphasizing structure and stressing processing, suggesting that trace durability was a direct consequence of the processes of encoding, with deeper and more elaborate encoding leading to more durable memory traces.

The classic illustration of this reversal of emphasis from structure to function was taken from a series of experiments carried out by Jenkins and his collaborators (Hyde and Jenkins 1969; Johnston and Jenkins 1971) using an incidental learning procedure in which subjects were required to process words in a prespecified way, and subsequently asked to recall or recognize them. The incidental learning procedure has the great advantage that subjects who are not expecting a subsequent recall are more likely to limit themselves to the type of encoding specified, with no temptation to introduce additional strategies for enhancing retention. Using this procedure, some subjects were required to perform what subsequently became known as a shallow encoding, for example deciding whether the word was written in upper or lower case letters; this led to very poor subsequent recall. Other subjects were asked to carry out somewhat deeper encoding, for example judging whether the target word (e.g. *dog*) rhymed with a specific comparison (e.g. *log*), and this led to somewhat better retention. Substantially better recall however occurred in subjects required to carry out some form of semantic or deeper judgement. An example of such coding would be judging the pleasantness of a word or deciding whether a word (e.g. *dog*) would fit into a particular sentence context (e.g. *The man kicked the . . .*).

Craik and Lockhart (1972) argued that much of the evidence accumulated in the study of long- and short-term memory could be fitted into a very simple but coherent framework. This assumes that learning material involves processing it through a succession of ever deeper stages, starting with the peripheral sensory stimulus and ending with an elaborate semantic integration of the material into the subject's existing knowledge. The deeper the processing, the better the learning.

Craik and Lockhart themselves assumed that the relevant processing was carried out by a primary memory system, and as such continued to maintain a dichotomous view of memory. Their approach was however, often assumed to obviate the need for a dichotomy, and used to support a reversion to the earlier unitary view of human memory (e.g. Postman 1975). Indeed, although Craik himself continued to be interested in primary memory or STS (cf. Craik and Levy 1977), experiments generated within the Levels of Processing framework were concerned almost exclusively with the role of coding in LTM. For the most part, those suggesting that Levels of Processing had made the need for a dichotomous view of memory obsolete, simply ignored the phenomena of short-term memory.

During the 1970s, the Levels of Processing framework itself began to run into difficulties. For the most part, these difficulties are concerned with Levels of Processing as a theory of long-term learning, and are not concerned with its primary memory component. However since we shall be concerned with the role of working memory in long-term learning, it is perhaps appropriate at this point to give a brief outline of some of the problems that have confronted Levels of Processing in recent years.

Troubles with levels

The essence of the original Levels of Processing approach was as follows. Information processing was assumed to follow a sequence of stages from the peripheral sensory level through to the deep semantic level. Each stage of processing was assumed to leave a memory trace, with the durability of the memory trace increasing with depth. Rehearsal was assumed to be of two kinds, *maintenance rehearsal* whereby an item is recirculated without changing the level of processing, and *elaborative rehearsal* whereby each successive processing increases the depth of encoding. It was assumed that learning proceeded exclusively via elaborative processing, whereas maintenance rehearsal, although ensuring that an item could be recalled and tested immediately, had no influence on long-term memory. As we saw earlier, this striking and counterintuitive assumption is not without empirical support (e.g. Craik and Watkins 1973). However exceptions to this generalization began to appear during the 1970s.

1. *Maintenance rehearsal and long-term learning.* Glenberg, Smith, and Green (1977) for example, and Nelson (1977) both presented evidence to suggest that long-term retention could be influenced by maintenance rehearsal, particularly when tested by recognition. A much earlier study by Mechanic (1964) had shown convincingly that in the case of nonsense syllables at least, maintenance rehearsal could substantially enhance subsequent recall. Mechanic carried out an incidental learning study in which his subjects were presented with nonsense syllables and required either to articulate them once, or to articulate them as often as possible in the time available. The repeated articulation condition led to substantially better subsequent recall. I myself obtained exactly comparable results in an unpublished incidental learning study where subjects were required to write out nonsense syllables either once or as often as possible in the time available. Repeated writing led to consistently better recall.

These and other results indicate that the simple generalization, that maintenance rehearsal does not enhance retention, is an oversimplification. It should however be pointed out that the amount of learning resulting from merely repeating an item is typically small, and dependent on the type of material. In the case of an item such as a nonsense syllable where the constituent letters or speech sounds are initially not well-integrated, repetition may well cause a substantial increment in the ability of the subject to recall the item as a whole, a phenomenon that Horowitz and Prytulak (1969) have termed *redintegration.* Similarly in the case of an already integrated item such as a word, repeated presentation may prime the representation of that word which may under certain circumstances substantially increase accessibility. What repetition does not appear to do is to build up complex associations between items, an important prerequisite of recall under many standard verbal learning paradigms. This distinction has been explored more fully by Mandler and his colleagues (Mandler 1980; Graf and Mandler 1984). In conclusion, the Levels of Processing distinction between maintenance and elaborative rehearsal is not so much incorrect as incomplete in suggesting that maintenance rehearsal has no effect on LTM.

2. *Shallow processing and durable learning.* The Levels of Processing framework suggests that encoding an item in terms of its superficial features will give rise to a memory trace that dissipates very rapidly. While as a rule of thumb, such a generalization appears to account for a great deal of the existing literature, important exceptions have been observed. For example Kolers (1976) trained his subjects to read passages of prose written in text that was transformed, for example by representing each letter as its mirror image. He found when testing subjects a year later, evidence not only of general learning as reflected in speed of reading transformed text, but also of specific learning as evidenced by particularly rapid reading of those particular passages that had been read a year earlier.

Morris, Bransford, and Franks (1977) made the important point that it makes little sense to talk about the encoding dimension without specifying the retrieval situation. They demonstrated that while the normal procedures used in the verbal learning laboratory seem to be particularly geared to semantic encoding, if the experimenter sets up a retrieval task whereby the subject needs to make subtle phonological distinctions, then phonological coding is found to lead to better long-term retention than semantic coding. They advocate the concept of *transfer appropriate processing* rather than depth of encoding as being the critical variable. This implies that the optimal method of encoding during learning will depend critically upon the retrieval cues available at retrieval, whether this be by recall or recognition; visual processing will be optimal when visual distinctions must be made, and semantic will be best when retrieval of meaning is crucial.

Craik's subsequent position is that retrieval cues are indeed critical, but that over and above this, semantic cues tend to be more effective over long delays than phonological or visual. At the very least however, the evidence for durable learning from shallow processing places a major constraint on Levels of Processing as a general theory. As we shall see below, it is by no means the only constraint.

3. *Discrete domains or a processing continuum?* One of the attractions of the Levels of Processing framework was that it appeared to replace a series of *ad hoc* generalizations about learning and memory with the concept of a continuum of processing depth. In theory at least, each encoding task would process material to a specified depth which in turn would determine the memorability of the items processed. In actual practice, this promise does not appear to have been fulfilled. Clear differences are indeed typically observed *between* processing domains, so that in the case of words, visual processing leads to poorer retention than phonological, which in turn is poorer than semantic; but differences

within domains do not appear to have been observed. In those studies where more than one type of encoding has been observed within a domain, no difference in subsequent retention appears to have been obtained (e.g. Craik and Tulving 1975; Graf and Mandler 1984). This suggests that a concept such as depth that implies continuity, is less appropriate than a more discrete concept such as that of a processing domain (see Baddeley 1982*b* for further discussion).

4. *The linear processing stages assumption.* Formulation of the Levels of Processing framework was strongly influenced by theories of perceptual processing that were current at the time. More specifically Craik and Lockhart attempted to produce a theory of memory that was compatible with the assumption that perception involved the processing of a stimulus through a linear succession of stages, each one deeper than the last. Such a view had the highly desirable characteristic of allowing the process of perception to be broken down sequentially, were the assumption to prove valid. Unfortunately all the evidence to emerge since that time suggests that perception involves the concurrent processing of many dimensions of a stimulus simultaneously, together with the transfer of information in both a bottom-up direction from the stimulus, and a top-down direction from the semantic characteristics of the likely percept.

Consider for example the presentation of a typed word; a simple linear interpretation of the perception of such a word might suggest that the graphemic form is first transformed into a phonological representation or speech sound, which is then mapped onto the meaning of the word, the three stages typically implied by most studies in the Levels of Processing framework. However, Marcel (1983) has shown that subjects may be sensitive to the meaning of the word at a time when subsequent pattern masking has made them unaware of the physical or phonological characteristics of that word. Similarly, evidence from deep dyslexic patients (Marshall and Newcombe 1966, 1973; Coltheart, Patterson, and Marshall 1980) indicates that certain brain-damaged patients can process the meaning of a printed word without being able to derive its phonological characteristics. Such patients show good evidence of semantic processing, tending to make errors that are similar in meaning to the printed word, rather than similar in sound, for example reading the word *prayer* as *church* and the word *paddock* as *horses*. Such patients thus appear to be able to derive a 'deep' encoding of a word while not being able to derive a 'shallower' phonological encoding, a result that is hard to fit into the sequential linear model underlying levels of processing. Parallel distributed processing models are now much more widely held than the simple sequential view of perception that underlies Levels of Processing (e.g. Hinton and Anderson 1981; McClelland 1979).

5. *The problem of measuring processing depth.* In its initial formulation, Levels of Processing took an existing phenomenon, the relationship

between encoding and memory, and proposed the concept of processing depth to account for that phenomenon. Subsequent research either tended to rely on further replications of the initial observations under various conditions, or else use subsequent learning as an indicator of depth of processing. This latter approach is obviously circular, and the only satisfactory way out of it is to provide an independent measure of processing depth.

Craik and Tulving (1975) offer one of the few attempts to tackle this crucial problem. Their research began promisingly with the observation that deep processing appeared to take longer than shallow. Could processing time therefore be used as an independent measure of processing depth? Unfortunately not. Craik and Tulving showed that it is quite possible to set up a shallow processing task which is nevertheless time-consuming, for example assuming that C means consonant and V vowel, does the word *rabbit* conform to the following pattern *CVCCVC*? Such slow but shallow processing does not lead to good recall.

A further puzzle for a simple Levels of Processing view emerged from the observation (Schulman 1974; Craik and Tulving 1975) that in the case of semantic categorization at least, those items evoking a 'yes' response are consistently better retained than those evoking a 'no' although they tend to be processed more rapidly. In order to account for this, Craik and Tulving suggest a further factor of *compatibility*, with those items that are compatible with the question asked being better retained than those that are incompatible.

In the same study, Craik and Tulving also noted that for a given processing depth, those items that were encoded more elaborately also seemed to be better recalled. Hence the sentence *The wizened old man hobbled across the castle courtyard and dropped the gold watch down the well* would lead to better cued recall than the simple statement *The man dropped the watch.* On the basis of this they suggest that degree of elaboration is a further determinant of long-term retention. Such a view is of course far from novel; William James for example suggested that 'Of two men with the same outward experiences and the same amount of mere native tenacity, the one who thinks over his experiences the most and weaves them into systematic relations with each other will be the one with the best memory' (James 1890). The addition of such further concepts however, does call seriously into question the capacity of Levels of Processing to provide a simple overall account of human memory.

6. *Applications of levels of processing.* Although it may have limitations as a theoretical account of human learning, there is not doubt that the concept of Levels of Processing does provide a useful rule of thumb that is capable of accounting for a great deal of the verbal learning literature. Might it not serve a similarly useful function when applied more widely?

I myself have attempted to use Levels of Processing in this way, but unfortunately with relatively little success (Baddeley 1982*b*). It appeared initially that the phenomenon of amnesia might conceivably be explicable in terms of the impaired capacity of amnesic patients to encode deeply (Cermak, Butters, and Moreines 1974). Unfortunately, direct tests of this hypothesis have been universally disappointing. Patients who are densely amnesic but otherwise intellectually unimpaired show no evidence of defective processing (Mayes, Meudell, and Neary 1980). Similarly, when amnesic patients are forced to process materials deeply under incidental learning conditions, they show, like normals, an enhanced degree of learning. The amount of enhancement observed however is by no means sufficient to compensate for their massive learning deficit and lends no support to the view that their memory deficit stems from a coding deficit (see Baddeley 1982*a* for a more detailed discussion).

A second area in which Levels of Processing appeared to offer a useful lead was that of face recognition. Bower and Karlin (1974) reported that subjects required to judge the sex of a person in a photograph (shallow processing) were much less good at subsequently recognising the photograph than subjects who had processed the face more deeply, judging the intelligence or pleasantness of the person portrayed. Unfortunately other interpretations are possible, for example that the amount of time one needs to look at a picture to judge its sex is much less than that required to judge the person's honesty or intelligence; longer processing would of course be expected to lead to more learning. When amount of processing time is equated, there does indeed remain a significant advantage to processing the face semantically rather than in terms of its physical features (Patterson and Baddeley 1977). Unfortunately however the magnitude of this effect is small, and appears to stem from the requirement to process the face as a whole rather than from the depth at which this processing occurs. Hence, judging whether the person portrayed is tall or short leads to just as good subsequent recognition as apparently 'deeper' judgments about their pleasantness or honesty (Winograd 1976). Attempts to increase processing depth and elaboration by presenting the subject with a character sketch of the person portrayed appear to have no effect on subsequent recognition (Baddeley and Woodhead 1982).

There is no doubt that the concept of Levels of Processing offered and still offers a simple rule of thumb that accounts for a good deal of empirical data. Unfortunately however it has not proved to be a concept that is easy to develop. The problem of measuring depth of processing has not been solved, while the simple distinction between maintenance and elaborative rehearsal has proved oversimplified. The domain in which material is processed has implications for its subsequent recall, but the initial assumption of a linear sequence of stages of ever increasing depth is almost certainly misleading. Finally, while the inital model assumed the existence of a primary memory serving many of the functions required of working memory, the way in which the framework has developed has led to the problems of short-term and working memory being at best neglected and at worst denied. By this point it will I hope be clear that the Levels of Processing framework does not offer a satisfactory alternative to an adequate model of working memory.

Part II

The concept of a general working memory (WMG)

3 Working memory and learning

As described in Chapter 1, research in short-term memory received a major boost in the 1950s with the development of new techniques (Brown 1958; Conrad 1964; Peterson and Peterson 1959) and of theoretical approaches based on information processing concepts (Broadbent 1958). This led to a wealth of studies during the 1960s coupled with a great deal of theoretical development often mathematically very sophisticated. By the early 1970s, the field appeared to be reaching a plateau with a bewildering proliferation of memory tasks and models. Although it is certainly the case that these models had much in common, nevertheless the field appeared to be fragmenting rather than developing in a coherent way.

In 1972, Craik and Lockhart presented what appeared to many as an elegant simplification of the situation. They suggested that the durability of a memory trace was dependent on the manner in which the stimulus was coded, with relatively shallow encoding, based for example on the visual appearance of a word, leading to very rapid forgetting, with somewhat deeper coding as for instance in terms of the sound of a word leading to rather more durable encoding, while deep coding, in terms of a word's meaning led to the most durable. While Craik and Lockhart themselves offer this formulation as part of a dichotomous theory, assuming both an LTM system and a temporary primary memory system, their views were popularly seen as a plausible alternative to a dichotomous view. Instead of a simple distinction between long- and short-term memory, the levels of processing approach appeared to offer a continuum with trace durability being a simple function of depth of stimulus encoding. Interest in short-term memory waned, being largely replaced in popular favour by empirical studies on the generality of the concept of levels of processing. Such an approach seemed to avoid many of the difficulties that were cropping up for earlier views of short-term memory, although, as discussed in the previous chapter, it encountered in due course equally difficult problems of its own.

At the same time as Craik and Lockhart were developing and elaborating their levels of processing approach to memory, Hitch and I were attempting to tackle the problem of developing an adequate model of short-term memory from a somewhat different viewpoint (Baddeley and Hitch 1974). In particular, we were concerned with the question of whether short-term memory acted as a working memory. The term

33

working memory implies a system for the temporary holding and manipulation of information during the performance of a range of cognitive tasks such as comprehension, learning, and reasoning. The apparently simple question of whether STM acts as a working memory proved to be surprisingly complex and rich. It has occupied a good deal of the research time of myself and a range of colleagues over the last decade.

What follows attempts to describe our work and to outline a tentative model, giving some indication of its generality and ecological relevance. The next two chapters discuss a series of experiments that attempted to explore the possibility that a single working memory system underlies many cognitive tasks including learning, retrieval, comprehension, and reasoning.

General and specific working memory: WMG and WMS

Before going further, it would probably be useful to distinguish two ways in which the term working memory is used in what follows. I have so far used the term in its general sense which I propose to abbreviate as WMG, the *General* concept of working memory. By WMG, I intend to refer to the temporary storage of information that is being processed in any of a range of cognitive tasks. This can be differentiated from the *Specific* working memory model, WMS, that attempts to offer a more detailed model of those structures and processes involved in performing the tasks requiring WMG. There would probably be considerable, though not universal agreement among cognitive psychologists on the usefulness of some concept such as WMG, but much less agreement on WMS, the particular model proposed by Hitch and myself (Baddeley and Hitch 1974), and developed in Chapters 5, 6, 7, and 10 of this book.

Is the assumption of a general working memory merely a tautology? I think not, although I suspect that most cognitive psychologists would probably subscribe to the view that some form of temporary storage is involved in information processing, albeit merely the temporary activation of some long-term memory system. Even if one places a further constraint on the definition of WMG, by assuming that it enables otherwise independent sources of information to interact, I suspect that there would probably still be relatively few cognitive psychologists who would argue against such a view. A third assumption, however, that I would wish to make might cause rather more dissent. I wish to assume that the concept of a working memory implies a common system that operates across a wide range of tasks. A distributed processing system comprising a set of independent processors would not constitute a working memory in this sense, even though the constituent subsystems were able to communicate with each other. For the concept of a unitary working memory to be useful, I would wish to argue that the system should be limited in capacity, and should operate across a range of tasks involving different processing codes and different input modalities. There is by no means complete agreement over this latter viewpoint, with for example Allport (1980) and Barnard (1985) arguing for a series of interacting, but relatively independent subsystems, and against the idea of a unitary working memory.

The sections that follow attempt to collect evidence on this point. It is in the nature of the question, that it is unlikely that such evidence will produce a logically compelling conclusion. However, if the concept of a single limited capacity working memory is to prove profitable, then it is necessary to establish two things: first that the capacity of the system is limited, and secondly that absorbing a substantial amount of the available processing capacity should have broadly comparable effects across a range of different cognitive tasks. The next two chapters describe experiments aimed at exploiting the plausibility of the assumption that a unitary WMG plays an important role in human information processing.

The strategy underlying the experiments that follow thus rests on the assumption that working memory has a limited capacity. If a substantial amount of that capacity is taken up by a supplementary task, then the WMG hypothesis predicts that performance will deteriorate substantially. It further predicts that such deterioration should be shown by a range of cognitive tasks even though such tasks do not have an obvious STM component.

Methodology

Choosing a secondary task

One of the practical difficulties in testing the WMG hypothesis arises from the problem of selecting a suitable secondary task that can be used to load the hypothetical WMG system. This problem stems from the lack of a generally agreed view of short-term memory. Fortunately, however, virtually all views of short-term or primary memory agree on two things. First, that the system has a limited capacity, whether this limit is set by number of items, amount of information, or time. Secondly, virtually all views agree that the digit span task depends on this limited capacity system, with longer sequences of digits occupying more of the available capacity up to a point at which the capacity is exceeded and errors begin to occur as the subject's digit span is reached. Graham Hitch and I therefore, opted to use immediate memory for digit sequences as our secondary task, manipulating the demand of this task by varying the number of digits to be retained.

We began with the assumption that WMG and the system responsible for memory span were broadly equivalent. This suggested that a digit sequence approaching span length should have devastating effects on performance since it would leave virtually no spare capacity for perform-ing the primary task. We began with sequences of one or two digits, and were surprised to discover virtually no effect of this concurrent load on primary cognitive task performance. We found that in order to observe clear and reliable effects, we needed to use sequences of about six digits, and typically have used this length for most, though not all of our studies. The exception to this is two studies in which length of digit sequence was systematically manipulated, and a number of experiments in which a card-sorting task was used rather than digits as an alternative means of loading the hypothetical WMG system. These variants will be described in more detail subsequently.

Our initial experiments used a preload technique whereby subjects were presented with a sequence of digits which they were instructed to retain. This was followed by the primary learning or reasoning task which the subject performed before attempting to recall the digit preload. This proved unsatisfactory however, since the subjects typically opted for a time-sharing strategy whereby they would first concentrate on rehearsing the digits rapidly, would then perform the primary task, and subsequently attempt to recall the digits, often unsuccessfully. The result was a constant increment in the time to perform the primary task that was independent of the difficulty of that task, and appeared to represent the amount of time the subject devoted to digit rehearsal before beginning the task. Furthermore, performance on the digit span task tended to be drastically poorer than under conditions when no primary task was required. We had, therefore, no reason to assume that the subject was at anytime performing the two tasks simultaneously, and since this was one of our criteria for WMG, the technique was clearly unsatisfactory (Baddeley and Hitch 1974). Fortunately, however, we were able to remedy this problem by the simple expedient of requiring the subject to continue to repeat the digit sequences out loud. Performance on the digit task improved to something approximating control memory perform-ance, while the effect of the digit load on performance changed from being constant regardless of item difficulty to an interaction, with diffi-culty reasoning problems being slowed down more than simple ones (Baddeley and Hitch 1974).

It is important to note, however, that requiring the subject to vocalize the digits continuously introduces another factor, the influence of con-current articulation. As we shall see later, there is abundant evidence to suggest that merely requiring a subject to utter a redundant sound such as the word 'the' will influence his performance on a range of tasks, even though the memory demands of such suppression are minimal. For that reason, we typically include a second control condition under which the subject suppresses articulation by uttering either a single word, or by counting repeatedly from one to six, both tasks that combine continuous articulation with a minmal memory load.

Does it matter what suppression task is used? Fortunately, this does not appear to be a major problem; in one of our studies, we compared the effect of requiring the subject to utter a single word, 'the', with that of requiring him to count repeatedly from one to six, a task which we argued would be likely to involve a substantially wider range of phonemes, and which hence might be expected to have a more dramatic effect on performance. We found no reliable difference, and have subsequently used whichever appears most appropriate. Hence, if we are comparing a digit load with suppression, we typically use counting, involving broadly equivalent phoneme generation in the two tasks.

In attempting to study the effect of articulatory suppression itself, however, we have occasionally contrasted it with other tasks. For example, it can be argued that the effects of articulatory suppression stem less from its articulatory nature than from the attentional demands of performing a rapid concurrent task, albeit a repetitive one. In order to explore this possibility, we have on occasion compared the effect of suppression of articulation with that of tapping with a finger at a comparable rate. In this case, since we used the movement of a single digit, it seemed most appropriate to suppress articulation by means of a single utterance. This incidentally appears to be the commonest procedure in the literature, with different investigators favouring different words ranging from 'the' (Murray 1968) and 'Blah' (Besner, Davies, and Daniels 1981) through a cheery 'hiyah'! (Levy 1971), to 'double-double' with its sinister implications of toil and trouble (Heim, personal communication) and 'Colacola' with its intriguing hint of possible commercial sponsorship (Slowiaczek and Clifton 1980). Fortunately, while it would be unwise to conclude that the nature of the utterance used in suppression is of no importance, it does not seem to be a major variable as evidenced either by our own limited direct comparison, or by the general comparability of results between laboratories.

A somewhat neglected factor that is probably of some importance is the rate at which the subject is required to articulate. We ourselves have tended to opt in a somewhat *ad hoc* manner for a rate at which a subject might be expected to rehearse, namely somewhere in the region of three or four items per second (Landauer 1962). As will be seen from the results of subsequent experiments, this is sufficient to produce clear effects of suppression on certain tasks, typically those involving phonological coding, while having little or no effect on the subject's general information processing as measured by his reasoning or semantic memory performance. However, as Besner, Davies, and Daniels (1981) have shown, concurrent articulation may have a more general effect when the subject is encouraged to articulate as fast as possible. It seems plausible to assume that when a subject is attempting to perform any task to the limits of his ability, there is likely to be a general attentional cost, if only from the task of monitoring performance, and correcting the errors that tend to occur when any task is performed at the limit. I would suggest that where the purpose of using articulatory suppression is to disrupt speech coding, it is advisable to use a rate that is sufficiently rapid to discourage the subject from inserting covert rehearsals of the primary material, but is not so demanding as to produce effects that extend beyond the articulatory system. We now typically opt for a rate of three to four items per second, using a metronome to practice the subject at this rate, but removing the metronome during the actual test, and relying on the experimenter to monitor the rate of articulation informally, prompting the subject if suppression becomes too slow or irregular.

One further problem should be discussed in relation to the concurrent memory load technique. We began with the procedure of presenting a single sequence of digits which the subject was required to continue to rehearse out loud while performing the primary task. So long as the primary task was relatively short, such as that involved in verifying a single sentence, this procedure was fairly satisfactory. A problem arose, however, when the primary task was more extended, as for example occurred when we were studying the free recall of a sequence of 16 words, which when presented at a two-second rate would mean that the subject was continuing to rehearse the same digit sequence for over 30 seconds. The evidence suggested that under these conditions, the repetition of the digit sequence became progressively more automated so that its demand on the subject decreased throughout the list, producing a much smaller effect on later than on early items.

Where the primary task was likely to take more than a few seconds, therefore, we modified the digit load task as follows. The subject was presented with a sequence of up to six digits at a rate of either one or two per second, and required to repeat them back immediately at the same rate, whereupon a fresh sequence of digits would be presented, recalled in turn and so on. In the control condition, subjects simply responded to each digit as they heard it, and performed no task during the recall interval. The position is therefore, one in which all conditions, required the subjects to hear and write down the same number of digits, but differed in the number of digits that had to be remembered before being written. The concurrent task would typically be started at a variable time in advance of the primary task; this avoided the problem that the start of the primary task would otherwise always coincide with the input stage of the secondary task and so forth. It should finally be noted that the concurrent digit task can, of course, be presented either auditorily or visually, and that either written or spoken responses can be used, as appropriate.

The attentional trade-off problem

We began this series of experiments over 10 years ago. In the intervening period there have of course been developments of both a conceptual and technical kind that should be considered before going on to discuss the experiments and their implications. The approach we took was of course a very simple one. We argued that if learning and/or retrieval were limited by the amount of available attentional capacity, then requiring a subject to perform a second attention-demanding task during learning or retrieval should cause performance impairment. Furthermore, we argued that the greater the extent to which a process was limited by available attention, the more susceptible it should be to disruption by an attention-demanding task. By coupling an attention-demanding secondary task with either learning or retrieval, we thus hoped to reveal the extent to which these two components of human memory were limited by the amount of attention available.

Three conceptual developments have subsequently occurred that bear on this approach. One of these is the distinction drawn by Norman and Bobrow (1975) between processes that are resource-limited and those that are data-limited. This development is consistent with the approach taken in the recent studies which are concerned with the question of whether learning and retrieval are resource-limited.

More problematic is the growing awareness of the importance of trade-off functions both *within* tasks (as for example in the case of speed–error trade-offs, e.g. Wickelgren 1977), or in dual task conditions *between* the performance of the two tasks (Navon and Gopher 1980). Current wisdom within this area would appear to advocate strongly that each of our experiments should attempt to plot performance operating characteristic (POC) curves for the influence of our various secondary tasks on the relevant components of memory. Although the initial reason for our not attempting such an approach was historical, I shall argue that such a research strategy is neither practicable nor necessary in the present case.

The experiments I describe later in this chapter are concerned with the role of WMG in verbal learning and retrieval. They typically study the effect of an attention-demanding secondary task such as concurrent digit span on the learning and/or recall of lists of words. Consider first of all the number of observations required to plot a POC curve. An accurate indication of list recall would probably require at least ten observations per point, while a satisfactory indication of the shape of the operating function would probably involve plotting at least five points along the curve. In a typical learning and retrieval study we would probably be interested in four different conditions (namely a concurrent load during learning only, during retrieval only, during both learning and retrieval, and during neither). This means that we should test each of our subjects on about 200 lists. Such a study not only places very heavy demands on the subjects, but also raises the further problem of whether or not their performance is likely to remain stable and their strategies unchanged over this marathon session of verbal learning. Even if subjects can successfully be encouraged to stick to a single strategy throughout, we know that learning-to-learn and interference effects will not remain constant, making it highly questionable whether the resulting data can legitimately be averaged to plot POC curves.

Implicit in the plotting of such curves is the assumption that the subject is behaving in a qualitatively similar way at each level of secondary task load. If the subjects are effectively performing a different task at different points, it is clearly not legitimate to interpret their performance on the assumption that the only difference is a differential trade-off of attention between two tasks.

We do have evidence from other studies that bears directly on this point. Hitch and Baddeley (1976) examined in detail the trade-off between performance on a memory span task and a concurrently performed reasoning task. We expected that for a given level of concurrent digit load, a subject could choose either to devote more attention to reasoning, hence making more memory errors, or the reverse. We therefore looked at the correlation for each subject between performance on reasoning and memory, predicting a negative correlation. Correlations in fact proved to be consistently positive: trials on which the subject made memory errors were typically associated with slower reasoning performance than those in which performance was perfect. It was as if the subject were capable of keeping both tasks running, provided everything went smoothly, but once she began to make errors on the memory task, then she appeared to need to switch attention away from the reasoning task, hence slowing it down. The process of error correction appears to be extremely attention-demanding, with the extent of that demand not being measurable in any simple way. Consequently, attempting to induce subjects to vary their rate of errors on the secondary sorting or digit span tasks seemed likely to introduce major difficulties in interpreting our results.

The technique we typically adopted avoids this problem by studying performance at two levels of attentional load, both of which are sufficiently low to avoid errors on all but a very small percentage of trials. This essentially gives two points on the hypothetical performance operating curve, both taken from an area over which observable differences in performance on the secondary task are minimal.

The fact that we were unable to observe performance on the secondary task in detail clearly creates a number of potential problems. The first of these concerns the question of whether the two levels of difficulty are sufficient to produce differential effects on performance. Fortunately, however, since we consistently obtain substantial effects on at least one of our conditions, we can rule out this possibility.

A second problem arises with the possible objection that subjects do not invest the same amount of attention in the secondary task across all conditions. By requiring virtually perfect performance, we are insisting on a minimal investment of attention, but it is possible that under some circumstances considerably more than this minimum is devoted to the task by our subjects.

Let us first consider the probable effect of the difficulty of the primary task. The most plausible assumption here is that as the primary task becomes more difficult, so the amount of attention given to the secondary task will be reduced. The effect of this will be to underestimate the difference in relative difficulty among primary task conditions since the attentional capacity taken from the secondary task will be used to help performance on the more difficult memory task. The effect of this will be conservative in that it will minimize differences; if we do observe differences between conditions, then they are likely to be underestimates rather than overestimates of the 'real' magnitude of the difference. Such differences would be exaggerated only if there were an *inverse* relationship between the attentional demands of the primary task, and the amount of attention the subject chose to bestow on that task, with subjects withdrawing more attention from the secondary task when the primary task is easier. This would seem to be a highly implausible strategy.

The reasons for our choosing a simple secondary task technique are historical — more complex POC measures had not been developed when we began our programme of research. However, given the major practical and theoretical problems raised by any attempt at rigorously plotting POC curves for our complex tasks, and the absence of any clear evidence so far that such techniques are likely to lead to new theoretical insights, I would argue that the approach we selected remains the most appropriate.

Learning and WMG

Free recall learning

We carried out a range of studies in which subjects were required to learn verbal material presented in one modality while at the same time being required to retain sequences of three or six digits presented using an alternative modality. One such experiment involved presenting subjects with lists of 16 unrelated words at a rate of one word every two seconds for immediate free recall (Baddeley and Hitch 1974). Subjects were given a concurrent load of either six digits, three digits, or performed a control condition under which they merely copied alternating sequences of three and six digits. As in the procedure just described, the digits were continually changed so as to maintain a relatively constant load throughout presentation of the word list. On half the trials, the sixteenth word was followed by a recall signal, whereupon the subject was required to abandon the secondary digit task and attempt to write down as many of the words as possible in any order. On the other half of the trials, the sixteenth word was followed by a sequence of 30 letters at a rate of one per second. The subject was required to copy these down, after which he was given a recall signal. By comparing immediate and delayed recall, it was possible to obtain a quantitative estimate of the magnitude of the short-term recency effect (Baddeley 1970*b*; Glanzer 1972).

What should we expect from such a study? The WMG hypothesis would predict that as the concurrent digit load increased, the amount learned should decrease. Over and above this, the modal model would predict first that the magnitude of the effect should be substantial, since a load of six digits approached the memory span for our subjects, and by implication should be sufficient to occupy most of the available STS capacity. Secondly, the modal model would predict that the recency effect would be virtually wiped out by a six digit concurrent load. This follows from the assumption that both the recency effect and the digit span task depend on the same limited capacity store.

Figure 3.1 shows the results of this study. The effect of a three digit load was to cause a small and marginally significant decrement overall in performance; a six digit load produced a clear and significant decrement in performance, but one which was by no means catastrophic in magnitude. It will be clear from Fig. 3.1 that the recency effect was not at all influenced by the concurrent load, a conclusion supported by a quantitative estimate of the short-term component. Such a result is strongly at variance with the predictions of the modal model, which would predict almost total obliteration of the recency effect by the six digit concurrent load. One possible way in which the modal model could, however, cope with these results is to argue that the recency effect in this case represents an auditory modality effect, based on a sensory store rather than the output of the modality-free STS.

There is, of course, clear evidence that STM for material presented in the auditory mode is considerably more durable and resistant to interference from other modalities than is visually presented material (Broadbent, Vines, and Broadbent 1978). We therefore repeated our experiment but reversed the assignment of tasks to modalities, presenting the words visually and the digits auditorily (Baddeley and Hitch 1977). On this occasion, we obtained no significant effect of three digits, but again observed a healthy decrement when subjects were required to maintain a concurrent load of six digits. The crucial issue, however, is the fate of the recency effect. We again observed a very healthy recency effect despite the requirement to maintain a sequence of six concurrent digits. There was, however, a subtle difference between the two recency effects. In our first study, the probability of recalling the last few items was virtually identical regardless of concurrent load whereas in our

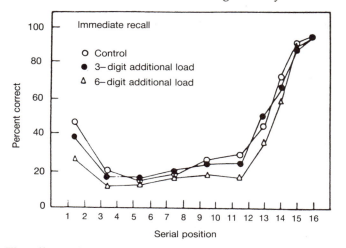

Fig. 3.1. The effects of a concurrent digit load on the immediate and delayed recall of auditorily presented word lists (Baddeley and Hitch 1974).

second study, the load condition ran parallel with, but consistently below the control condition throughout the curve.

This latter result is what one might expect on the assumption of two separate and independent components, a long-term or secondary memory component that operates throughout the curve, together with a recency effect which influences only the last few items. The results of the first experiment are not open to this interpretation, since the last few items are recalled no better under control than under load conditions. This suggests that subjects may have been using a different strategy with auditory presentation, and relying exclusively on some form of auditory memory for the immediate retention of the last few items. As mentioned earlier, there is indeed good evidence to suggest that auditory presentation does give rise to a particularly durable memory trace which resists disruption by visual material, whereas material that is presented visually appears to be readily disrupted by subsequent auditory material (Broadbent, Vines, and Broadbent 1978). In general, however, despite the minor complication of a modality effect, our results are very clear in showing an effect of a concurrent digit load on the LTM component of the serial position curve, hence providing general support for the WMG hypothesis. At the same time, however, our results raise problems for the modal model both because the magnitude of the overall effect is less than would be expected, and because the concurrent load does not appear to interfere with the recency effect, regarded as one of the central indicators of the short-term component of the modal model.

Further experiments showed comparable effects of concurrent load on learning across a range of other tasks, including paired-associate learning (Baddeley, Eldridge, Lewis, and Thomson 1984) and the retention of prose (Baddeley and Hitch 1974).

An equivalent decrement in amount learned can also be produced using card sorting rather than immediate memory as a concurrent task. Murdock (1965) required his subjects to sort playing cards while attempting to memorize lists of unrelated words. He varied the load imposed by the sorting task by manipulating the number of categories into which the cards had to be sorted. The greater the number of sorting alternatives, the heavier the concurrent load and the poorer the subsequent free recall performance. In a replication and extension of this study, Baddeley, Scott, Drynan, and Smith (1969) showed that concurrent load did not affect the recency component, a result exactly analogous to that observed with concurrent digit span. Finally, a number of experimenters have shown that concurrent tracking or reaction time tasks may impair long-term memory performance as tested both by free recall and paired-associate learning (e.g. Martin 1970). It appears then that as the WMG hypothesis would predict, learning is impaired by a concurrent load, this effect being characteristic of a wide range of learning procedures and secondary tasks.

Working memory and retrieval

Our initial studies concentrated on learning, and only subsequently did we attempt to explore the role of WMG in retrieval. We began this exploration reasonably confident that we would obtain clear and reliable effects of a concurrent load. It seemed plausible to assume that a process as subtle and fallible as retrieval would be readily susceptible to disruption, a view that is consistent with a number of versions of the modal model which assumes that one of the functions of STS is to hold retrieval plans and strategies (Atkinson and Shiffrin 1968; Rumelhart, Lindsay, and Norman 1972).

Direct evidence for such a view came from a range of studies which attempted to measure the additional demand of learning and retrieval by means of secondary tracking or reaction time tasks. Subjects might for example, be required to learn and recall word sequences at the same time as monitoring a light and responding as rapidly as possible when the light came on (Martin 1970). In another series of studies subjects performed a tracking task in which they were required to keep a spot of light on a target while listening to and recalling words (Trumbo and Milone 1971). The results of these, and a range of other studies by Martin, Trumbo, and their colleagues were consistent in suggesting that both learning and retrieval are attention-demanding, with retrieval apparently demanding more attention than learning.

However, these studies used a somewhat different procedure from our own in that they measured performance on the secondary rather than the primary task, and used latency rather than accuracy measures. This raises the possibility that their results might be influenced by an artifact. There is considerable evidence to suggest that subjects are virtually incapable of emitting two unrelated responses at the same time; if two responses are required, then the second is almost invariably delayed, the phenomenon of refractoriness (Welford 1967). Since recall involves emitting responses, and since subjects were instructed that the memory task was of principal importance, it is conceivable that the secondary task effects previously observed are largely those of refractoriness. There is no reason to assume any refractoriness problem during learning, since the subject is not required to make overt responses. This could well explain why smaller effects on latency were observed during the acquisition than during the retrieval stage. We, therefore, decided to explore the matter further.

Free recall and card sorting

Our first experiment used free recall as the primary task and card sorting as a secondary task, studying the influence of concurrent sorting during both retrieval and learning. We used two card sorting conditions, a load condition in which subjects had to sort playing cards into the four suits with each response requiring a decision, and a control condition in which the subject was handed the cards face down and merely required to deal them sequentially into four locations; a task involving an action sequence and minimal decision. Subjects sorted or dealt at a paced rate of one card every two seconds, a rate at which subjects were able to perform both tasks perfectly. We hoped that the dealing control would minimize bias due to refractoriness since subjects were required to emit the same number of responses in both conditions, the difference being the presence or absence of a sorting decision.

The results obtained are shown in Table 3.1. They were clear but unexpected. While we obtained the usual substantial effect of concurrent

TABLE 3.1

Mean percentage of words recalled as a function of secondary task load during free recall learning and retrieval (Baddeley, Eldridge, Lewis and Thomson 1984).

		Load during retrieval		
		Low	High	Mean
Load during learning	Low	41.3	37.9	39.6
	High	27.0	30.6	28.8
	Mean	34.2	34.3	—

load on learning, we found no effect of sorting on recall. Since this result was inconsistent with both the modal model, and with the results of Martin, Trumbo, and their colleagues, we felt a clear need to replicate this study before drawing any firm conclusions. We therefore carried out a further study in which we manipulated an additional variable, the nature of the lists to be recalled.

The modal model suggests that one of the functions of STS is to hold retrieval plans. It seemed possible that our lists of unrelated words simply offered too little scope for the formation of such plans, whereas this would surely not be the case with lists made up of groups of words from different semantic categories. We therefore compared performance on random lists with lists of 20 categorized words comprising four items from each of five taxonomic categories—for example four animals, four vehicles, four precious stones, four flowers, and four diseases. Our results which are shown in Table 3.2 were again fairly straightforward. Subjects were indeed able to take substantial advantage of categorization with or without concurrent load. They showed the usual clear effect of sorting load during input, but little effect of output load on either random or categorized lists.

At this point, we began to be somewhat concerned about the discrepancy between our results and those of Martin and of Trumbo. It occurred to us that our comparison between learning and retrieval might be an unfair one since learning occurs under paced conditions, where the rate of presentation is set by the experimenter, whereas recall is unpaced, with the subject free to emit his responses as and when he wishes. There is evidence that unpaced performance can give rise to higher levels of information processing than paced (Conrad 1960*b*) and it therefore seemed desirable to carry out further comparisons in which both input and retrieval were paced, or were both unpaced.

Pacing of learning and recall

We therefore carried out two further studies. The first of these removed the pacing element from free recall learning by simply displaying all the words to be learned on a single card that was exposed for 60 seconds. This should allow subjects to distribute their learning time as they wished. Presentation was followed by a filled interval in order to remove the recency component, followed by a further 60 seconds for free recall. In this study, we reverted to using the concurrent digit load task, with letter copying as the intervening task used to eliminate recency. Results were clear, once again showing a highly significant effect of concurrent load during input, but no effect during recall. Such a result implies that our input effect is not due to pacing; it does not, of course, rule out the possibility that pacing will produce an output effect. This was tested in the next experiment.

TABLE 3.2

Mean percentage of words recalled on random and categorized word lists in Experiment II as a function of secondary task sorting load and memory stage (Baddeley, Eldridge, Lewis, and Thomson 1984).

Random lists

		Load during retrieval		
		Low	High	Mean
Load during learning	Low	20.2	17.3	18.8
	High	15.4	13.3	14.4
	Mean	17.8	15.3	—

Categorized lists

		Load during retrieval		
		Low	High	Mean
Load during learning	Low	41.5	37.6	39.6
	High	32.5	30.1	31.3
	Mean	37.0	33.9	—

As its name suggests, free recall is a technique in which the subject is unconstrained and can respond at will. In order to introduce a comparable degree of pacing during learning and retrieval, we shifted to a paired-associate procedure in which the subject was presented with five pairs of words which were tested immediately afterwards by presenting the first word of each pair and requiring the subject to recall the second. In order to ensure a reasonably high recall rate, we used compatible adjective–noun pairs such as *sharp–sword* and *evening–star*. Presentation and test both occurred at a rate of 4 seconds per pair, and subjects performed the concurrent digit span task which involved either hearing and recalling successive sequences of six digits, or merely copying them. Subjects had either the load or the control condition during input, recall, both, or neither on different trials.

The results showed our usual significant effect of concurrent load on learning. There was no significant effect of load on recall, but there was a significant interaction indicating that subjects who learned under control conditions recalled better under control conditions than under concurrent load. This at least suggested some trace of a retrieval effect. We interpreted it as suggesting that subjects who are unencumbered by the digit load during learning were more likely to come up with relatively complex links between stimulus and response; links that cannot be used quite so effectively at retrieval when carrying a concurrent digit load.

In general however, despite some rather unconvincing traces of concurrent load on retrieval, our results overwhelmingly suggest that learning is much more susceptible to the effect of a concurrent task than is recall, a result that is diametrically opposite to those obtained by Martin, Trumbo, and their colleagues. Both their and our results appear to be highly consistent across the range of both learning and concurrent tasks. How should we explain this discrepancy?

There are two major procedural differences between our technique and that used by Martin *et al.* First, Martin and his colleagues used performance on the secondary task as their measure, whereas we studied performance on the primary task, while adding a secondary task which we set at a level that allows the subject to perform it virtually perfectly. Secondly, whereas we consistently used an accuracy measure, they consistently used latency. A suggestion that latency might be giving a different result from accuracy came from a further study in which we measured the influence of concurrent card sorting on free recall, but at the same time measured the regularity of the sorting response. We found that although the sorting or dealing task was paced, inter-response times did in fact fluctuate, with the more demanding concurrent task of sorting leading to a more variable inter-response interval than the easier task of merely dealing the cards face downwards. Furthermore, when we studied the effect of the memory task on sorting regularity, we observed that sorting was slightly but significantly less regular during retrieval than during learning (Baddeley, Eldridge, Lewis, and Thomson 1984). When performance was measured in terms of amount recalled however, we obtained our usual results; an effect of concurrent load at input, but not at retrieval. We had in one study, therefore, produced evidence supporting both our own previous results using an accuracy measure and results analogous to those of Martin with a timing measure. Since we had not instructed the subjects to regard the sorting response as any less important than we had in previous studies, this seemed to point to the difference between latency and accuracy as being crucial, rather than instructions regarding division of attention.

Concurrent load and retrieval latency

We explored the difference between accuracy and latency measures of performance in a final experiment where we moved from recall to recognition. If the accuracy–latency distinction is crucial, we would expect to obtain our usual results on accuracy, namely no effect of concurrent load, while at the same time reproducing Martin's observation of a clear effect of load on retrieval when a latency measure is used. Subjects were therefore presented with a learning list of 32 words. The subsequent recognition test required them to make a 'yes' or 'no' response to each of a sequence of 48 words comprising the 16 'old' words and 32 'new' ones. Subjects were given no secondary task during learning, but performed the recognition task under each of three conditions, one involving a concurrent load of six digits, a second involving articulatory suppression but no memory load, while the third comprised a control condition under which they were free of any supplementary task. All subjects learned three lists of words and were tested on one list in each of the three conditions. The results obtained are shown in Table 3.3.

Once again we obtained no effect of concurrent load on accuracy. There was, however, an interaction between concurrent load and response bias. Subjects appeared to be more prepared to press the 'yes'

TABLE 3.3
Mean percentage correct detections, false alarms, d's, and response latencies as a function of secondary task load during recognition (Baddeley, Eldridge, Lewis, and Thomson 1984)

	Control	Articulatory suppression	Memory load
Correct detections (%)	88.5	87.5	92.4
False alarms (%)	7.4	8.2	12.5
d′	2.94	3.07	3.10
'Yes' latency (sec)	1.04	1.12	1.14
'No' latency (sec)	1.11	1.23	1.54

key with a concurrent digit load than under suppression or control conditions. As Table 3.3 shows, however, there is no difference in memory performance as measured by d′ scores across the three conditions, suggesting no basic effect on retrieval efficiency. The occurrence of a significant interaction between load and response bias is useful in showing that our lack of a main effect is not due to insensitivity of the study due to ceiling effects; if this were the case, we would not expect to be able to detect such an interaction.

Moving on to the latency measure, as Table 3.3 shows, we do have a clear effect of concurrent task on time to respond; latency is slightly but significantly increased by articulatory suppression, and is very clearly increased by a six digit concurrent load. It appears then that a secondary task will influence the latency to retrieve an item, but does not appear to influence accuracy. Such a result is consistent with a separation of retrieval into two components, one involving access to a relevant response, and the other involving the emission of that response. Our results suggest that the process of accessing a response may be relatively automatic, but emitting that response does depend on some limited capacity system resembling a WMG.

Use of the concurrent technique in connection with retrieval produced some very unexpected results, suggesting that the probability of retrieving an item from long-term episodic memory is not impaired to any substantial extent by a concurrent secondary task. This point is clearly shown in Table 3.4 which reports the percentage of variance accounted for by imposing a concurrent attentional load during learning and during retrieval. While the attentional demands of learning are clear and substantial, accounting for a mean of 28 per cent of the variance, the

TABLE 3.4

Percentage of variance accounted for by an attentional load during learning and during retrieval for Experiments 1 to 5 (Baddeley, Eldridge, Lewis, and Thomson 1984)

Experiment	Task	Locus of supplementary load	
		Learning	Retrieval
1	Free recall	42.8***	0.0
2	Free recall (random)	27.0***	9.0**
2	Free recall (categorized)	25.2***	3.4
3	Free recall	35.8***	8.9*
4	Paired associates	24.2**	3.4
5	Free recall	14.4***	1.8
Mean		28.2	4.4

$*p < 0.05; **p < 0.01; ***p < 0.001.$

effects of an attentional load on retrieval accuracy are small (4.4 per cent) and unreliable. While the effect of a supplementary task on learning is totally expected, the absence of an effect at retrieval might seem both implausible and inconsistent with prior data. There is, however, little or no good evidence to suggest that the actual process of accessing a memory trace does demand attention or the operation of WMG. Indeed, if one were designing a cognitive system, there is a great deal to be said for allowing its retrieval operations to go ahead without placing major demands on the central processing system, which can then be left free to concern itself with monitoring the present situation and planning for the future.

Consider the simple task of carrying on a conversation. It is clearly advantageous to have a language generation system which will come up with the appropriate words when required without the need for attention-demanding lexical search. This is not always possible, as for example in the case of an aphasic patient, where accessing the right word at the right time is a major problem, and where fluent conversation ceases to be possible. It is certainly the case that we do 'rack our brains' in trying to remember for example a name, suggesting that we *believe* at least that increasing the amount of attention given to retrieval will pay dividends. It is, however, notable that such 'racking of brains' is often quite unsuccessful, with the name in question popping up apparently spontaneously at some later time, strongly suggesting that the retrieval process is going on unattended.

Do our results then mean that deliberate attempts to retrieve an item are simply a waste of time? That would almost certainly be going too far. As has been suggested elsewhere (e.g. Baddeley 1982*b*; Nickerson 1980), retrieval probably involves two separate processes, one appears to involve automatic access to the relevant memory trace given the appropriate stimulus cues, the phenomenon studied extensively by Tulving and his colleagues in connection with the encoding specificity hypothesis (Tulving 1983). The other, which among other things has been termed recollection (Baddeley 1982*b*), involves the active setting up of potentially fruitful retrieval cues and the evaluation of the results of such cues. Conscious retrieval strategies do seem to occur, for example trying to remember a person's name by going through the alphabet or using a spouse's name as a cue. Rationally checking the plausibility of what has been retrieved, using other associated evidence is another instance of the process of recollection, a process which it seems likely will make attentional demands and hence is likely to be interfered with by concurrent mental activity. However, this remains merely a speculation, in contrast, to the substantial evidence we have accumulated on the comparative invulnerability to a concurrent load of retrieval in standard laboratory tasks, when measured in terms of recall probability.

We have so far been concerned with accuracy as a measure of performance. When latency measures are used, however, it is clear that retrieval performance *is* influenced by concurrent load. Similarly, when performance on a secondary tracking or reaction time task is used as the measure, the results of Martin, Trumbo, and their colleagues again suggest an effect of concurrent retrieval on performance. Indeed, their results suggest that retrieval has a more dramatic effect than learning. How can we explain this apparent discrepancy?

Suppose we begin by considering the role of time in both learning and retrieval. In learning, there is abundant evidence for what Cooper and Pantle (1967) have termed the *total time hypothesis*. This simply states that the amount learned is a direct function of the amount of time spent learning; if learning time is doubled, the amount learned is doubled. It seems plausible to assume that the crucial factor here is not time *per se* but amount of processing. Presenting material at a slower rate will only be advantageous if the extra time is actually used for learning; if, as in the case of patients suffering from dementia, subjects merely read each word and then wait passively for the next, increasing the presentation time does not increase amount learned (Miller 1975). Most subjects in learning experiments however do use the available time productively; hence the total time hypothesis. By analogy, a secondary task that diverts the subject's attention from learning will tend to impair performance, with the degree of impairment increasing as the degree of diversion increases, exactly the result obtained by Murdock (1965) and by our own studies of the effect of concurrent tasks on learning.

There is, however, no evidence to suggest that retrieval is tied to temporal factors in this way. In a typical free recall task, the subject produces an initial flurry of responses which gradually tapers off, leaving most of the recall period devoid of activity. Doubling the recall period would be unlikely to produce more than one or two additional items. Consequently, time during retrieval is much less precious than time during learning, and using some of this for performing the secondary task is unlikely to be very costly in terms of correct recalls.

Taken at face value this might suggest that subjects under concurrent load conditions would produce as many items but do so in perhaps twice the time. Detailed recording of our subjects' response patterns suggests however, that this is not the case. The overall rate of production of responses is broadly comparable in control and concurrent load conditions. What does seem to be disturbed is the microstructure of retrieval. Our study involving episodic recognition memory and two semantic memory studies that will be described in the next chapter both indicate that subjects take longer to retrieve responses when carrying a concurrent load. It is as if a bottleneck occurs between accessing a response and emitting it, the phenomenon usually referred to a refractoriness

(Welford 1967). Since the slowing effect of a concurrent digit load is greater than that of articulatory suppression, despite the fact that both involve the same number of responses, it seems likely that the process of response selection is crucial here rather than merely that of response execution. Selecting a novel sequence of random numbers in the digit span task is presumably more demanding than running off the highly overlearned counting sequence. The reason why the secondary task studies of Martin *et al.* appear to show more marked retrieval than learning effects presumably reflects the fact that during the learning stage, subjects are not required to make responses, hence avoiding the problem of refractoriness.

   Finally, it is perhaps worth noting at this point the danger of relying excessively on one type of measure of attentional-demand, be it latency to perform a secondary task or its influence on the accuracy of the primary task. In the present instance they provide opposite results, and it is only by considering both that we are likely to get a balanced picture.

4 Working memory and comprehension

It is frequently asserted that the comprehension of both written and spoken language depends on some form of working memory (e.g. Atkinson and Shiffrin 1968; Kintsch and Van Dijk 1978). In particular, the model of comprehension developed by Kintsch and Van Dijk (1978) assigns an important role to a temporary store of limited capacity. Kintsch and Vipond (1979) point out that changing the assumed capacity of this store within their model has important implications for the predicted comprehensibility of different samples of prose. They compare the speeches made by two presidential candidates, Eisenhower and Stevenson during the 1950s campaign in which Stevenson appeared to make by far the better speeches, but Eisenhower won the votes. They show that although the speeches do not differ markedly on such standard readability measures as word frequency and mean word length, their model predicts that adequate comprehension of Stevenson's speeches demanded a short-term store of greater capacity than was the case with Eisenhower. As such many voters might have failed to understand Stevenson.

However, elegant though the work of Kintsch and his colleagues is in demonstrating that some form of WMG is a useful conceptual tool, it does not provide direct empirical evidence for the importance of such temporary storage. As such, this work is complementary to our own more pragmatic approach.

Prose comprehension and WMG

We began by carrying out two studies in which subjects were required to listen to passages of prose while at the same time maintaining sequences of zero, three, or six digits (Baddeley and Hitch 1974). The first study used passages of text, some involving narrative others description and others argumentation. In the memory load conditions, subjects were presented with six spoken digits before each sentence and required to recall them after hearing the sentence. In the control condition, each sentence was followed by six digits which the subjects were required to recall immediately, after which the next sentence was presented. Hence, total amount of recall was equated, but in one condition subjects were required to remember the digits at the same time as they were listening to the prose, while in the control condition they were able to switch between the two tasks, devoting attention in turn to comprehension and digit retention. Comprehension was then tested using the Cloze procedure (Taylor 1953), in which the original text was typed out with every fifth word deleted. The subject's task was to attempt to fill in the blanks, the underlying assumption being that the deeper his understanding of the text, the better would be his subsequent ability to perform the Cloze test. Our subjects correctly completed a mean of 51.9 per cent of the items under control conditions, and 45.4 per cent under a six digit load, a difference that was statistically significant.

Although this result was encouraging, it was subject to a number of difficulties. In particular, performance on the digit recall task was relatively poor, a mean of 56.2 per cent correct sequences in the six digit condition compared to a mean recall of 82.4 per cent under control conditions. While this is not perhaps surprising in view of the difference in delay between the two conditions, it did nonetheless suggest that subjects might have been diverting their attention from the digit preload to the comprehension task, thereby producing an underestimation of the concurrent load effect. A second and perhaps more significant objection is that in both control and load conditions, the text was split up into sentences with a major disruption of processing between each sentence. Since the essence of prose is that the meaning extends across successive sentences, this is clearly undesirable. Recent experiments by Glanzer and his colleagues has shown that interpolating a rehearsal-preventing task between the sentences of a passage does indeed impair comprehension, as measured by reading speed (Glanzer, Dorfman, and Kaplan 1981).

The next experiment, therefore, moved from the preload technique to a concurrent load procedure in which subjects were presented visually with sequences of three or six digits while listening to a prose passage. In the load condition they recalled and wrote down each sequence before being presented with the next random digit sequence and so on. The control condition merely involved copying the random digits as they were presented. In this experiment we used questions to assess comprehension rather than the Cloze test. The texts used were taken from the 12- and 13-year old level of the Neale Analysis of Reading Ability. Mean number of questions answered correctly fell from 73 per cent under control conditions to 70 per cent with a load of three digits and 60 per cent with a six digit load. Statistical analysis indicated that comprehension was not significantly impaired by a concurrent load of three digits, but was reliably impaired by a six digit load (Baddeley and Hitch 1974).

So far, our comprehension results resemble those obtained in our studies of working memory and learning, suggesting a clear decrement in performance when the subject is holding a six digit memory load, but little or no decrement when the load is reduced to three digits. Our comprehension results are, however, open to the objection that on both occasions our measure has relied on memory, so that we may merely have a further demonstration of the influence of concurrent load on learning. At this point, we therefore shifted to measures of comprehension based on verification latency rather than retention of information. This has the advantage that the material to be comprehended can be continuously present so that there is no necessary involvement of memory.

Semantic memory and WMG

Sentence verification

We went on to carry out a series of experiments using the technique devised by Collins and Quillan (1969) whereby the subject is presented with a brief sentence describing some commonly known aspect of the world. A typical sentence might be *Canaries have wings*, or some equivalent but obviously false statement such as *Canaries have gills*. The subject is required to decide on the truth of each sentence and press a 'true' or a 'false' key as rapidly as possible.

The task was initially devised to test a specific theory regarding the structural storage of knowledge in semantic memory. This assumed a hierarchy with general concepts such as *LIVING THINGS* being split into more specific concepts such as *ANIMAL* or *PLANT*, some of which themselves split into such subconcepts as *BIRDS, FISH, TREES*, and *FLOWERS*, which in turn led to particular instances such as *CANARY* or *ROSE*. It was suggested that features that apply to most examples of a category, for example that birds have wings, are stored with that category rather than with each individual instance. This was assumed to lead to economy in storage space, but to have a cost in retrieval time. Verifying that a canary has wings for example involves two steps, verifying that a canary is a bird and then verifying that birds have wings. In contrast, a statement about canaries that is peculiar to canaries, for example *Canaries are yellow*, was said to involve fewer steps and hence, to lead to faster responding.

Our experiments intended to explore the role of WMG in comprehension using a range of examples involving different numbers of hypothetical steps. Unfortunately, however, we, like others failed to replicate the original Collins and Quillan hierarchical effect (see Baddeley 1979; Baddeley and Lewis 1981; Conrad 1972). However, provided one merely treats the sentences as broadly equivalent, then speed and accuracy of verification can be used as a convenient general measure of the efficiency with which subjects can interrogate their knowledge of the world. We have found the test to be highly reliable, and sensitive to a range of stressors including alcohol (Baddeley 1981), high pressure (Logie and Baddeley 1983) and brain damage (Sunderland, Harris, and

Baddeley 1983). This test also appears to provide a plausible example of general semantic processing in so far as our as yet unpublished results indicate that it correlates highly with both the Mill Hill vocabulary test, and with verbal fluency as measured by performance on a task involving generating items from a given semantic category.

Although we have carried out a number of experiments using the Collins and Quillan technique (Baddeley 1979; Baddeley and Lewis 1981), for the present purpose a single experiment will suffice, a study in which the subjects attempted to verify visually presented sentences while holding a load ranging from zero to eight digits spoken at a rate of one per second. We used a mixed design whereby on any given trial, a subject did not know in advance how many digits she would be required to hold. Her task was to listen to the experimenter and repeat whatever sequence she heard, continuing to articulate the sequence until after she had completed the sentence verification response. The sentence was always presented after the subject had begun to repeat the spoken digits. Where no digits were to be repeated, the experimenter said the word 'nothing' whereupon the subject was instructed to remain silent.

Sentences were typed on index cards which were stacked behind a shutter. When the shutter opened a timer was started. The subject's task was to decide whether the sentence was true or false, and press a left or right key accordingly. As soon as she did so, the shutter dropped and the clock stopped, whereupon the experimenter recorded the time and replaced the card. A total of 14 female subjects were tested on a random mixture of 20 sentences at each level of concurrent load.

Performance on this task is shown in Fig. 4.1. Overall, latency increased with concurrent digit load. There is, however, a slight paradox in that the zero load condition is in fact slower than the condition involving the rehearsal of a single item. It is probable that this stems from the fact that the zero load condition was the only one in which the subject was not required to repeat what the experimenter said. Since the subject did not know in advance what condition to expect, and since this occurred on only one occasion in every nine, it seems likely that the need to obey this atypical instruction caused some slight slowing in sentence processing. The most appropriate baseline would, therefore, seem to be the one digit load condition which is equivalent to a condition of articulatory suppression. When this is used, we find that a digit load of even two items is marginally significantly slower than that of one, three items clearly slower and so forth, with each additional digit causing an increase in response latency (for further details see Baddeley, Eldridge, Lewis, and Thomson 1984).

The question arises as to whether increasing digit load produces a continuous or discontinuous function. This has obvious implications for the underlying theory of what produces the effect. It might, for example,

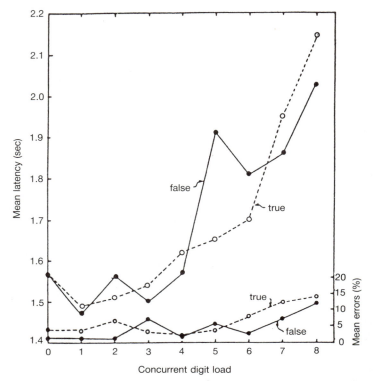

Fig. 4.1. The effects of a concurrent digit load on speed and accuracy of sentence verification (Baddeley, Eldridge, Lewis, and Thomson 1984).

be the case that no effect occurs until some relatively passive store is overloaded, at which point performance begins to deteriorate. The fact that we have obtained either a very small or no effect of two or three digits in earlier studies seemed to point in this direction. However, the more systematic data from this experiment do not support the view of a discontinuous function. It should, however, be borne in mind that such a discontinuity would only become apparent in group data if the assumed passive store had about the same capacity for all subjects. If different subjects had different capacities, then the discontinuity would appear at different points; averaging subjects might well produce what appeared to be a continuous curve. However, in the present study neither the individual nor the group curves show any obvious discontinuity. Individual curves themselves are, of course, based on averages, and as such should be interpreted with some caution. As far as they go, however, they give no apparent support to the discontinuity hypothesis.

This generalization is less obviously true in the case of error data, also shown on Fig. 4.1. Unlike latency, errors are not significantly impaired by the concurrent task until the load approaches six items, while loads of seven or eight items both have a highly reliable effect on error probability. It is, of course, possible that this merely reflects the lower sensitivity of the error measure, based as it is on relatively small numbers of erroneous responses. It does, however, resemble the result obtained from the previous comprehension tasks, both of which used a percentage correct measure, and from the previously described learning studies which again used accuracy rather than latency, and which typically show little or no effect of digit loads of less than six items.

This experiment showed that a concurrent task involving retaining sequences of digits consistently slows down the verification of simple sentences. Although subjects vary as to how steep the function is, the same characteristic effect is shown by all our subjects. These results certainly suggest that some aspect of comprehension is dependent on a limited capacity WMG, but give little evidence as to the more detailed nature of the interference. More specifically, the observed disruption might occur at the level of the processing and comprehension of the sentence, or of the retrieval of the appropriate response, or of the overt execution of that response, or indeed all of these processes might be impaired. We had initially hoped that the use of different types of sentence involving different degrees of the hierarchical processing suggested by Collins and Quillan (1969) would bear directly on this issue. However, since the expected inter-sentence differences did not materialize this was clearly not feasible. The next experiment therefore, selected two phenomena within the area of semantic memory that were known to be replicable, one of which seemed likely to reflect the process of accessing a given concept, while the other was based on the difficulty of the subsequent categorization decision.

Semantic categorization

One of the most commonly used tasks for studying semantic memory involves presenting the subject with a category, for example *animals*, and an instance, for example *horse*, and requiring him to decide whether the instance does or does not belong to that category. Using this procedure, Wilkins (1971) showed that the time to verify such a statement is a function of the instance frequency or saliency of the item within the category. If people are asked to produce as many items as possible from a given category such as *birds*, then items such as *robin* and *sparrow* which are in some sense more salient or typical birds are produced earlier and by more subjects than less typical items such as *ostrich, penguin,* or *chicken.* It seems plausible to assume that accessing such atypical items from the category is more demanding than accessing more salient instances. If this is so, and if the process of moving from category to instance uses some limited capacity WMG system, then one might expect a concurrent load to be particularly disruptive of performance on the more difficult low saliency items. If on the other hand, previously observed concurrent load effect impairs some other component process, such as category access or response selection, then there is no reason to assume an interaction between the effects on latency of instance saliency and of concurrent load.

The second phenomenon to be studied in the experiment concerns the nature of the negative instances. Schaeffer and Wallace (1969) showed that given a category such as *trees*, a negative item from a similar category e.g. *daffodil*, would take longer to reject than an item from a very different category e.g. *kettle*. This presumably reflects the increased difficulty of the decision; trees and flowers have much more in common than trees and kitchen utensils. If this decision process is dependent on a limited capacity WMG, then once again one might expect the difficult negative responses to be more impaired by a concurrent memory load than the easier negatives based on items from categories that are clearly different.

It is perhaps worth pointing out, however, that both this and the previous prediction are made purely on the basis of general plausibility. There is no logical necessity to assume that two operations that place demands on the same system will necessarily lead to an interaction between their effects, nor that the absence of such an interaction necessarily means that the two processes affect different aspects of the system (see Broadbent 1984 and McClelland 1979 for a discussion of this). However, as we shall see in the case of a subsequent reasoning task, interactions between linguistic variables and concurrent load are sometimes observed, and their presence or absence may provide an important cue to the underlying processes, albeit not a completely unequivocal one. However, this issue will be discussed in more detail later.

The task we used therefore, was as follows. The subject was first presented with a category name (e.g. *trees*), which was then followed by an instance (e.g. *pine*). In the case of positive instances, half were taken from the items generated most frequently by subjects in a category generation task (Battig and Montague 1969) and half were from those generated least frequently. In the case of the negative items, half came from categories that were similar to that presented, for example a bird category might be tested with an animal as a negative instance. The remaining half comprised negatives from categories that were clearly different, for example the category animal paired with a kitchen utensil. The procedure involved presenting a sequence of six random digits which the subject was required to continue to repeat until he had completed the category judgement task. This was compared with an articulatory suppression control condition in which the subject was required to count repeatedly from one to six. The primary comprehension task involved a series of index cards, on each of which was typed a category name and an instance. The card was placed behind a shutter which was raised as the subject began to articulate either the digit load or the counting task. This started a timer which was terminated when the subject pressed a 'yes' or 'no' key with her left or right hand respectively. The experimenter then noted the time, the subject's response and changed the card. A total of 18 female subjects were tested.

The results of the study are shown in Fig. 4.2, from which it is clear that there is an overall effect of concurrent load, as one would expect from the previous study. The two additional variables also had the expected effect, with low saliency items taking consistently longer to verify than high saliency, and similar negative instances taking longer to reject than dissimilar. However, although there is a general tendency for the concurrent load to slow down the negative responses somewhat more than the positive, neither the salience of positive items nor the similarity of negative items interacts significantly with concurrent load. We thus have no evidence that the limited capacity WMG system is particulatly involved in either the item access, or the decision components of the task.

The error scores for the various conditions were also analysed. There were significant effects on error rate of both saliency in the case of positive instances, and of similarity in the case of negatives, but no effect

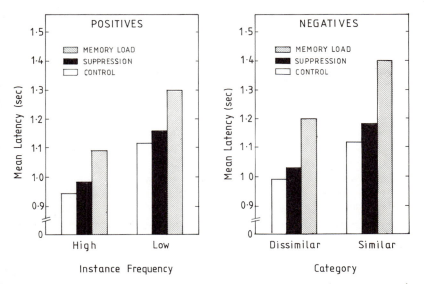

Fig. 4.2. The effects of memory load and articulatory suppression on categorization (Baddeley, Eldridge, Lewis, and Thomson 1984).

of concurrent load. Once again we find that when measured in terms of items correct, concurrent load has no effect on retrieval. When measured in terms of latency, an effect is observed, but this does not appear to interact with the difficulty of the retrieval task. Before going on to discuss this, however, one further study will be described.

Our data suggest unequivocally that a concurrent load will impair comprehension in some way. On the other hand, evidence on the retrieval component of comprehension, like that of the retrieval component in our learning studies suggests that a concurrent task may influence latency but not accuracy. It is as if the retrieval process itself proceeds independently of available WMG capacity, but that WMG is necessary for initiating the response.

It could however be argued that our comprehension data are irrelevant to this question since all the studies we have so far conducted have involved the subject in both processing the input and retrieving the response. It is conceivable that all the effects we have observed stem from the input process, with none of the comprehension effects based on retrieval *per se.* The next experiment explores this possibility by requiring subjects to generate items from specific semantic categories. Since the category name is given in advance, no input processing is involved in this task. Consequently, if the previously observed effect of concurrent load on semantic memory stems purely from input, we would expect no influence of a secondary task on generation performance. On the other hand, if item retrieval is dependent on some aspect of WMG, we would expect subjects to generate fewer items per unit time under concurrent load conditions.

Category generation

The procedure used in this experiment was relatively straightforward; subjects were required to write down as many instances as they could of a given category within a period of 2 minutes. Subjects performed this task either while hearing and repeating back sequences of six random digits, while hearing and repeating back the number sequence *1 2 3 4 5 6,* or in silence. In order to plot the rate of production of items over time, every 15 seconds the experimenter gave the signal 'mark', whereupon the subject drew a line under the last item he had written. Subjects generated items from categories under each condition in counterbalanced order (Baddeley, Eldridge, Lewis, and Thomson 1984).

The mean output functions are shown in Fig. 4.3. Considered overall, there was a clear tendency for concurrent load to impair performance to a greater extent than the articulatory suppression counting condition, which in turn led to poorer performance than the silent control. This latter difference should, however, be treated with caution since although suppression appeared to have a clear effect at the beginning of the

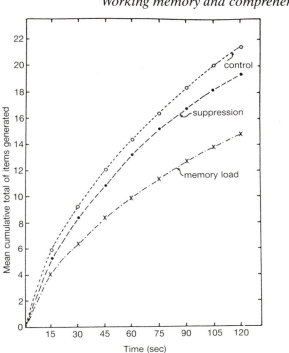

Fig. 4.3. The effects of memory load and articulatory suppression on category generation (Baddeley, Eldridge, Lewis, and Thomson 1984).

experimental session, those subjects tested in the counting condition at the end of the experiment showed no difference between suppression and control. While this result should be treated with circumspection since comparison across groups was involved, nonetheless it suggests that subjects are capable of coping with the problem of simultaneously generating items and counting. This was not the case with the concurrent digit load which continued to lead to very significantly poorer performance throughout the experimental period.

Interpretation of the functions in question depends on one's particular theory of how the task is performed. A range of models has been proposed (c.f. Indow and Togano 1970; Nickerson 1980). Many such theories do, however, tend to involve such simplifying assumptions as random sampling from the category. Sampling is however, clearly not random. A subject's output tends both to reflect category saliency, with certain items emerging consistently before others, and clustering, with items from a given sub-area of the category tending to emerge together, (e.g. *household pets, farm animals, African animals,* etc.). Both of these phenomena suggest that sampling is non-random.

We therefore, doubt whether any of these models is sufficiently developed to throw useful light on our data. What we can do, however, is to ask the more general question of whether the effect of concurrent load is constant throughout the 2-minute period of generation. It is conceivable for example that the task begins by being dominated by a relatively automatic retrieval process and then switches to the more attention-demanding recollection procedure (Nickerson 1980). If so, one might expect the effect of the concurrent load to be slight during the initial phase, but substantial during the later phase of generation. Since subjects generate about 1.4 items in the control condition for every item they generate under concurrent load, we can test the stability of the concurrent load effect by multiplying each point on the curve by the same amount, 1.4. If item generation switches from a relatively automatic retrieval process to attention-demanding recollection, one might expect an over correction of the early points on the curve and an under-correction of later points, producing a much flatter function. This does not occur, suggesting that the effect of concurrent load is relatively constant throughout. It would be of interest to explore this point further by manipulating the nature of the generation task. It seems likely that some tasks such as generating palindromes, words like *nun* or *minim* which are identical whether spelled forward or backwards, would place much heavier demands on the active recollective process and would therefore be more susceptible to the influence of a concurrent load. We have not, however, so far explored this possibility.

Reasoning and WMG

We have so far shown a clear effect of concurrent load on a range of learning tasks, and on comprehension, at least when measured in terms of latency. Our results for retrieval are less straightforward, and we have suggested that there may well be at least two components, an automatic search process, together with a more active recollective component that has some resemblance to problem-solving, and which is dependent on the operation of a limited capacity WMG. The last two experiments to be described in this section explore this possibility further by studying a syntactic verification task selected so as to place relatively heavy demands on the subject's reasoning capacity. The task in question is the grammatical reasoning task devised as a means of presenting subjects with a large number of simple and overlearned reasoning questions in a short period of time (Baddeley 1968b). It takes advantage of the considerable psycholinguistic literature suggesting that subjects are faster at processing affirmative than negative sentences and faster at processing actives than passives (Wason and Johnson-Laird 1972). The test correlates highly with intelligence, is highly reliable and very sensitive to a range of stresses (Baddeley 1968*b*). It gives rise to consistent effects of both active vs passive voice and positive vs negative response, together with the well established interaction between these, and although subjects show consistent learning on this task, the learning function is relatively linear with the result that a test in which subjects perform the task for only one minute is sufficient to give a good and stable measure of their reasoning performance (Carter, Kennedy, and Bittner 1981).

We have carried out a number of experiments on the influence of concurrent load on this task (Baddeley and Hitch 1974; Hitch and Baddeley 1976), but will confine discussion here to two studies. The first of these (Baddeley and Hitch 1974 Experiment III) used the concurrent digit load task, comparing the effect of a concurrent load of six random digits with an articulatory suppression condition involving counting repeatedly from one to six, and a silent control. The digits whether random or sequential, were presented auditorily and the reasoning task visually using the shutter device described previously. Subjects were required to continue to rehearse the random digits while verifying a range of sentences claiming to describe the order of two subsequent letters, A and B. The sentences ranged from simple activity declaritives such as *A follows B—BA* to which the subject should respond by pressing the 'true' button through passives such as *A is preceded by B—AB* (false), negatives such as *B does not follow A—BA* (true) and combined negative passives such as *A is not preceded by B—AB* (true).

Figure 4.4 shows the mean time taken by our subjects to verify sentences of these various types as a function of concurrent task. The results indicate first of all that the nature of the sentence has a clear influence on verification latency, secondly, that latency is consistently slowed down by the concurrent digit task, with subjects being significantly slower in this condition than when suppressing articulation, which is in turn marginally significantly slower than the silent control. Finally, we observed an interaction between sentence type and concurrent load, with the more difficult sentences showing a greater decrement than the simpler. These results are clearly consistent with the concept of a WMG which is of limited capacity. Taking up some of that capacity by means of a secondary task impairs reasoning performance, with the effect being particularly great for the more demanding sentences.

The final experiment in this sequence is one in which we explored the reasoning effect in rather more depth by studying seven female subjects over five days, and systematically varying the load from zero to eight digits on each day. The design used was essentially that employed in the previous study of semantic processing under zero to eight concurrent digits. The major difference was that we were interested in collecting sufficient observations to draw reliable conclusions about each of the four types of sentence. In addition, the longer period of testing allowed

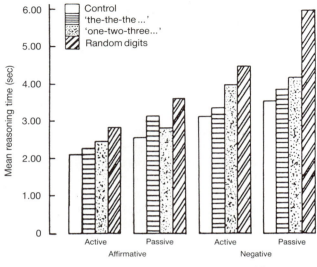

Mean reasoning time (sec)

Control
'the-the-the ...'
'one-two-three...'
Random digits

Active   Passive   Active   Passive
  Affirmative   Negative

Grammatical form of reasoning problem

Fig. 4.4. The effects of memory load and articulatory suppression on speed of grammatical reasoning (Baddeley and Hitch 1974).

us to study the effects of practice and also to obtain a clearer indication of individual differences and performance on this task.

Figure 4.5 shows the overall effect of concurrent load on verification time. It is clear from this, that the effect of concurrent load on RT is replicated. We observed a very substantial practice effect over days, but this did not remove or interact with the influence of concurrent load. A simple index of this is the percentage increment to the verification time under control conditions produced by the maximum load of eight digits. If we calculate this over the five successive days, mean increment is 32, 30, 41, and 41 per cent respectively. In short, although our subjects are improving very substantially on this task, they do not appear to be escaping the deleterious effect of a concurrent digit load.

In one respect however, our results differ from those of the previous study; although there are clear and highly significant effects of the active/ passive and positive/negative variables, these did not interact with concurrent load. It is far from clear why this should be, or indeed what are the implications of interaction effects, or their absence. Specifying such implications demands a more detailed model of the underlying process than has so far been proposed (c.f. Broadbent 1984; McClelland 1979).

Figure 4.5 also displays the error data for the sentence verification task. It is noteworthy that subjects appear to be able to maintain a

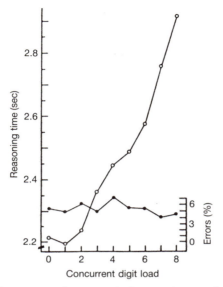

Fig. 4.5. Speed and accuracy of grammatical reasoning as a function of concurrent digit load (Baddeley and Lewis unpublished).

constant error rate of about 5 per cent regardless of concurrent digit load. This is fortunate since it suggests that subjects are continuing to treat the sentence verification task in a consistent way, and are not trading off reasoning accuracy in order to perform the digit task. Verification times for erroneous responses tended to be slower than for correct ones, with an overall mean latency of 3.99 seconds. However, those erroneous responses on which a digit error also occurred did not appear to be substantially different from those in which digit recall was perfect.

Analysis of the secondary digit task indicated that subjects were succeeding remarkably well in carrying out the concurrent task, with a substantial error rate occurring only in the eight digit load condition (See Table 4.1). Since five of our seven subjects had a span of eight or less, this represents virtually no decrement in memory as a result of the concurrent reasoning task. Even allowing for some improvement in span over the five days of practice, this is a remarkable result creating a major problem for any concept of working memory relying on the modal model, which would presumably predict that a difficult reasoning task performed with a 95 per cent accuracy should have a disastrous effect on a subject's concurrent ability to remember a digit sequence equivalent to her span.

Table 4.1 also gives the mean verification time for those sentences that were processed correctly, but associated with an error on the concurrent

TABLE 4.1
Digit memory errors and their relationship to speed of performance on the reasoning task

	1–4	5	6	7	8
Percent incorrect memory sequences	0	2.0	3.1	9.4	19.3
Correct reasoning time when memory errors occurred (sec)	–	3.42	3.75	4.15	3.95
Correct reasoning time when memory task was errorless (sec)	2.31	2.48	2.58	2.76	2.93

digit memory task. Mean latency for correct responses when digits were also correct is given for comparison. These cases are interesting because of their implications for the underlying processing. For example, if subjects were sharing a limited pool of processing resources between the digit and the reasoning tasks, one might expect a negative relationship between performance on the two. On those trials when more capacity was devoted to reasoning, less would be left for the memory task, so faster reasoning should be associated with a higher rate of memory errors. Table 4.1 however suggests just the opposite. Memory errors are associated with slow, not rapid reasoning.

This pattern of results also was observed in the previously described experiment using this procedure (Hitch and Baddeley 1976). It suggests that the interference between the memory and reasoning tasks occurs, not because they continually draw from the same limited pool of capacity, but rather that interference is intermittent. It may be the case for instance that when the memory task is running smoothly it places only moderate demands on working memory. When errors occur however, they demand immediate heavy resources in order to maintain performance. This in turn will lead to slower reasoning. Reasoning accuracy however appears not to be influenced by the accuracy of the digit memory task, since reasoning errors are essentially the same for sequences of 4 digits or less, which are always recalled correctly, as they are for 8 digit sequences, which show an error rate of about 20 per cent. In short, for the reasoning task subjects are able to maintain accuracy despite the demands of the concurrent digit memory task, but only at the cost of increased processing time.

Evidence for a general working memory

This is perhaps a good point to review the results obtained so far using the concurrent load technique, and discuss their implications both for the concept of WMG and for the modal model as a specific instantiation of such a working memory system.

The series of experiments just described had three major aims, to explore the plausibility of the WMG hypothesis, to explore the limits of the modal model as one candidate for WMG, and thirdly it was hoped in asking these questions, to come up with serendipitous new information about the role of STM in learning, comprehending and reasoning.

When we began this line of research, we expected that the concurrent digit load task would be a very blunt instrument with which to bludgeon what we imagined to be some relatively sensitive cognitive processes. We found the cognitive system to be much more robust than anticipated. Furthermore, when disruption did occur, it did not always happen in the way we expected. These unexpected features of our results encouraged us to continue to use the apparently crude concurrent load technique and it is perhaps worth briefly reviewing some of these findings in the light of their implications for the assumption of a general working memory.

We have now examined the effect of a concurrent memory task on a range of cognitive functions, each of which was previously assumed to rely on a limited capacity working memory. Do our results suggest that we should retain such a concept, and if so, should our system be assumed to resemble the modal model? In order to justify such a concept, we require adequate evidence that absorbing some of the subject's short-term capacity will have consistent and coherent deleterious effects on performance of a range of cognitive tasks that do not obviously in themselves involve short-term retention. In the case of learning verbal materials, there is abundant evidence that this does occur. The case for retrieval is less clear cut, since somewhat surprisingly the effects of concurrent load on retrieval accuracy appeared to be small and unreliable, although clear latency effects are found. Comprehension and verbal reasoning on the other hand again show strong and consistent effects on both speed and accuracy. Considered overall then, despite the unexpected results for retrieval, our data are consistent with some form of limited capacity memory system that influences learning, comprehension and reasoning. In short they are consistent with the concept of a General Working Memory.

Do our results support the modal model? In detail, they clearly do not. In particular the magnitude of the interference effects are far smaller than would be expected if one assumes that the same limited capacity short-term system is responsible for digit span and also for performance of the various cognitive tasks we have studied. The final reasoning experiment bears particularly strongly on this point since it shows that subjects with digit spans of seven or eight items are capable of holding this number of digits at the same time as performing a difficult reasoning task with 95 per cent accuracy, albeit somewhat more slowly. The modal model would surely suggest that a subject who is loaded to the limit of his span with digits should have so little processing capacity left that his reasoning performance should disintegrate. A general pattern of clear but limited decrement characterizes all the tasks we have studied, suggesting that the system responsible for digit span overlaps with the assumed WMG system but is by no means synonymous.

At a more detailed level, two of our results appear to be at variance with the modal model. The first and clearest of these is the observation that the recency effect is quite unaffected by concurrent load. Since the modal model assumes the recency effect to be based on the output of the limited capacity short-term store that forms the core of working memory, one would expect it to be completely obliterated by a load of six concurrent digits. Secondly, and less crucially, our evidence for the insensitivity of retrieval accuracy to the effects of a concurrent digit load is inconsistent with the modal model, insofar as it suggests that STS plays a crucial role in retrieval by holding and operating retrieval plans. Loading the STS heavily should surely interfere with retrieval by displacing such retrieval plans.

Before going on to consider alternative models, it is perhaps worth mentioning again the other sources of evidence against the modal model. Probably the most dramatic of these is the observation that certain patients with grossly impaired digit span can nonetheless learn quite normally. This is, of course, inconsistent with the view that a single unitary short-term memory is essential for long-term learning. A second difficulty for the modal model stems from the various observations that an item may be maintained in short-term memory for a considerable period of time without it apparently being transferred to long-term memory, a result that conflicts with the simple assumption that the route into long-term memory is via maintenance in STS. Finally, the evidence on the nature of coding in memory has proved to be much more complex than at first seemed probable; in particular, it is no longer reasonable to assume a short-term store which operates using a purely phonological code, and a long-term store relying only on semantic coding.

An alternative to the modal model of working memory

In an attempt to produce an alternative model, Graham Hitch and I abandoned the view of working memory as a single unitary store. We substituted the idea of a number of subsystems controlled by a limited capacity executive system. The danger here, of course, is to produce a system that is so complex as to be untestable and unproductive. The problem with a multiple system is to ensure that one does not simply invent another store or control process whenever an embarrassing result occurs. Such an approach would of course rapidly become unproductive. We therefore chose to operate initially with a tripartite system, comprising a supervisory controlling system, the *Central Executive* aided by two slave systems, one which was specialized for processing

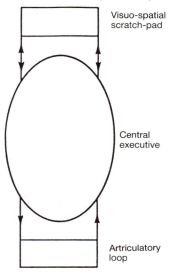

Visuo-spatial
scratch-pad

Central
executive

Artriculatory
loop

Fig. 4.6. A simplified representation of the working memory model.

language material, the *Articulatory Loop* and the other concerned with visuo-spatial memory, the *Visuo-Spatial Scratch Pad or Sketch Pad.*

A simple representation of such a model is shown in Fig. 4.6. There is a considerable amount of evidence to suggest separate verbal and spatial systems, indicating that we were not being excessively unparsimonious in starting with such an assumption. Our strategy in general has been that of testing our model to destruction, by systematically exploring the detailed working of these two subsystems, being willing to complicate the model only when it becomes obvious that the current version is clearly inadequate.

We have so far devoted most of our research activity to the peripheral slave systems, primarily because we regard these as offering simpler and more tractable problems than the central executive. Similarly, in analysing the central executive, we have where possible tried to split off modules which can be regarded as operating as separable sub-systems. In that respect, the central executive could be regarded as the residual area of ignorance about working memory which we are consistently attempting to reduce. We have assumed that the central executive has attentional capacities and is capable of selecting and operating control processes. We have as yet done little to explore the way in which this might be done.

We tend to assume a single central controller, but this is not essential to the model. If the control functions could be shown to be carried out by the interaction of the various cognitive subsystems, as for example Barnard (1985) suggests, we would be happy to accept this. At present, however, the concept of a central executive with peripheral slave systems appears to be a more manageable one. The following two chapters are concerned with attempting to fill out the details of this specific working memory model, WMS. The next chapter is concerned with the speech-based slave system, the *Articulatory Loop*, while the following chapter concerns the *Visuo-spatial Sketch Pad*, a system involved in generating and manipulating visuo-spatial images. Some applications of these concepts are then described in subsequent chapters before returning to the thorny problem of understanding the Central Executive.

Part III

A specific model of working memory (WMS)

5 The articulatory loop

Why an articulatory loop?

As we have seen, subjects are capable of holding a substantial number of digits in some form of short-term storage at the same time as performing the complex cognitive operations involved in learning, comprehension or reasoning. Such results are not consistent with the concept of working memory as a unitary short-term store with a capacity of only six or seven digits. One way out of this dilemma is to assume that the system involved in storing digits is not synonymous with the system involved in reasoning. The fact that the various tasks studied show clear effects of a concurrent digit load argues for a link, but the fact that such effects are far from catastrophic indicates that the system underlying digit span is not synonymous with WM. We therefore decided to explore the hypothesis that the task of retaining digits was carried out largely by a separate sub-system of WM, one that was controlled by the same central processor as was responsible for reasoning and learning, but which was specifically adapted to retaining speech-based material, while placing minimal demands on the central executive processor.

We opted for a speech-based system since there is a great deal of evidence to suggest that some form of speech code plays an important role in short-term memory. We assumed that the peripheral slave system rather than the central executive was speech-based for two main reasons. First, we suspected on general theoretical grounds that the central processor would be modality-free, acting as a link between a number of modality-dependent peripheral systems. Secondly, experiments concerned with the role of speech coding in reasoning and comprehension had suggested that some form of phonological coding played a genuine, but relatively small part in these tasks. I shall sketch in some of the sources of evidence for speech coding in short-term memory and then outline the first version of the Articulatory Loop model. This will be followed by a description of further evidence that convinced us that this initial model was no longer tenable, and this will be followed by an account of the revised version of the Articulatory Loop.

Evidence for phonological coding in STM

In what follows, I shall use the term 'phonological' in a purely neutral sense as meaning speech-based. The term 'articulatory' will be used when the coding is assumed to be based on the subject's speech production

75

system, while the term 'acoustic' will be used when the coding is assumed to be based on the subject's speech perception processes.

The phonological similarity effect

The first convincing evidence of the importance of phonological coding in STM was produced by Conrad (1964) who studied the errors made when subjects attempted to recall sequences of consonants. He observed that when a given letter was misrecalled, the error tended to be phonologically similar to the correct item, for example *B* would be more likely to be recalled as *D* than as *R*. Since the letter sequences were presented visually, the phonological confusion had presumably occurred in immediate memory, not in perceiving the letter. In exploring this phenomenon further, Conrad (1964) showed a high correlation between the probability that one letter would substitute for another in memory, and the probability that those two letters would be confused in a listening task in which the subject was required to write down consonants spoken in noise.

In a subsequent experiment, Conrad and Hull (1964) compared the immediate memory of sequences of consonants that were phonologically similar such as *B, G, V, P, T* with memory for dissimilar sequences such as *Y, H, W, K, R*. Errors occurred substantially more frequently with the phonologically similar set, an effect which Wickelgren (1965) subsequently showed to be largely attributable to the difficulty in recalling the order of presentation of the letters in question.

In a subsequent study, I myself used sequences of words in order to compare the effects of phonological and semantic similarity. I observed a clear phonological similarity effect with sequences of similar sounding words such as *mad, man, cad, mat, cap* being correctly recalled on only 9.6 per cent of occasions, whereas dissimilar words of comparable frequency within the language such as *pit, day, cow, sup, bar*, were correctly recalled 82.1 per cent of the time. Similarity of meaning had very much less of an effect, with a sequence such as *large, great, huge, long, big*, being recalled 65 per cent of the time and a semantically dissimilar strings such as *old, wet, strong, thin, deep*, being recalled on an average of 71 per cent of occasions. When the situation was changed to one requiring the long-term learning of sequences of ten items, with the short-term component minimized by following each presentation of the words with an interpolated task, the pattern changed dramatically, with similarity of meaning becoming the crucial variable and phonological similarity ceasing to be important (Baddeley 1966a, b).

This general pattern of results, indicating the importance of phonological coding in immediate memory tasks, appears to be very replicable and has been demonstrated in a wide range of situations (see Baddeley 1976, pp. 114–20 for a review).

Initial studies tended to refer to the phonological similarity effect as acoustic, implying that the crucial factor was the similarity of sound of the items being remembered. It was subsequently, however, suggested that the coding might be articulatory rather than acoustic. Hintzman (1967) carried out a detailed analysis of memory errors and argued that they were more consistent with an articulatory than with an acoustic interpretation. However, as Wickelgren (1969) pointed out acoustic and articulatory codes are highly similar, and it is not feasible to make clear predictions as to the nature of acoustic confusions without specifying the nature of the background noise against which the acoustic discriminations are made. In the case of short-term memory, the precise characteristics of this presumed neural background noise is not known, it is therefore not possible to produce a satisfactory auditory analogue that would allow a meaningful analysis along the lines suggested by Hintzman.

Rather more convincing evidence for articulatory coding came from a study by Conrad (1970) of congenitally deaf children. He observed that despite never having being able to hear, some such children showed phonological confusions in remembering consonant sequences. He was then able to demonstrate that children showing this effect were those rated by their teachers as good speakers. This result argues for the possibility of articulatory coding, but does not, of course, necessarily rule out the possibility that normal hearing subjects also code acoustically. Evidence of more direct relevance to normal memory, however, was provided by the phenomenon of articulatory suppression.

Articulatory suppression

In a detailed examination of the role of speech in memory, Murray (1965) carried out a series of experiments in which he varied the strength of overt vocalization required of the subject. One experiment looked at STM for digit sequences as a function of strength of articulation, requiring his subjects to either remain silent, mouth the items, whisper them, or speak them out loud. In general, he found <u>the greater the amount of articulation, the better the performance</u>. In another experiment, Murray (1967) presented his subjects visually with a sequence of digits, and prevented the subject from subvocally rehearsing them by requiring him to utter an irrelevant sound, the word 'the' throughout presentation. Performance was significantly poorer when relevant articulation was suppressed in this way. However, while this effect could be attributable to the suppression of articulatory coding, it could also be argued that the articulation of an irrelevant sound merely acted as a general distractor. This interpretation is not, however, adequate to explain a later result in which Murray (1968) showed that subjects required to remember sequences of consonants presented visually show no evidence of a phonological similarity effect when they are required to suppress articulation. This is an important finding, which has been replicated several times; Levy (1971), Estes (1973), and Peterson and Johnson (1971) all observed that the phonological similarity effect vanishes when items are presented visually and the subject prevented from subvocal rehearsal by means of an articulatory suppression task.

The word length effect

At about the time that we were developing the initial working memory model, we discovered another source of evidence for speech coding in STM, namely the word length effect (Baddeley, Thomson, and Buchanan 1975). Subjects who are asked to repeat back sequences of words are much more likely to do so correctly if the words are short such as *sum, wit, hate,* than if they are required to remember long words of equal frequency in the language, such as *opportunity, university, aluminium.* We were at first concerned that this might reflect linguistic rather than durational differences between the two sets, since our short words tended to be relatively simple and probably of largely Anglo-Saxon origin, in contrast to the more complex Latinate long words we had used. We therefore repeated the experiment using country names, a type of material which one would not expect to differ systematically between long and short items. Hence, we might compare memory for a sequence such as *Chad, Burma, Greece, Cuba, Malta* with a sequence such as *Czechoslovakia, Somaliland, Nicaragua, Afghanistan, Yugoslavia.* Subjects averaged 4.17 words out of 5 for the short names and 2.80 for the long names, a highly significant difference.

A subsequent study attempted to tease out whether the crucial factor was the duration of the spoken word, or its length in terms of syllables. Either might be plausible. A trace decay hypothesis might suggest that duration is important since longer words take longer to say and hence, allow the memory trace to be refreshed less frequently, leading to more forgetting. An interference theory or displacement model might argue that the crucial feature is number of syllables. A number of theorists have argued that one component of STM is a system containing a limited number of slots or memory locations; when the number of items to be remembered exceeds this number, forgetting occurs. If each slot were to hold a fixed number of syllables, then polysyllabic words would overload the system more rapidly than monosyllables.

In order to decide between these two hypotheses, we compared immediate memory for two sets of words. Both comprised two syllables, but in one set, spoken duration was relatively brief e.g. *bishop, wicket,* while for the other group spoken duration was relatively long, e.g. *harpoon, Friday.* We observed a consistent tendency for subjects to do better on the short-duration words, despite the fact that the two sets were matched not only for number of syllables, but in a second study also for number of phonemes.

A very neat extension of this result was produced by Ellis and Henneley (1980). They had noticed that the Welsh language version of the Wechsler intelligence test contained a puzzling anomaly, namely that the digit span norms for Welsh children were quite substantially below those for the original American norms. Ellis and Hennelly point out that Welsh digits, although containing the same number of syllables as English, nevertheless tend to contain longer vowel sounds and hence, take longer to articulate. They therefore explored the hypothesis that the observed difference in norms could be due to this difference in spoken duration. They used as their subjects bilingual students for whom Welsh was their first language. They showed first of all that these subjects had a longer digit span in English than in Welsh. They then measured the time taken by their subjects to articulate digits in English and then in Welsh, observing as anticipated that producing the Welsh digits took longer. When this information was used to measure the memory span of their subjects in the two languages in terms of spoken duration, then their English and Welsh spans became equal. Finally, when subvocalization was prevented by articulatory suppression, the difference between the digit span of their subjects in English and Welsh again disappeared. It appears to be the case that Welsh digit span norms are inferior to US norms simply because Welsh digits take longer to articulate. Preliminary evidence suggests that a comparable state of affairs may occur quite commonly in languages such as Italian, where most digits involve at least two syllables.

The fact that word duration is a crucial variable in memory span is consistent with a trace decay hypothesis rather than the interpretation in terms of a limited number of storage slots. Let us suppose that the presentation of an item leaves a memory trace which decays over time. Re-presentation of an item either by the experimenter, or by the subject himself rehearsing the item will refresh the trace and arrest the process of decay. Amount retained will therefore be a joint function of decay rate and rehearsal rate. With very few items, the subject will be able to rehearse the complete sequence in less time than it takes the memory trace to decay, hence allowing him to maintain the sequence indefinitely (Vallar and Baddeley 1982). As the length of the sequence increases, so will the time needed by the subject to rehearse the entire sequence, until a point is reached at which the decay time for an individual item is less than the time to rehearse the total sequence. When this happens, errors will begin to occur.

Looked at in this way, it is possible to express the memory span in terms of either the number of items or the total spoken duration. Whereas a span measured in terms of numbers of item is likely to depend on the duration of those items, the total recall of.time should be constant. We tested this hypothesis using the long- and short-duration disyllabic words described previously. We measured articulation rate in two ways, by presenting the words as typed lists and requiring the subject to read them as rapidly as possible, and by presenting subjects with groups of three words that they were required to articulate a total of ten times as rapidly as possible. Reading and articulation rate were then used to convert the observed memory spans into temporal spans. The results suggested that a subject's span for long words was equivalent to the amount he could read in 1.62 seconds for long words and 1.67 seconds for short words, a difference which did not approach significance. When measured in terms of articulation rate, long words gave a span of 1.33 seconds of articulation and short a span of 1.31 seconds, again indicating no difference as a function of word length.

In order to explore the temporal duration hypothesis over a wider range, we carried out an experiment in which subjects attempted to recall sequences of words of 1, 2, 3, 4, or 5 syllables. The words were matched for frequency and category membership, the set being shown in Table 5.1. Subjects were tested at each length on sequences of five words, presented visually at a rate of 2 seconds per word. Reading rate for each set of words was determined by requiring the subjects to read lists of 50 words, each of which comprised five occurrences of each item in the relevant set. Subjects read each list four times and were timed by stop-watch.

TABLE 5.1
Set of words used in Experiment II

Set No.				
1.	mumps	measles	leprosy	diphtheria	tuberculosis
2.	stoat	puma	gorilla	rhinocerous	hippopotamus
3.	Greece	Peru	Mexico	Australia	Yugoslavia
4.	Maine	Utah	Wyoming	Alabama	Louisiana
5.	zinc	carbon	calcium	uranium	aluminium

Figure 5.1 shows the mean recall and reading rate scores for the various sets of words as a function of length. As expected, word length has a very pronounced effect on both reading rate and memory, with each condition being significantly different from each other. A more crucial issue, however, is the question of the relationship between reading rate and span. It will be recalled that the decay hypothesis predicts that this should be constant. Figure 5.1 shows the result observed, a linear relationship between reading rate and recall that is described by the equation $S = c + kR$, where S is the memory span, R is reading rate and k

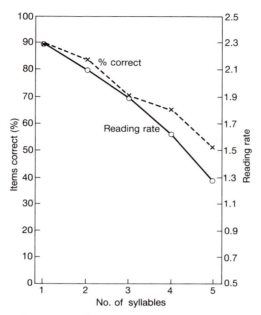

Fig. 5.1. Mean reading rate and percentage correct recall of sequences of five words as a function of length.

and *c* are constants. This suggests that the relationship predicted by a simple decay hypothesis does indeed hold for the group results. We next explored the question of whether it also held for differences between individuals; in short, are fast articulators good rememberers? Our data suggest that they are since we obtained a substantial correlation between memory span and reading rate ($R = 0.685$, $p < 0.005$).

The evidence so far then hangs together very neatly in suggesting some form of phonological store that relies on a fading trace which can be maintained by subvocal rehearsal. The question then arises as to whether the phonological store implied by the word length effect is the same as that suggested by the phonological similarity effect. If this is the case, then one might expect that the influence of articulatory suppression on the word length effect would be just as drastic as its effect on phonological similarity. We therefore carried out a further experiment in which subjects were presented visually with sequences of five words from either a short word set comprising monosyllables, or a set comprising words of five syllables. Under one set of conditions, subjects were left free to rehearse while in the other, rehearsal was prevented by requiring the subject to count repeatedly from one to six. The results were clear; the standard word length effect was present under control conditions but was abolished by articulatory suppression.

So far then, all the data seemed to fit into the simple concept of a time-based loop, somewhat analogous to a closed loop on a tape recorder. The loop was assumed to be based on articulation and to consist of a bank of articulatory programmes which were able to feed the process of articulation. This in turn refreshed the stored articulatory programmes and prevented them from fading. Such a simple device seemed to be capable of handling all the results we have so far described. The phonological similarity effect was assumed to be due to confusion among articulatory programmes, with items involving similar sounds also involving similar articulatory patterns. Murray's observation that the more intense the degree of articulation the better the recall also fitted, given the assumption that more intensive articulation laid down clearer or stronger articulatory traces. The effect of articulatory suppression fitted in neatly since a set of irrelevant speech sounds would tend to pre-empt the articulatory system, disrupting its use for short-term storage, while the evidence for phonological confusions in congenitally deaf children who are good articulators also fits in particularly neatly with such a view. The first articulatory loop model, therefore, was essentially a simple tape loop analogy.

Problems with the initial articulatory loop model

Although the initial model appeared to offer a simple explanation of a wide range of data, there remained a cluster of results that did not fit this model. Although the phonological similarity effect is disrupted by articulatory suppression, this is only the case when material is presented visually. With auditory presentation, the phonological similarity effect withstands suppression. In a final experiment in our initial word length paper (Baddeley, Thomson, and Buchanan 1975), we observed a similar effect for word length; although articulatory suppression removed the word length effect with visual presentation, when material was presented auditorily a clear word length effect was observed even when subjects were suppressing articulation. If articulatory suppression pre-empts the articulatory loop, then it should abolish the phonological similarity and word length effects regardless of whether presentation is visual or auditory. The next section describes how this apparent anomaly, together with data from other paradigms led to a modification and elaboration of the initial articulatory loop model.

In a previous study concerned with rate of presentation we had observed a difference in the effect of articulatory suppression on performance depending on whether suppression occurred only during input or during both input and recall (Baddeley and Lewis 1984). It appears to be the case that with moderately rapid presentation, subjects are able to use rehearsal during the recall period to maintain items of memory. It seemed possible at least that the word length effect observed under auditory presentation and suppression might have been dependent on this. While this may not seem particularly likely on *a priori* grounds the issue was sufficiently important theoretically to merit exploring this possibility.

Giuseppe Vallar and I therefore carried out an experiment in which subjects heard and attempted to recall sequences of five words comprising either one syllable or five syllables each (Baddeley, Lewis, and Vallar 1984, Experiment 4). Subjects were either free to rehearse, or required to suppress articulation by counting rapidly from one to eight throughout both input and written recall. In order to equate writing time, we allowed subjects to abbreviate items to their first three letters. The results of the study are shown in Fig. 5.2. The highly significant word length effect that occurred under control conditions was reduced to a nonsignificant trend under suppression, a difference that was reflected by a significant interaction between word length and suppression.

In view of the importance of this result to the Articulatory Loop model, it clearly merited replication. An experiment by Muriel Woodhead and myself repeated the study using sequences of 4, 5, or 6 words, again drawn from sets comprising words of one or five syllables (Baddeley, Lewis, and Vallar 1984, Experiment 5). The results were virtually identical with the previous study, with a significant word length effect under control conditions, a significant interaction between word length and suppression, but no significant effect of word length when subjects suppressed articulation during both input and recall. There was, however, in both studies a slight trend in the direction of a word length effect under suppression, which though not significant, suggests that it would be unwise to conclude that suppression completely abolishes the

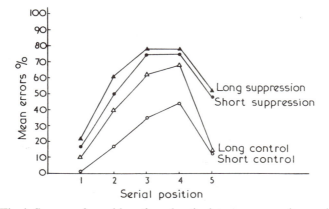

Fig. 5.2. The influence of word length and articulatory suppression on immediate memory for auditorily presented words. Suppression occurred during both presentation and recall (Baddeley, Lewis, and Vallar 1984).

effect of word length. However, even if the effect did reach significance, it might simply reflect a tendency for subjects to intersperse an occasional subvocal rehearsal between suppression responses.

In general however, these results suggest that the word length does indeed stem from the process of articulatory rehearsal *per se*; long words take longer to rehearse and allow more forgetting. If rehearsal is prevented, then word length ceases to be an important variable (Baddeley, Lewis, and Vallar 1984). The result does, however, raise two further questions. First, why is suppression during input enough to abolish the word length effect with visual presentation? Secondly, what happens to the phonological similarity effect when items are presented auditorily and suppression occurs throughout input and recall? If the phonological similarity effect manifests itself through the process of articulatory rehearsal, one might expect it to be abolished by suppression provided this occurs throughout the input and recall. If on the other hand, the phonological similarity effect operates through some other component of the system and is not dependent on articulation for its occurrence, then one might expect it to survive the effects of continuous articulatory suppression. Two experiments exploring this point will be described before going on to reconsider the Articulatory Loop hypothesis.

We carried out a total of three experiments in which material was presented auditorily, and the influence of phonological similarity was studied with and without articulatory suppression (Baddeley, Lewis, and Vallar 1984, Experiments 1–3). The results of all three were consistent in showing that similarity continues to have a marked effect whether suppression is at input only or at both input and recall. This results contrasts with the case of visual presentation, where suppression eliminates the phonological similarity effect (Estes 1973; Levy 1971; Murray 1968; Peterson and Johnson 1971).

A revised articulatory loop model

The available evidence, therefore, suggests that the phonological similarity and word length effects reflect different components of the articulatory loop system. The word length effect appears to reflect the process of articulatory rehearsal, and is based on the simple fact that longer words take longer to say, hence reducing the rate at which an item can be rehearsed. Cutting out the process of rehearsal by articulatory suppression appears to be sufficient to remove this effect.

The phonological similarity effect on the other hand appears to be a function of the short-term store which is maintained and refreshed by the process of articulation, and which can in turn be used to feed the articulatory process. This store appears to be accessible either through auditory presentation or by the articulatory coding of visually presented material. However, although auditory presentation seems to provide direct access to this phonological store, it does not appear to guarantee rehearsal. If it did, then overall level of performance should not be impaired by articulatory suppression, provided materials were presented auditorily. As we have seen, decrement does occur under these conditions (e.g. Baddeley and Lewis 1984).

We are left then with a very simple system comprising a phonological store and an articulatory control process. The sections that follow describe the application of this simple model to a number of further issues. These cause some additional development, and suggest other components of the working memory system, but on the whole the revised articulatory loop model appears to offer an adequate and useful account of the available evidence.

The inner voice and the inner ear

While the articulatory loop component of working memory is probably the one that has been most extensively explored, we are left with at least one major loose end. It may be recalled that articulatory suppression impairs the retention of visually presented words, eliminates the phonological similarity and word-length effects and obliterates the influence of unattended speech. All these results suggest that articulatory suppression prevents visually presented items being phonologically encoded.

On the other hand, subjects appear to be quite capable of making judgements of rhyme or of homophony on visually presented words while suppressing articulation. Indeed not only are subjects capable of continuing to perform this task, they do so with little impairment in speed or accuracy (Baddeley and Lewis 1981; Besner *et al.* 1981). Further evidence that articulatory suppression does not prevent phonological coding comes from a study by Besner and Davelaar (1982). This involved two experiments, one concerning phonological similarity and the other word length. In the first experiment subjects were tested for immediate serial recall of sequences of items that were either pseudo-homophones (e.g. *phood, newd, chood*) or were non-homophones (e.g. *thude, snude, beued*). Furthermore, the sequences were either phonologically similar or dissimilar, and were remembered under either control conditions or under articulatory suppression. As would be expected, a phonological similarity effect occurred under control conditions but was abolished by articulatory suppression. On the other hand, items that were pseudohomophones were easier to recall under both control and suppression conditions. A second experiment was equivalent except that length of item, rather than phonological similarity was manipulated. Again, presentation was visual and subjects performed under control or suppression conditions. Pseudohomophones were easier than non-homophones under both conditions, whereas the effect of item length was present only in the control condition. Besner and Davelaar conclude that

'There are at least two different phonological codes driven by print and they subserve different functions in the reading process. The first code can be used for lexical access, and is not prevented from operating by suppression. The second phonological code is prevented from operating by suppression, and functions as a durable storage medium for retaining serial order information; this aids verbatim recall and comprehension.' (Besner and Davelaar 1982, p. 708).

These two separate phonological storage systems were loosely described by Baddeley and Lewis (1981) as the *inner voice* and the *inner ear*. The inner voice was assumed to be the articulatory loop system, requiring either subvocal speech or an auditory input for items to be encoded. Such a sytem is assumed to maintain speech-coded material by means of subvocal rehearsal but not be usable for visually presented items if subvocalization is prevented by articulatory suppression. The inner ear was assumed to involve some form of acoustic image. It was assumed to be independent of articulation, and to be capable of setting up a phonological representation, but not one that is sufficiently robust to be useable in a memory span task.

It is possible to avoid the assumption of two separate systems, provided one is prepared to accept the assumption that different types of input to the store will set up traces of different strength or durability. On this assumption, the strongest trace is set up either directly by auditory presentation or indirectly through subvocal articulation. If material is presented visually and subvocalization prevented by articulatory suppression, then both these routes are blocked. However a third route is possible via LTM. As a result of learning to read and to name objects, a route is built up whereby the phonological representation of a name or a word can be accessed from LTM, leaving a comparatively weak trace within the phonological store. If one assumes that such a trace is sufficient to allow judgements of homophony, but not sufficiently durable to support memory span, then the available data can be accommodated. Whether it is more parsimonious to assume two separate stores, or two representations within a single store is a moot point. However, although cogent empirical evidence is still lacking, this aspect of the articulatory loop would certainly appear to merit further investigation.

Applications of the articulatory loop

The modality effect

It has been known for many years that the modality of presentation influences the probability that items will be recalled. In particular, auditory presentation leads to enhanced recall of items within the recency portion of the serial position curve (Conrad and Hull 1968; Crowder and Morton 1969). Such a phenomenon clearly ought to be explicable within a working memory framework. Initial interpretations suggested that the modality effect represented the contribution of a temporary acoustic store, termed by Crowder and Morton (1969) the Precategorical Acoustic Score (PAS). Subsequent research has shown that this effect is not limited to the last item in a list (Frankish 1985), and is indeed not peculiar to auditory presentation, since enhanced recency effects are shown when subjects are recalling sequences of items in sign language (Shand and Klima 1981) or via the lip-reading of spoken items (Campbell and Dodd 1980). Similarly, asymmetries occur in the extent to which material presented auditorily is disrupted by subsequent visual material, and vice versa (Martin and Jones 1979). However, while a complete model of the working memory system would certainly incorporate this interesting and productive area of research, the model has at present little to say on these phenomena. Not having worked in this area myself, my view of it coincides closely with that presented by Gardiner (1983) in a recent review, namely that 'Much of the evidence reviewed is of a somewhat preliminary nature and is as yet unexplained by any theory of memory. The need for additional converging experimental tests is obvious; so too is the need for theoretical development'.

Noise, unattended speech and cognitive performance

There is no doubt that people tend to find unwanted loud noises unpleasant, and there has been considerable discussion over the question of whether noise impairs a person's ability to perform cognitive tasks. It is slightly ironic that at a time when noise pollution is increasingly becoming regarded as undesirable, the evidence for cognitive impairment seems to be less and less convincing. There appears to be good evidence that exposure to noise above 90 dbA for long periods of time is likely to cause physiological damage to the auditory system. More controversial, however, is the question of whether exposure to noise at a lower level than this causes relatively slight impairment in cognitive performance (Broadbent 1979), or whether these effects can be attributed to factors other than noise (Poulton 1979).

One area in which there does seem to be some agreement on performance decrement is that of short-term verbal memory, where a number of investigators have shown effects that are significant. Even here however, noise effects are typically small, and even vary in direction of effect, with some studies showing an impairment in performance (e.g. Salame and Wittersheim 1978), while others suggest that performance may be enhanced (e.g. Wilding and Mohindra 1980). Poulton (1979) has suggested that the deleterious effects of noise on STM may be due to a tendency for the noise to mask a subject's inner speech, a view that implies that this issue might be one that could usefully be tackled within a working memory context. The opportunity of working in this area cropped up with the arrival of Dr. Pierre Salame to spend several months at the Applied Psychology Unit, Salame and Witersheim (1978) having previously shown that immediate memory for sequences of visually presented digits was impaired if each digit was accompanied by a burst of white noise.

Salame was interested in extending his work to examine the effect of unattended concurrent speech on short-term memory. He predicted that if the unattended auditory material were meaningful, the disruption would be substantially greater. I myself had previously conducted some rather informal experiments in which I tried to disrupt performance on the previously described semantic sentence verification task by accompanying it with excerpts from a radio soap opera. The results were discouraging and I predicted that subjects would be able successfully to ignore unwanted spoken material. There was in fact published evidence on this point (Colle and Welsh 1976) which we both should have known but did not, so we agreed to conduct an experiment to see who was right.

Our experiment involved presenting subjects with sequences of nine digits, presented one at a time on a visual display unit. We had three conditions, one in which each digit was accompanied by a spoken word (e.g. *BID*, or *POT*) which the subject was instructed to ignore. In a second condition, the words were replaced by spoken nonsense syllables, the syllables being selected so as to comprise the same phonemes as the words (e.g. *PID, BOT*). The third condition was a silent control under which no distracting sound occurred. Salame predicted that the words, being meaningful, would be much more distracting than the nonsense syllables. I predicted that we would obtain no reliable differences. We were both wrong. Subjects showed an increase in errors of approximately 40 per cent when attempting to ignore either words or nonsense syllables, which did not differ in their effect on performance. Our unattended speech effect was very consistent, and rather substantial compared to the typical small and unreliable effects of white noise, despite the fact that the sound level used, 75 dbA was substantially below the level at which one might expect white noise to impair performance.

We therefore carried out a second experiment in which we compared the effect of unattended speech at the previous moderate level of 75 dbA with bursts of white noise of a similar intensity and duration. We also decided to test one possible interpretation of our result. When a sudden event such as a noise occurs, there is a tendency for it to capture the subject's attention briefly, the so-called orienting reflex (Sokolov 1963). It seemed possible therefore that our decrement was due to directing the subjects' attention towards the sound and away from the visual stimulus just as the stimulus digit was appearing. It is not implausible to assume that this would interfere with the encoding of the stimulus sequence resulting in poorer subsequent retention.

We tested this hypothesis by desynchronizing the occurrence of the visual digits and the unwanted auditory stimuli, so as to alternate them and hence presumably minimize any tendency for the orienting reflex to distract the subject from perceiving the stimulus. On this interpretation, we might expect no decrement from either unattended speech or un- attended noise in our second desynchronized study.

Our results were inconsistent with the attentional interpretation, with subjects showing just as great a decrement between control and the unattended speech condition (46 per cent), as in the previous study. The noise bursts had a much smaller and marginally significant effect (19 per cent decrement), suggesting that speech was much more disrupting than white noise.

Suppose we attempt to use the articulatory loop model to explain our results. Our subjects were presumably subvocally articulating the visual digits, and hence utilizing the phonological store. We know from the previous experiments on phonemic similarity and spoken material that speech appears to have direct access to this store, at least when the subject is attending to the spoken message. If we make the further assumption that spoken material has obligatory access to this store, and can not be shut out by the subject, then we have a possible interpretation of our unattended speech effect. Our subjects are presumably relying on the phonological store to help them retain the visual digits. The irrelevant spoken material will corrupt this store and hence disrupt retention of the wanted digits.

At about the same time as we were completing our second experiment, we came across a related study by Colle and Welsh (1976) who tested their subjects' STM for sequences of visually presented consonants, and observed that performance was substantially better in silence, than when the task was performed against a background of continuous speech in a foreign language that was unfamiliar to the subjects.

Encouraged by the Colle and Welsh results, we decided to test the articulatory loop hypothesis more directly by studying the effect of un- attended speech under articulatory suppression. The prediction here is straightforward. Visually presented material will only enter the articula- tory phonological store if the subject is able to articulate it. Under articulatory suppression, the visually presented digits should not gain access to the phonological store, consequently there is no reason to suppose that corrupting that store with irrelevant information will further impair performance. One can contrast this for example with a general attentional explanation. This might argue that, despite the evidence in our second experiment that synchrony of the wanted digit and the unwanted sound is unimportant, it is still possible that some of the subject's limited attentional capacity is taken up in filtering out the unwanted speech. On such a hypothesis, one would expect that adding a further load by requiring the subject to suppress articulation, would if anything exacerbate the attentional problem, causing even more overload. We have then two divergent predictions, the articulatory loop hypothesis predicts that suppressing articulation will abolish the irrelevant speech effect, whereas the attentional interpretation predicts that the effect should be at least as great, and probably even greater under suppression.

We tested this by again visually presenting subjects with sequences of nine random digits, accompanied on half the occasions by synchronized spoken words which the subject was instructed to ignore, while the other half of the trials proceeded in silence. Within each of these conditions, subjects were required to suppress articulation by counting repeatedly on half the trials, and were free to rehearse on the remainder. The results are shown in Fig. 5.3. As the articulatory loop hypothesis predicted, suppression had its usual effect of impairing overall performance, but in addition, removed the unattended speech effect.

Our results then suggested that unattended speech impairs performance by corrupting the phonological store, not by serving as a general distractor.

The final experiment in this particular series used the unattended speech effect to explore the nature of the phonologial code. We had already shown that the system appeared to accept speech regardless of

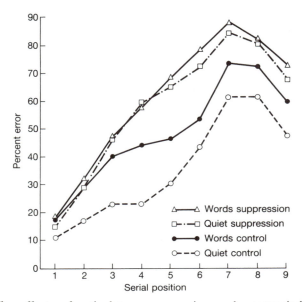

Fig. 5.3. The effects of articulatory suppression and unattended speech on memory for sequences of visually presented digits (Salame and Baddeley 1982).

whether or not it comprised meaningful words, but was relatively un-influenced by white noise. It seemed possible, however, that although any spoken item would be disrupting, subjects might be expected to be parti-cularly affected when visually presented digits were accompanied by different auditory digits. Such an effect might occur, however, for either of two reasons, depending on the nature of the store. If the store com-prises a set of lexical representations of items, then problems will occur because of confusion between visually and auditorily presented digits. On this interpretation, one would expect less disruption from non-digit items, even though these are made up from the same phonemes as digits, producing words such as *tun* and *woo* instead of digit names such as *one* and *two*. If on the other hand, the store operates at a purely phonological level, then both these sets of distractors would be equally damaging. Part of our experiment, therefore, compared these two types of distractors, irrelevant unattended digits, and unattended words made up from the phonemes contained in digits.

Suppose, however, we obtain no difference between these two condi-tions. We would still be left with the question of whether our result meant that both types of distractor were equally disruptive, or that irrelevant speech simply discourages the subject from making any use of the phonological store. We, therefore, included a third distractor condition in which the irrelevant words were selected as being phonologically dis-similar to digits. We used disyllabic words with short vowels such as *jelly* and *tipple*; hence, although the spoken duration of the three sets of irrelevant words were approximately equal, the disyllabic words were phonologically easier to distinguish from the monosyllabic digits with long vowels than were the *tun, woo* set. The results we obtained are shown in Fig. 5.4, from which it is clear that both digits and words made up from the same phonemes were approximately equally disruptive. Disyllabic words on the other hand caused a clear impairment in performance, but were significantly less disruptive than digits or their phonologically equivalent words. Our results, therefore, support the view that the phonological store operates at the level of the individual phoneme or syllable, rather than the word.

It seems then that our attempt to tackle a somewhat practical problem concerning the effect of noise on cognition has produced some interest-ing theoretical results. We acquired a new technique for manipulating the articulatory loop system, and were able to use it to learn more about coding within the phonological store. But what of our original practical question? The main practical implication of our results is probably methodological. In the past, attempts to study the influence of noise on performance have overwhelmingly opted to use white noise. This has the characteristic of being easy to specify and produce and of having known masking properties. However, its effects on performance tend to be

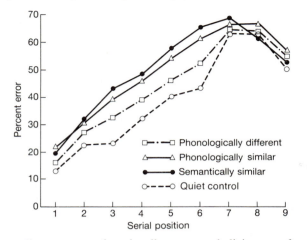

Fig. 5.4. Immediate memory for visually presented digits as a function of the phonological and semantic characteristics of unattended speech (Salame and Baddeley 1982).

minimal, at least at levels which are physiologically safe. Our data suggest that speech has a much more disruptive effect, at least in the case of short-term memory. Subsequent research by Colle (1980) suggests that the magnitude of the disruption is not dependent on the intensity of the speech. Further work by Salame and myself is consistent with this conclusion (Salame and Baddeley 1983); we compared the effect of unattended white noise with that of continuous Arabic speech at 75 and 90 db. We found the same effect at both intensities, namely a clear effect of unattended speech, but no effect of noise.

In conclusion then, our results, and those of Colle suggest that the study of cognitive performance in noise might benefit substantially from switching attention away from a preoccupation with sound intensity towards a concern with the qualitative characteristics of the unwanted sound.

The trace decay assumption

The assumption of a decaying phonological trace plays a central role in the articulatory loop model. In that context it is clearly a useful and plausible assumption, but the question arises as to how plausible it is within a broader context. As discussed in Chapter 1, the assumption of trace decay in short-term memory was seriously challenged in the 1960s. While the claims to disprove trace decay in STM are themselves far from convincing, nonetheless the assumption is not one that would enjoy universal support in the 1980s. For that reason it is necessary to examine the assumption carefully at this point.

There are at least two trace decay hypotheses, a strong version which attempts to attribute all forgetting to trace decay, and a weaker version which argues that trace decay is one component of forgetting in STM tasks. It is clear that other factors such as retrieval and temporal discrimination play an important role in short-term as well as long-term memory, and for that reason I would not wish to defend the strong decay hypothesis. I would regard the short-term forgetting shown in the Peterson task as primarily attributable to retrieval factors (see Baddeley 1976, pp. 122–131) and would use a similar temporal discrimination model to account for recency effects in free recall (see Chapter 7). The articulatory loop hypothesis does however regard trace decay as an important factor in memory span. Why then is there no simple prediction that rapid presentation leads to better span performance?

The first reason has been mentioned earlier, namely that a crucial factor in determining trace decay is not the rate at which the experimenter chooses to present the material, but rather the rate at which the subject is able to refresh the memory trace by rehearsal. The evidence suggests that merely exhorting subjects not to rehearse is not an adequate way of providing such control (Reitman 1974), although the results of Hockey (1973) suggest that such instructions do interact with rate of presentation; slowly presented items are retained more poorly than rapidly presented items when subjects are induced to adopt a passive learning strategy and avoid rehearsal.

Another way of attempting to control rehearsal is through articulatory suppression. Baddeley and Lewis (1984) presented digits auditorily at a rate of one per half second or one per 2 seconds, and studied the effect of articulatory suppression during digit presentation only, or throughout both presentation and recall. There was one condition in which rapid presentation appeared to be highly advantageous, that in which suppression occurred during presentation but not recall. It is argued that this is consistent with the concept of trace that decays in 1 or 2 seconds. With slow presentation, virtually none of the trace will be left by the beginning of the recall phase; with rapid presentation, material will be available, but unless it can be rehearsed, it will fade during the relatively slow process of written responding. In the critical condition, the subject is assumed to perform a rapid rehearsal of the material remaining, before and during recall, hence preventing any further decay.

More direct evidence comes from studies using prefix and suffix effects. It may be recalled that Conrad (1958) showed that when telephonists were required to insert a prefix before dialling a telephone number, performance declined quite markedly, despite the fact that the delay was less than a second. However, although delay represents one possible interpretation of the result, it is not the only one; it may for example be that remembering an additional action simply increases the amount of information that must be stored, hence overloading the system and producing errors. I tested this directly some years ago in an unpublished experiment in which subjects were read out sequences of digits, followed by the instruction 'left' or 'right'. They had a response sheet with two sets of response locations, and were instructed to write their answer in the response location specified by the spoken suffix. Two groups of subjects were tested. The 'random' group did not know from trial to trial where they would have to write their response, and hence needed to process the instruction. The 'redundant' group however were told in advance that the response location would regularly alternate—left, right, left, right, etc., so the instruction conveyed no further information. The redundant group performed significantly better than the random group.

So far we have broadly replicated the Conrad effect, but our result like his is open to two possible interpretations, temporal decay or informational overload. The temporal decay interpretation might suggest that the difference arose because the redundant group were able to begin responding as soon as the last digit had been presented, whereas the random group had to wait until they had heard and processed the instructional suffix. The information overload interpretation on the other hand would suggest that the random group performed more poorly because of the greater information processing demand of the random suffix.

These two hypotheses were tested by making a small modification to the procedure. Instead of waiting until the last digit had been presented before giving the left-right instruction, the instruction was inserted just before the presentation of the final digit. On a temporal decay interpretation of the previous result, the difference between the two conditions should disappear, since the digit span procedure forbids subjects to begin responding until the last digit has been presented. The informational load hypothesis would however still predict a difference, since the random group still have an additional processing demand. Preposing the suffix instruction removed the difference between the two conditions, providing clear support for the temporal decay interpretation rather than the informational overload hypothesis.

The evidence so far then suggests that a brief delay between presentation with the digit sequence and its recall may be sufficient to produce marked forgetting. This possibility was explored more extensively in a series of experiments on prefix and suffix effects carried out by Audrey Hull and myself (Baddeley and Hull 1979). We argued that suffix effects were of two types, modality-specific effects that are limited to the last one or two items presented, and modality-free effects that extend throughout the list of items recalled. The first type of modality-specific effect occurs most clearly with auditory presentation. Under these conditions, there is a marked recency effect, with the last one or two items being extremely well recalled. The recency effect however is virtually obliterated by the presentation of a single spoken suffix. The initial phenomenon was demonstrated by Conrad and Hull (1968) but was elegantly explored subsequently by Crowder and Morton (1969) who proposed that the last few spoken items were held in a peripheral sensory storage system, the precategorical acoustic store. The nature of this storage remains controversial (see Crowder 1983 and Gardiner 1983). Since it is peripheral to the working memory system it will not be further discussed.

The study by Baddeley and Hull (1979) was primarily concerned with the second type of suffix effect, an effect that is modality-free and that extends across the serial position curve. More specifically the study was concerned first with whether the phenomenon could be interpreted in terms of temporal decay, and secondly with whether the same mechanism could be used to account for both suffix effects, and for prefix effects such as those involved in the previously described study of redundant versus random suffixes.

A number of experiments were carried out in which a sequence of digits was presented, the subjects required to utter a predetermined prefix before vocally recalling the digit sequence. In the first experiment, subjects were required to prefix their response with one of two Welsh town names, *Rhyl* or *Abergavenny*. Conditions were blocked so that there was no uncertainty as to which town name was to be emitted at any given time. The results showed that the requirement to prefix a response with a town name impairs performance, with the impairment being greater for the longer town name. The effect characterizes the whole of the serial position curve with one exception; the last item shows at least as much disruption by the short name as by the long, a phenomenon that occurred in all the experiments in this series. Since depression of performance on the last item by a spoken suffix is the classic index of the Crowder and Morton PAS effect, our results suggest that PAS disruption does not increase with the length of the prefix or suffix. Indeed there is a significant tendency in our own results and in related results by Crowder (1982b) for a long suffix to cause less impairment of performance on the last item than a short suffix, arguing strongly for the proposed separation between modality-specific and modality-free suffix effects.

A further experiment systematically varied the length of the suffix word from one to five syllables. Overall performance declined as suffix length increased. In the next study subjects were required to utter a prefix before recalling sequences of seven digits. As prefix length was increased from one to five syllables, recall accuracy decreased. The results of this and the equivalent suffix study are shown in Table 5.2. These results can readily be explained by assuming a rapidly decaying memory trace; both prefix and suffix impair performance by introducing a brief decay that is

TABLE 5.2

Effects of prefix or suffix length on recall of seven-digit sequences (per cent erroneous digits) (Data from Baddeley and Hull (1979)).

| | Control (0) | Prefix/Suffix Length (Syllables) | | | | |
		1	2	3	4	5
Prefix experiment	11.8	25.4	29.2	29.9	33.5	34.0
Suffix experiment	11.3	23.3	25.4	25.5	26.5	29.7
Mean	11.6	24.4	27.3	27.7	30.0	31.9

too short to allow coherent rehearsal, and which hence leads to forgetting. The longer the prefix or suffix, the longer the delay, the greater the decay and the poorer the retention.

In conclusion, although trace decay does not offer as full an account of short-term forgetting as was claimed by its early advocates, there is evidence to suggest that a decay assumption is a plausible as well as a useful assumption within a more complex model of short-term forgetting. Such a model is offered by the articulatory loop hypothesis.

Neuropsychological evidence and the articulatory loop

STM patients and the articulatory loop

As we saw earlier, neuropsychological evidence from patients with defective short-term memory but normal long-term learning presented one of the major reasons for dissatisfaction with the modal model of STM. In general, such evidence fitted well with the working memory hypothesis, since it could be argued that such patients had suffered damage to one of the subsidiary slave systems of working memory rather than to the central executive. The obvious candidate for the locus of such damage was the articulatory loop. Since patients with STM deficits have lesions within the area of the brain normally associated with speech, and since aphasia is frequently accompanied by impaired memory span, the evidence seemed to fit reasonably well.

There were, however, three points at which the initial Baddeley and Hitch (1974) version of the working memory appeared to be at variance with neuropsychological data. First, such patients typically have a substantially better span for visually presented material than for auditory, the reverse of normal subjects (Shallice and Warrington 1970); this suggests the existence of some form of visual STM capable of storing *sequences* of items, and as such somewhat different from the Visuospatial Sketch Pad suggested by Baddeley and Hitch. Secondly, such patients show a reduced recency effect (Shallice and Warrington, 1970; Basso *et al.* 1982), a result that suggests a positive association between span and recency rather than the disassociation showed in the Baddeley and Hitch free recall data. Both these points will be discussed in detail later.

The third problem concerns the specific nature of the deficit in STM patients. The first version of the loop model suggested that it should be articulatory in nature, whereas Shallice and Warrington argue for a defect in an auditory input store. This interpretation was supported by two major pieces of evidence. The first was based on the absence of any apparent articulatory deficit in at least one STM patient, J.B. A detailed analysis of her spontaneous speech by Shallice and Butterworth (1977) indicated that her fluency was well within the normal range, as measured by the pattern of pausing during continuous speech. While this presented a problem for the articulatory interpretation, it was by no means conclusive evidence. Although J.B. did show impressively normal speech, she herself commented that people had occasionally suggested that her speech was slightly unusual. Common observation suggests that there is a very wide variation in pause structure among normal speakers, indicating that this might not be a particularly sensitive test of articulatory capacity. Finally, J.B. was atypical in having no apparent speech impairment, since most patients with impaired span are also somewhat aphasic. Furthermore, at the time of testing she had had many years to learn to cope with any speech difficulties, and had in fact shown a steady tendency for her digit span to improve. The Shallice and Butterworth result was therefore, worrying but not crucial.

A further source of evidence against the articulatory interpretation came from a study in which Shallice and Warrrington (1974) compared memory span for spoken words with that for environmental sounds such as a creaking door or a barking dog. In order to prevent subvocal rehearsal, which would presumably tend to favour the words, they required subjects to suppress articulation. The STM patients showed a deficit in span for words, but not in the case of environmental sounds. This is not simply because such sounds are easier, since the control subjects actually did significantly worse on sounds than words. While at first sight, this result fits well into the working memory model, suggesting that the STM deficit is peculiar to spoken language, a problem arises when we bear in mind the fact that subjects were suppressing articulation during this study. If the storage of the speech items was articulatory in nature, then suppression should equate performance of patients and controls by removing the one component that differentiates the patients from the controls. The fact that the difference between groups remains suggests that the patients show a deficit in an acoustic rather than an articulatory store. The fact that no decrement occurs for environmental sounds suggests that the defective store is speech-based.

To summarize, at a time when the evidence from normal subjects still seemed to fit reasonably well with a concept of an articulatory code, the neuropsychological evidence was suggesting that some form of auditory input store might be more plausible. I regarded the neuropsychological evidence as worrying but not sufficiently strong on its own to cause the abandonment of the simple articulatory model in favour of a more complex system. As we saw earlier however, subsequent data from experiments on normal subjects forced us to elaborate the model, separating out the phonological store and articulatory control process. How well does the revised articulatory loop model fit the neuropsychological data?

If we assume that patients such as JB who have defective STM together with fluent speech suffer from a defect in the phonological store while having the articulatory control processing intact, then the various results fit neatly into place. If the phonological store is primarily concerned with *input*, then damage to such a store is entirely consistent with continued fluent speech. Our experiments on the influence of irrelevant speech on memory suggest that the store can be accessed directly by spoken material, but not by noise, a result that is consistent with Shallice and Warrington's data suggesting that it is used to hold sequences of words but not environmental sounds.

One could also make a number of predictions about the behaviour of such patients, but unfortunately pure cases with normal speech are extremely rare. I did have the opportunity to test J.B., but her span continued to increase, and on two occasions when I tested her, her behaviour was inconsistent, showing no evidence of word length effect on the first session, together with both a word length effect and overt evidence of subvocal rehearsal on the second.

The opportunity then occurred of testing a new case P.V., (Basso *et al.* 1982) with an Italian colleague Giuseppe Vallar. We began with the study of the effect of phonological similarity on memory span using both auditory and visual presentation. Fortunately, Italian letter names resemble English in being easily divided to those that are mutually confusable and those that are not. What might one predict from this study? If P.V. is totally devoid of a phonological store, then one might expect no similarity effect with either spoken or visual input. If on the other hand she has a phonological store but is unable or unwilling to operate the articulatory rehearsal process, one might expect a similarity effect with spoken but not with visual presentation. This is what we observed, as Table 5.3 shows.

If the articulatory control process is not being used, one might make the further prediction that articulatory suppression would not have its usual deleterious effect. We therefore conducted a second experiment in which sequences of letters were presented visually, and the subject was either free to rehearse or required to suppress articulation by repeatedly

TABLE 5.3
Probability of correctly recalling phonologically similar and dissimilar consonant sequences

AUDITORY PRESENTATION

Sequence Length	Control		Similar	
	Sequences	(Items)	Sequences	(Items)
2	1.0	(1.0)	0.60	(.75)
3	0.40	(0.73)	0	(.23)
4	0	(0.32)	—	—

VISUAL PRESENTATION

Sequence Length	Control		Similar	
	Sequences	(Items)	Sequences	(Items)
2	1.0	(1.0)	1.0	(1.0)
3	0.80	(0.87)	0.90	(0.93)
4	0.70	(0.85)	0.50	(0.75)
5	0.10	(0.54)	0.60	(0.76)

counting from one to six. Supression had no effect on performance.

This result is interesting for two reasons. First, because it reinforces the previous conclusion that P.V. does not use subvocal rehearsal to aid her STM performance, and secondly because it suggests that the general attentional demand of repeated counting is not sufficient to impair memory performance. This is relevant to the objection that is sometimes raised to drawing conclusions from suppression experiments, namely that the effects might stem from the general attentional demands of repeated counting rather than from interfering specifically with phonological processing. P.V.'s results suggest that the attentional demands of suppression at moderate rates are minimal (c.f. Besner, Davies, and Daniels 1981).

The evidence then is consistent with the view that P.V. takes little advantage of subvocal rehearsal, at least with visually presented material. It could, however, be argued that rehearsal may occur with auditory presentation. Subvocal rehearsal might be more necessary under these conditions, as the subject would have to cope without the aid of a visual short-term store, and it is conceivable furthermore that rehearsal might be easier with auditory presentation. There is evidence that suggests that the verbal repetition of heard speech is a particularly compatible response (Davis, Moray, and Treisman 1961; McLeod and Posner 1984). We, therefore, used the word length effect combined with auditory presentation to explore this possibility.

Two sets of words were used, one comprising words of two syllables and the other five-syllable words. P.V. was familiarized with the two sets of words, and it was ensured that she could pronounce all without difficulty. Her memory span for the two sets of words was then tested using spoken presentation. No word length effect occurred, indeed the difference was marginally in favour of the long words.

All our results so far then are consistent with the hypothesis that P.V. does not use subvocal rehearsal. We are still, however, not able to distinguish whether this is because she is *incapable* of the necessary rapid articulation, or because she *chooses* not to use this strategy. The obvious way of testing this might have been to attempt to teach her various memory strategies. We were, however, reluctant to risk confounding any future results by teaching particular strategies. There was no evidence to suggest that any such training might be necessary or useful therapeutically, and consequently we decided not to risk influencing the subsequent behaviour of this particularly pure and rare case.

We chose instead to measure P.V.'s articulatory skill directly by having her count repeatedly from one to ten, and then articulate the alphabet repeatedly. We timed her performance and compared it with that of normal control subjects of similar age and educational background. She was quite unimpaired on this task.

We explored two further articulatory tasks which seemed more likely to involve the phonological store (Vallar and Baddeley unpublished). In one condition, she was required to read out lists comprising either the two-syllable or five-syllable words used in the word length study. She showed a slight impairment on this task. This is consistent with the evidence, to be discussed in a later section of a phonological component in reading.

A clearer impairment showed in the third task we studied, that of shadowing sequences of spoken words. We again used the two- and five-syllable items, and presented them at various rates. While she was able to perform this task at slow rates, as speed increased, her performance fell behind that of controls. Since this task probably used the phonological store as a buffer to avoid temporary overload at faster rates, the observed decrement is unsurprising.

To summarize, our results are consistent with the view that P.V. has a defective phonological store. With auditory presentation, she presumably has no option but to use this store, despite the fact that it appears to have a capacity of only two items. Her use of the store is reflected by a clear phonological similarity effect. When presentation is visual, however, she appears to have access to a more efficient system with a capacity somewhere in the region of four items. Bearing this in mind, there is presumably little advantage in attempting to transfer information to the defective phonological store. Earlier studies on this patient (Basso *et al.* 1982) showed that even when the sequence to be retained comprises only a single digit, rate of forgetting is extremely rapid with auditory presentation. If, as the word length effect suggests, memory span is a joint function of rate of decay and rate of rehearsal, then it seems unlikely that rehearsal would be a useful strategy, since by the time she has articulated three or four items, the trace of the first item will have decayed beyond retrieval.

The view that P.V. chooses not to use articulatory rehearsal, rather than that she is incapable of such rehearsal is supported by her unimpaired capacity for reciting well-learned sequences such as the alphabet and numbers. If we assume that subvocal rehearsal involves reading out items from a phonological store, articulating them and thereby refreshing the phonological trace, then we have not demonstrated that this complete process is still available to P.V. However, since we know that the articulatory processes themselves appear to be relatively intact, if the control process is defective it must presumably be at the point of reading out from the phonological store, or feeding back into it. We already know from the studies using the Peterson short-term forgetting task, that rate of forgetting is particularly rapid. Since we have positive evidence of defective phonological storage, the assumption of further deficits for which there is no evidence seems neither necessary nor desirable.

The role of STM in comprehension

We have so far attempted to use the concepts and techniques of working memory to understand a neuropsychological deficit, the STM impairment shown by P.V. Given that this stage is successful, then it opens the way for a second stage of investigation in which the performance of the patient on a range of new tasks is used to gain some insight into the role of working memory in those tasks.

In the case of P.V., we have gone on to study her comprehension of spoken and written text in the belief that this will throw light on the role of the phonological store in normal comprehension (Vallar and Baddeley 1984*b*). This line of research is still ongoing; while P.V.'s auditory comprehension has been explored in some detail, we are still at a relatively early stage in studying her reading performance.

We began by testing P.V.'s capacity for phonological processing, presenting pairs of spoken consonant and vowel syllables, and requiring her to say whether successive items are the same or different (e.g. *pa-ba* (No) or *pa-pa* (Yes)). Her performance on this task was normal. She also proved able to comprehend individual spoken words by pointing to one of a range of pictures in a shortened version of the Peabody Picture–Vocabulary Test, and was successful with words ranging from short easy items such as 'house' to long and relatively difficult ones (e.g. 'entomology').

We next tested her syntactic comprehension using a test in which sentences were spoken and she was required to indicate which of a pair of pictures matched the sentence. She proved able to perform this task virtually perfectly even when the sentences were semantically reversible (e.g. *The cat is chased by the dog* versus *The dog is chased by the cat*). Saffran and Marin (1975) report that their patients had difficulty in dealing with sentences of this type. However they tested comprehension indirectly through repetition, a task relying heavily on memory. They also used somewhat longer sentences than those in our syntactic test. Furthermore their patients had a smaller sentence span than P.V. whose span for meaningful words in a sentence was 6 words.

We then went on to test the capacity of P.V. to verify sentences varying in complexity. The simplest condition we presented required her to verify statements about the world (e.g. *Plants grow in gardens* versus *Plants are people*). A second condition involved taking simple sentences and elaborating them by adding verbiage (e.g. *There is no doubt that champagne is something that can certainly be bought in shops* versus *It is true that physicians comprise a profession that is manufactured in factories from time to time*). The final condition involved complex sentences in which the erroneous sentence was produced by reversing the order of two of its constituents. Examples are *It is fortunate that most rivers are able to be crossed by bridges that are strong enough for cars* (true) versus *The world divides the equator into two hemispheres the northern and the southern* (false).

The results of this latter test proved clear-cut. Whether tested for auditory comprehension or reading, P.V. had no difficulty in accurately categorising either the simple sentences or those sentences elaborated by adding verbiage. Her performance on the last type of sentence however was virtually at chance for both spoken and written presentation.

In a subsequent as yet unpublished study, we have gone on to investigate the capacity of P.V. to deal with inconsistencies of anaphoric reference within spoken passages. She appears to be capable of dealing with anaphora within a sentence even though the two constituents are separated by several phases. In a between-sentence case, she appears to be reasonably accurate at detecting mismatches of gender, but much less good at detecting discrepancies of number. Interpretation of this awaits the testing of suitable controls which is proceeding at present.

In general however P.V.'s comprehension of spoken discourse appears to be remarkably good, with one or two striking exceptions, including her performance on the Token Test and on the highly complex sentences just described. She appears to operate by rapidly accessing a semantic code with the result that she runs into difficulties only when the semantic code needs to be supplemented by a representation of the surface structure that extends beyond the half dozen or so words of connected text that she retains phonologically. In this respect her processing is consistent with views of comprehension such as that presented by Marslen-Wilson and Tyler (1981) who assume that the normal comprehension of spoken discourse involves the rapid and continuous mapping of the auditory input onto a semantic representation.

We have also begun to study P.V.'s reading comprehension and have established that she is able to read and accurately verify both short sentences and sentences lengthened by adding verbiage. There is however some evidence that her reading is slow, and somewhat surprisingly appears to involve marked subvocalization. When asked to read while suppressing articulation she at first declared that she was unable to do so. On a subsequent occasion however she was prepared to make judgements on individual words while suppressing articulation. Her speed of performance was unaffected, as was her capacity for making semantic judgements by categorising words into 'living' versus 'non-living'. We tested her phonological coding of written words by requiring her to judge the stress in a series of Italian words. Trisyllabic Italian words may have the stress on either the first syllable (e.g. *macchina*) or on the second (e.g. *ragazza*). She was able to perform this task virtually perfectly under control conditions but made many errors when suppressing.

There is no doubt that we need to explore P.V.'s reading more carefully before drawing any firm conclusions. It is possible the impairment in her phonological store is such that even a relatively undemanding storage task such as judgement of stress requires the additional boost of subvocal rehearsal in order to create a trace that is strong enough to support a phonological judgement task. Her auditory memory span results indicate of course that such a subvocal boost is not sufficient to increase her span substantially.

Short-term memory in the absence of speech

If we agree with Shallice and Warrington that both K.F. and P.V. suffer from a defective phonological input store, the question arises as to whether other patients exist with defects to other parts of the articulatory loop system. It is almost certainly the case that they do since the aphasias are often associated with defected STM performance (Allport 1984; Ostergaard and Meudell 1984). The actual nature of the defect, however, is likely to depend on the type of aphasia, and while this seems to be potentially a very fruitful area of study, the evidence at present is still somewhat fragmentary. Interpretation is further complicated by the fact that the classification of patients is still controversial, and cases rarely pure. Further complications arise because aphasia is frequently associated with more general language disturbance, including comprehension difficulties. Hence, although the relationship betw een working memory and aphasia is a very promising field, it is still at a very early stage of development, and will not be discussed further here.

A rather simpler situation, however, occurs in the case of patients whose general linguistic abilities are unimpaired, but who are unable to speak as a result of damage to the system involved in the relatively peripheral control of the speech musculature. Such patients tend to be classified as *anarthric, aphemic,* or as suffering from *subcortical motor aphasia.* They raise the interesting question of the extent to which the articulatory loop is dependent on the adequate operation of the relatively peripheral articulatory processes, and to what extent the system can operate without peripheral feedback.

Barbara Wilson and I were recently able to study such a patient (Baddeley and Wilson 1985). He was a 21 year old Oxford University student who had been badly injured in a car crash a year before. He recoved consciousness after three weeks but was grossly disabled, suffering from spastic quadriplegia. He had recovered to a point at which he could move around unaided using a wheelchair but was totally unable to speak apart from uttering a single inspiratory sound, resembling something between a laugh and a groan. His speech deficit was attributed to brain stem damage. He was, however, able to communicate by means of a Canon Communicator, a hand-held device with a QWERTY keyboard and a printed tape output. His verbal IQ was 109 and performance IQ 90. These are both lower than one would expect of an Oxford undergraduate, and that together with the verbal-performance discrepancy suggests some brain damage.

Evidence from both detailed test performance and his general behaviour suggested some probable frontal damage. There was, however, nothing to suggest language impairment. His vocabulary score on the WAIS was above average (a scaled score of 13, where the population average would be 10), and he expressed himself in a grammatical and articulate if somewhat verbose way using his communicator. In view of the somewhat laborious process of typing out all communication, one might expect his output to be somewhat telegraphic. Instead, it tended to be grammatical, but rambling and often slightly off the point. For example, when asked 'What does this saying mean—*Still waters run deep?*' he typed 'Profundity lies in action—the louder you talk, the less you know'. His performance on the Token Test, which involves obeying increasingly complex instructions was virtually perfect, suggesting no comprehension difficulties. He appears then to be someone with no capacity for producing *speech*, but with no deficit in either comprehension or the manual production of *language.*

What might one expect the effect of this speech deficit to be on his STM performance? This, of course, depends crucially on whether adequate functioning of the articulatory loop depends on the capacity to generate speech. If it does, then one would expect him to perform in an analogous way to a normal subject under articulatory suppression. Hence, one would expect some impairment in memory span, a phonological similarity effect with auditory but not visual presentation, and no word length effect. On the other hand, if the articulatory loop operates at a level above that of actual speech production, and does not rely on feedback from articulation, then one would expect his memory performance to be comparatively normal.

We began by considering his digit span score. This was six items, about average, but rather lower than one would expect to find in an Oxford student. Since some subjects certainly do have a digit span under supression of six items, this in itself was inconclusive. We next studied his memory span for phonologically similar and dissimilar letters, using both auditory and visual presentation at a rate of one letter per second. A clear phonological similarity effect occurred, with both auditory and visual presentation. This strongly suggests that phonologically encoding a visually presented letter is not dependent on the ability to pronounce it.

In order to gain some indication as to whether he was able to rehearse, we compared his memory span for auditorily presented words of one and five syllables. Again, we used pointing as a response with the sets of words typed out on cards. Since there was some evidence that he was using visual location as a cue, we discouraged this by removing the card during presentation and only exposing it at recall. He was tested on ten sequences of five words taken from each of two sets, one comprising ten words of five syllables and one comprising ten monosyllables. There was a clear word-length effect with only two of the ten sequences of long words being recalled correctly compared with five of the short word set; if measured in terms of correct items 29 long as against 39 short. This seems to suggest then that he was capable of some form of subvocal maintenance rehearsal.

We next explored his ability to make phonological judgements, requiring him to perform three homophone judgement tasks. The first of those required him to decide whether a word and non-word would sound the same when pronounced, examples being *ocean–oshun* (yes) and *harbour–harbut* (no). A second task involved deciding whether two non-words would or would not sound the same, e.g. *frelame–phrelaim* (yes), and *lopor–lupper* (no) while a third condition involved deciding whether each of 15 non-words would sound like a word if pronounced, e.g. *philthee* (yes), *lonnot* (no).

We compared the performance of G.B. with that of a sample of 16 members of the Applied Psychology Unit subject panel. The results showed that G.B. is able to perform all three tasks at well above chance level, and in terms of accuracy at least is within the range of normal performance on all three. Speed of performance, however, was considerably slower than that observed in any of our normal controls. In terms of both speed and accuracy, his performance appeared to be better in that condition where one of the two items is a real word, and worse in the condition in which each judgement involves two non-words, neither of which sounds like an English word.

Results so far suggest that G.B. is able to make rhyme judgements accurately if somewhat slowly. Unfortunately, since all three tests involved phonological judgements, we have no means of knowing whether this slowness is peculiar to rhyme judgements or whether it represents a general slowing down in performance. In order to test this further, we required him to perform three similar tasks devised by Coltheart (Coltheart and Patterson in Press), one involving judging whether regular words do or do not rhyme, one making similar judgements about orthographically irregular words, while the third involves synonym comparison. If G.B.'s slowness is due to his general motor and intellectual problems, we would expect this third semantic condition to be slowed down as much as the two phonological tasks. If on the other hand, rhyme judgements present a special problem, we would expect less slowing in G.B.'s ability to judge synonyms. Performance on these three tests demonstrated that G.B. was able to make rhyme judgements accurately if slowly, with performance being unimpaired by irregular orthography. His performance on the synonym task was well within the range of normal accuracy, supporting the previous contention that his comprehension was good. Again, however, he performed very slowly, suggesting that the slowness in making rhyme judgements that we observed previously represents a general impairment rather than a particular difficulty in phonological processing.

G.B. is the purest case we have studied, but we have been able to explore the generality of our results using a further five cases who for one reason or another were less pure in their anarthria. The pattern of results was substantially identical (Baddeley and Wilson 1985).

Having collected these data we then came across a closely related paper by Nebes (1975) who also studies a patient with a severe articulatory deficit. His 72 year old female subject also had a normal memory span of six digits, and appeared to have good language comprehension as measured by the Token Test and the Peabody picture vocabulary test which involves selecting a picture associated with an orally presented word. She could communicate in writing, typically producing sentences that were short and telegraphic but grammatically correct, apart from the fact that words were omitted, particularly articles and prepositions.

Her ability to make phonological judgements about printed words was tested in a number of ways, including indication of number of syllables and judgement of rhyme. She showed good evidence of phonological coding.

A final experiment concerned the role of phonological similarity in memory. She was presented with a string of four letters one at a time at a rate of two per second. The letters were taken from a set of ten comprising five phonologically confusable pairs (*db, iy, sx, qu, jk*). She was given a total of 80 trials, and those 17 cases in which only a single intrusion error occurred were analysed further. Given the nature of the material, one would expect by chance about 3 of the 17 intrusion errors to be similar to the correct item. In fact, 12 of the 17 were phonological confusions. It appears then that she like our patient has normal memory performance, shows good ability to make rhyme judgements and a clear tendency to encode visually presented letters phonologically. Finally, a broadly similar conclusion has been reached following an as yet unpublished series of studies carried out by Vallar and his colleagues on two anarthric Italian patients.

In conclusion then, it appears that in the case of previously normal adults, the ability to speak is not essential either for the phonological encoding or written material or on the basis of our word-length results, for subvocal rehearsal. This suggests that the loop and its rehearsal processes are operating at a much deeper level than might at first seem likely, apparently relying on central speech control codes which appear to be able to function in the absence of peripheral feedback. If this is the case, it is perhaps not surprising that attempts to study inner speech through the electro-myographic monitoring of the peripheral speech musculature have had only limited success.

Is the control of inner speech internalized automatically, or does it only develop as speech becomes an increasingly overlearned skill? It would in this connection be interesting to study the role of inner speech in the memory performance of congenitally anarthric children, some of whom can apparently have well-developed language skills. I know of no evidence on this point, but suspect that subvocalization develops from overt speech, relying initially on peripheral articulation to a much greater extent than appears to be necessary in adults. We shall however return to the question of the development of working memory in a later chapter.

6 Imagery and visuo-spatial working memory

A second area in which we have proposed a slave system of WM is in the processing of visuo-spatial material. There is considerable evidence for a separation of visual and verbal processes, stemming both from studies of normal memory and from neuropsychological research (De Renzi 1982; Milner 1971; Paivio 1971). We ourselves have explored one aspect of visual processing in some detail and to account for our results in the area of generating and manipulating visuo-spatial images have proposed a system that we refer to as the *visuo-spatial scratchpad* or *sketchpad*. There are in addition, a number of further areas where there is good evidence for some form of visual STM. While it is still far from clear how these areas are related to each other, or to the visuo-spatial sketchpad, they will be described, and their interrelationship discussed.

The visuo-spatial sketchpad

At about the same time as Hitch and I were starting to explore the possible role of WM in verbal reasoning, Gerard Quinn and I were beginning to investigate visual imagery using interference procedures. We carried out a number of experiments which unsuccessfully attempted to disrupt the use of visual imagery in remembering verbal stimuli by the subsequent requirement to process visual material. After working on this for one year I left Sussex, where Quinn was a research student, to move to the University of Stirling. With the help of a colleague, Neil Thompson, and two students Sandra Grant and Elspeth Wight, I decided to have one last try. Our experiment produced remarkably clear results, and led to a line of work that concerns itself with what I subsequently began to refer to as the visuo-spatial scratchpad, a name that was meant to suggest a system especially well adapted to the temporary storage of spatial information, much as a pad of paper might be used by someone trying for example to work out a geometric puzzle. Quinn has subsequently suggested that scratchpad is probably not quite the right word, suggesting as it does verbal notes at least as much as visual shapes. He suggested that the term 'sketchpad' would be better. I agree, and propose subsequently to refer to this hypothetical system as the 'visuo-spatial sketchpad', abbreviated as VSSP.

To return to our last desperate attempt to produce visual imagery interference effects: Our earlier experiments had basically been concerned with studying words of high or low rated imageability, and represented a series of attempts to replicate a striking phenomenon reported by Atwood (1971). He carried out an experiment in which subjects heard either highly imageable phrases such as *Nudist devouring bird*, or highly abstract phrases such as *The intellect of Einstein was a miracle*. Each phrase was followed by a simple classification task involving the presentation of the digits *1* or *2* either auditorily or visually. Atwood reported a marked tendency for the imageable phrases to be disrupted much more by processing the visually presented digits, while the abstract sentences were disrupted more by auditory processing.

We were unable to replicate this result as were a number of other investigators (Bower personal communication; Neisser personal communication), although Janssen (1976) has subsequently produced clear evidence of a similar though much weaker effect. I decided to move away from the Atwood paradigm trying instead to explore a phenomenon I had experienced that seemed to have implications for the nature of visual imagery. While in the US I developed an interest in American football, and on one occasion tried to listen to a game on the car radio while driving along a Californian freeway. I noticed that as my image of the field of play and course of game developed, my steering became more erratic, and I rapidly switched to a less hazardous music programme.

In our attempt to replicate this effect in the laboratory, we moved away from our previous policy of using high and low imageability words and phrases, and opted instead for two tasks which had already been shown by Brooks (1968) to involve visuo-spatial and verbal imagery. The spatial task involved showing the subject a block capital letter, with the bottom left hand corner marked with a star. His task was to look away from the letter and, holding it in his minds eye, to go around the letter from the star responding 'yes' if the corner in question was at the top or bottom, and 'no' otherwise. Hence for the letter *F,* the response would be 'yes' 'yes' 'yes', 'no' 'no' 'no' 'no' 'no' 'no' 'yes'. The verbal task devised by Brooks involved presenting the subject with a sentence, for example *A bird in hand is not in the bush.* The subject's task was to hold this in memory, and then successively categorize each word as either a noun (in which case he should respond 'yes'), or a verb, ('no'). Hence for that particular sentence the sequence would be 'no' 'yes' 'no' 'yes' 'no' 'no' 'no' 'no' 'yes'. Brooks used two methods of responding, either spoken or manual, this involved pointing to a series of 'yeses' or 'nos' scattered irregularly down the response sheet. He observed a clear interaction between type of memory task and mode of response, with the visual letter task being performed more accurately when the response was spoken than when it involved pointing, while the reverse was the case for the sentence task.

We chose to simulate the task of driving with the simple task of tracking, using a pursuit rotor in which a spot of light followed a circular path. The subject attempted to keep a stylus on the spot, his performance being measured by the total amount of time on target. Subjects were instructed to regard the classification tasks as primary and so avoid errors. This they did quite successfully. The results of the experiment are shown in Table 6.1 from which it is clear that the spatial letter-processing task disrupted tracking performance, an effect shown by all subjects tested, whereas the verbal task caused only slight and nonsignificant impairment.

TABLE 6.1
Influence of visual and verbal memory tasks on visual pursuit tracking

	Control (No memory task)	Verbal memory	Visual memory
Mean per cent time on target	90.8	88.0	78.0
S.D.	5.7	4.6	11.6

Having shown that a visuo-spatial memory task was capable of disrupting tracking performance, our next experiment reversed the procedure in order to determine whether tracking would interfere with memory. We again utilized a technique developed by Brooks, this time involving a modified memory span procedure (Brooks 1967). In it, the subject is first shown a four by four matrix with the second cell on the second row marked as the starting square (see Fig. 6.1). The subject's task is to repeat back exactly what the experimenter says. One set of statements involve a series of spatial adjectives which allow the sequence to be mapped onto the matrix as a particular shape or path. The second type of sequence is formally equivalent with the exception that the spatial adjective *above, below, left,* and *right* are replaced by the non-spatial adjectives *good, bad, slow,* and *quick* (see Fig. 6.1).

Sequences are read out at the rate of one item per 2.5 seconds, a rate which allows the spatial adjectives to be encoded using the matrix, but is too rapid to allow subjects to perform the much more arbitrary recoding that would be required to remember the nonsense sequences spatially. Our subjects, like those of Brooks found the spatial sequences easier than the nonsense, but provided they were represented with sequences of eight spatial items and only six nonsense items, overall probability of recalling the sequence completely correctly was approximately equal for the two types of material.

In our first experiments using this procedure, we required our subjects to listen to and recall visuo-spatial and nonsense sequences, both under

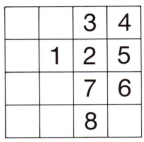

		3	4
	1	2	5
		7	6
		8	

Spatial material	Nonsense material
In starting square put a 1.	In the starting square put a 1.
In the next square to the *right* put a 2.	In the next square to the *quick* put a 2.
In the next square *up* put a 3.	In the next square to the *good* put a 3.
In the next square to the *right* put a 4.	In the next square to the *quick* put a 4.
In the next square *down* put a 5.	In the next square to the *bad* put a 5.
In the next square *down* put a 6.	In the next square to the *bad* put a 6.
In the next square to the *left* put a 7.	In the next square to the *slow* put a 7.
In the next square *down* put an 8.	In the next square to the *bad* put an 8.

Fig. 6.1. Example of stimulus material developed by Brooks and used in experiments on the visuo-spatial sketchpad.

control conditions, and while performing our pursuit-rotor tracking task. Fig 6.2 shows the effect of tracking on performance. There is a very marked tendency for tracking to disrupt the visuo-spatial memory task, while having no effect on the nonsense task which presumably relies on rote verbal memory.

Visual or spatial memory?

We had tended up to this point to attribute our results to *visual* imagery. They were, however, equally explicable in terms of a purely spatial and non-visual code, or indeed a code involving both. Our next experiment attempted to decide between these two possibilities (Baddeley and Lieberman 1980). We did so by comparing two potentially disrupting secondary tasks, one involving spatial but not visual processing, while the other involved visual judgements with a minimal spatial component.

We again used the Brooks matrix test as our index of visuo-spatial memory. The non-visual spatial task involved a somewhat complex procedure that led to the study being known as the pit-and-the-pendulum experiment. Subjects were blindfolded and seated in front of a pendulum suspended from the ceiling. At the end of the pendulum was a sound source that emitted a steady tone. The pendulum also contained a photo cell and when a flashlight was shone on this, the steady tone changed to a discontinuous bleep. The room was darkened, the pendulum swung and the subject was instructed to attempt to keep the hand-held flashlight

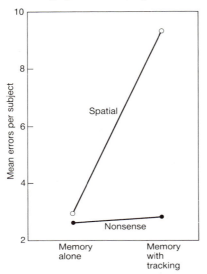

Fig. 6.2. The influence of concurrent tracking on memory span for visualizable and nonvisualizable sequences (Baddeley *et al.* 1974).

focused on the bob of pendulum, receiving feedback when on target from the change in tone that it emitted. We have then, an auditory but spatial tracking task. Since the subject was blindfolded, he was devoid of peripheral visual input. Hence if the disruption of imagery represents a *visual* effect, it should not be observed using this non-visual technique.

Our second disruption technique involved a series of brightness judgements. The subject was seated in a darkened room and required to observe a screen on which a slide projector exposed a series of blank slides. The slides provided illumination at two different brightnesses, and the subject was required to press a single key whenever a bright slide was presented. After suitable practice on the secondary tasks, our subjects were required to combine them with the previously described matrix memory task. Our results showed a clear tendency for the non-visual pendulum tracking task to disrupt the retention of spatially coded material more than that of the nonsense sequence.

In contrast, the brightness judgement task caused significantly more disruption of performance of the nonsense than the spatial task: spatial task disruption by the brightness judgement did not in fact reach statistical significance. This crossover effect, although not a necessary prediction of the spatial hypothesis, nonetheless was a very fortunate result since it allowed us to rule out the possibility that our spatial disruption effect occurred simply because the spatial task was more sensitive to the effects of disruption than the nonsense task.

Phillips and Christie (1977*a*, *b*) have argued that our results do not necessarily argue for separate visuo-spatial and verbal coding, but could reflect one of these systems, together with a limited-capacity central executive. On this argument, our demonstrations of the disruption of performance using the spatial task might simply reflect a heavier reliance of this task on the central executive, rather than its dependence on a specifically spatial code. Our demonstration of the greater sensitivity of the nonsense task in the last experiment makes this interpretation unlikely, though unfortunately does not rule out the possibility that one of the two effects we are showing depends on the central executive rather than a slave system. One might for example explain our results in terms of a visuo-spatial system together with the central executive, the brightness judgement task for some reason stressing the executive more than the tracking task done.

Logically speaking, the existence of two separate systems can be demonstrated using the double dissociation procedure whereby one situation is shown in which Factor A is affected while Factor B is unaffected while a second demonstrates the opposite, a disruption in Factor B while Factor A is unaffected. A good example here is the neuropsychological evidence for two types of memory, resting as it does on the occurrence of patients with quite normal STS, coupled with grossly defective LTS, and on the other hand patients with normal LTS and defective STS (see Chapter 1). While this is an excellent procedure for separating two components, when the number of components exceeds two, it becomes increasingly impracticable to attempt to apply such a disassociation procedure. In the case of a dichotomy this gives four conditions, components A and B both normal, or both impaired (neither of which allows separation of the two), or the two crucial conditions in which A is normal and B impaired and vice versa. However, once *three* components are assumed, the number of permutations rises to eight, of which six involve the type of partial impairment necessary for teasing out the separate components. It is virtually never possible to find tasks or patients characteristic of all six. With four components there is a total of 16 combinations of processes. It therefore seems likely that the application of the strict logic of the dissociation method is likely to become totally impracticable for a modular system as complex as WM.

One is, therefore, forced to opt for the rather looser validation technique of using converging operations, taking whatever opportunities one can devise for testing hypotheses in different ways and in different situations, with the aim of producing a coherent network of results that taken together, rule out most, if not all competing hypotheses. Since I assume that the working memory system will ultimately prove to comprise considerably more than two or three subcomponents, I myself believe that this is currently the only practicable way of experimentally investigating a system as complex as working memory.

Eye movements and the VSSP

The evidence we have collected so far is consistent with the assumption of a slave system that is capable of using auditory information to construct a spatial code. There is evidence from our own studies to suggest that a concurrent spatial tracking task will disrupt the utilization of this system, while the work of Brooks (1967) and Byrne (1974) suggests that requiring the subject to indicate his response by pointing will also disrupt performance, unless the pointing response is compatible with the spatial demands of retrieval. Hence Byrne showed that when subjects were required to recall an array of pictures arranged in a circle, their recall was disrupted if they were required to point in a counter-clockwise series of steps while recalling in clockwise order, but was enhanced when the direction of pointing and recall was the same. These results and others (e.g. Wright, Holloway, and Aldrich, 1974) are consistent with the view that the system is spatially based, and disrupted by spatially determined motor tasks.

There is, however, a cluster of findings which do not fit at all obviously into this pattern. These are essentially studies that show that the act of reading disrupts visuo-spatial imagery more than the act of listening. For example Brooks (1968), using the matrix task previously described, presented the material either auditorily or as a sequence of written statements. He found that the spatial matrix task was performed best under auditory presentation, while the nonsense task was best performed when presented visually.

At first sight this seems puzzling, since reading appears to be a visual rather than a *spatial* task. It is, however, necessary in normal reading to maintain a relatively precise spatial framework if one is not to lose one's position in the text, and it has indeed been suggested that visuo-spatial memory plays an important part in normal reading (Kennedy 1983). In a study of eye movements in reading, Carpenter and Just (1977) note that in reading ambiguous sentences, subjects' eyes often back-track to precisely the source of ambiguity, implying that they have retained an accurate spatial representation of at least the last few words.

One possibility then is that reading interferes with utilization of the VSSP because of the requirement to maintain a visuo-spatial frame of reference during reading. It is, however, not entirely clear why this should be incompatible with the performance of the matrix task. Furthermore, Eddy and Glass (1981) found that reading interfered with the comprehension and judgement of high imagery sentences even when the sentence was presented sequentially with each successive word being added to the previous words on a CRT. The spatial demands here one would have thought were fairly minimal.

An alternative possibility that has been suggested on a number of occasions (e.g. Hebb 1968) is that eye movements are an important factor in either setting up images as Neisser (1976) suggests, or possibly in subsequently scanning them as is suggested by Kosslyn and Schwartz (1981). There have been a number of attempts to measure eye movements during the performance of tasks involving imagery, but although some of the reported results are positive (e.g. Antrobus, Antrobus, and Singer 1964), the magnitude of the effects tends to be small and their reliability low (e.g. Marks 1973). While this is discouraging for an eye movement hypothesis, it is not devastating evidence against such a view.

As we saw earlier, there is abundant evidence for the importance of subvocal speech in certain memory tasks, and yet if the only source of this evidence were from EMG recordings, it would be difficult to rule out the interpretation that subvocal articulation is merely an epiphenomenon that sometimes occurs in certain memory and reading tasks. Our study of the anarthric patient G.B., showed that the capacity for overt articulation is unnecessary for the control process of subvocal rehearsal to occur. It therefore seems likely that the peripheral manifestations of articulatory rehearsal are a relatively faint and unreliable index of the details of the process itself. By analogy, one might reasonably expect that an imagery control process based originally on eye movements, may in the practised adult be only weakly reflected in the overt movement of the eyes. In the case of subvocal articulation, we circumvented this problem by using suppression techniques. These presumably work because the subject is required to utilize both the deep and peripheral components of the articulatory process. The next series of experiments, carried out by Idzikowski, Dimbleby, Park, and myself (in preparation) attempts to apply an eye movement suppression technique to the study of visual imagery.

Eye movements and imagery

This series of experiments stemmed from a conversation I had with John Bransford of Vanderbilt University. He described an experiment by one of his students, Nancy Vye, in which he mentioned that the use of a visual imagery mnemonic had been substantially disrupted by what he termed 'optical nystagmus'. This intrigued me since it has obvious implications for the analysis of imagery. I unthinkingly interpreted the word 'nystagmus' in terms of my own most frequent contact with the word which stemmed from my interests in head injury and in diving. In both these contexts it refers to the involuntary movement of the eyes that occurs when cold water is poured into the ear, either unintentionally as occasionally occurs in diving, or intentionally, as when this technique is used to investigate the ocular reflexes of a deeply unconscious patient. (It does of course refer to involuntary eye movements from a much wider range of causes.) The result described by Bransford seemed intriguing, though apparently based on a somewhat drastic technique, and we decided to try to replicate it using a slightly more benign form of nystagmus, the post-rotational nystagmus that occurs after a subject has been spun around a few times (Idzikowski *et al.* in preparation).

Our first experiment therefore involved requiring our subjects to perform both the spatial and nonsense matrix tasks on each of two days. On one of these, the subject was rotated in a chair driven by an electric motor for 45 seconds before each sequence. Electro-oculography indicated that this was sufficient to produce optical nystagmus of at least five degrees range following each trial. Of the 8 subjects tested, one had to be replaced because of nausea. Half the subjects underwent the rotational condition on the first day, while the remainder began with the stationary control condition. The results of all this dizzy activity were initially somewhat disappointing. There was no significant effect of rotation on performance. If anything, the nonsense condition showed more signs of deterioration than the spatial, exactly the opposite to that predicted.

Our experiment seemed to have demonstrated that the involuntary movement of a subject's eyes was entirely consistent with the formation and utilization of visuo-spatial imagery. This result is open to two plausible interpretations. The first of these is that eye movements are simply irrelevant to the operation of the VSSP. The second is that the feature of eye movements that is crucial for imagery is the central system whereby the subject *controls* the eye movement. On this argument, the subjects in the previous experiment could have been using the internal central eye movement control system and ignoring the involuntary reflex peripheral activity of the eyes. While at first sight this may sound implausible, given that the eyes have the task of monitoring the outside world at the same time as the subject is utilizing imagery, there would be an obvious advantage to a system that was able to decouple any peripheral automatic activity of the eyes from the utilization of the eye movement control system in connection with internal imagery.

We decided, therefore, to run a second experiment in which we attempted to suppress imagery by means of *voluntary* eye movements. We designed the experiment that follows, and I wrote to Bransford describing our work, and received from his student, Nancy Vye, a preprint describing a study that was in fact more similar to our second experiment than our first. It appears that I had misunderstood Bransford's use of the term 'nystagmus'; Vye's study had involved eye movements induced by an oscillating visual stimulus. The image of Vanderbilt's students' with ears full of icy water was it seems entirely a figment of my imagination. Paradoxically then, our first experiment which we

thought was a replication turned out to be original, our second which
designed believing it to be original turned out to be closer to a rep
tion. Vye had indeed found effects of eye movements by the subject'
an imagery task in at least one of her studies. The effects were, howe
still far from convincing, the eye movements were not monitored, ar
was unclear to what extent the eye movements were voluntary and
what extent reflex. We therefore felt that it was well worthwhile cont
ing with our own study.

The crucial condition in our experiment was one in which the subj
were required to track with their eyes a bell shaped stimulus mo'
sinusoidally across a TV screen. In order to ensure that subjects were
lowing this instruction, we required them to watch for a change in
shape, from a bell to a square. When this happened, they had to pre
reaction time key as rapidly as possible. As a further insurance that
movements were occurring, we recorded them using electro-oculogra
The basic comparison was between the scanning condition and on
which the bell shape remained stationary. Both displays had a ba
ground of stationary lines to serve as a visual reference for the subject.

At this point in the experimental design, it occurred to us that
positive results could be explained in either of two ways. One might c
clude that the disruption came from the movement of the *eyes*, on
other hand one could argue that the *background* moving relative to
eyes might possibly act as some sort of visual mask, disrupting the vis
spatial image. We therefore incorporated two further conditions; in
first of these, the target bell was stationary but the background mov
On a simple visual masking hypothesis, this should cause as much disr
tion as the first condition in which the bell and the eyes moved acros
stationary patterned background. The last condition was one in wh
both bell and background moved. The masking hypothesis should pred
no disruption here since stimulus and background should both be k
focussed on the same part of the retina by the tracking of the eyes.
eye movement hypothesis would however predict clear disruption.

Our results are summarized in Fig. 6.3. We obtained a significant eff
of eye movement, an effect which interacted with type of material
1,23 = 9.68, $p < 0.01$). As Fig. 6.3 suggests, this results from a highly si
nificant decline in performance on the spatial task when the eyes a
required to move, coupled with a small and non-significant decline
performance on the nonsense task. In contrast to the clear eye moveme
effect, there was no trace of an effect of background movement.

Analysis of the reaction time data indicated that the requirement
track the moving target increased RT substantially, from 611 to 811 ms,
highly significant effect. Background movement also increased RT to
smaller but still significant extent, from 717 to 775 ms. There was, how
ever, no effect of type of memory task on RT, nor was there any differ

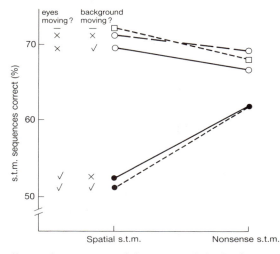

Fig. 6.3. The effects of movement of the eyes and the background on the use of visuo-spatial imagery: x=fixed, √=moving; —=free (data from Idzikowski *et al.* unpublished).

ence between RT's tested during presentation and during recall; the results obtained by Martin (1970) and discussed in Chapter 3 might have predicted a greater decrement in RT during recall than during learning. However, both the magnitude of this effect and the lack of difference between the effect during input and retrieval is consistent with our earlier interpretation of Martin's data, namely that concurrent RT will be very sensitive to the need to perform two response activities at the same time. In the present study, the eye movement and RT responses are required at the same time during *both* learning and recall.

Our second study then has given a clear indication that concurrent arbitrary eye movements can interfere differentially with the use of visuo-spatial imagery, and as such suggests that the central components of voluntary eye movements may be involved in some way as a control process in the VSSP.

The next experiment aimed to collect further information that might throw light on what aspects of the generation of utilization of images is disrupted by concurrent eye movements. Neisser (1976) suggests that images are the products of an anticipatory phase in perception. This might suggest that eye movements would interfere with the construction of images. Kosslyn and Shwartz (1981) suggest that images are scanned in a way that is similar to scanning a real visual scene, in which case one might expect disruption to occur principally at retrieval. A third possibility is that eye movements reflect a process involved in rehearsing or maintaining the image, in a way analogous to that in which articulation is assumed to maintain the phonological short-term trace. In this case, one would expect impairment at both input and recall.

Our third experiment therefore studied the effect of requiring the subject to track the moving bell shape either during input only, during recall only, during both or during neither. Results of the 24 subjects tested suggested that concurrent eye movements had a marked effect on performance in the spatial condition whether they occurred during input, recall or both.

It would clearly be premature to draw firm conclusions from the result of a single experiment. However, the disrupting effect does not appear to be confined either to input or retrieval, suggesting either that both these processes depend on similar control processes to eye movements, or else that the eye movement system is used to rehearse and maintain the image.

We should, however, perhaps consider a different interpretation based on that suggested by Phillips and Christie (1977b). They suggest that interference with visualization occurs because the visualizing process makes heavy general demands on a system analagous to the central executive in WM. They might argue that our concurrent eye movement task was in fact a means of loading up this central executive component, and that the memory task involving visualization tended to be particularly sensitive to this. Evidence from our second experiment might seem to support this, since the time to respond to a change in shape of the tracked target was substantially greater when the target was moving. However, if it were indeed the case that the spatial task made heavier demands on some central processor than the nonsense task, one might expect this also to be reflected in the reaction time task. It may be recalled there was absolutely no difference in latency to respond to a change in the visual stimulus being tracked depending on whether the subject was simultaneously performing the spatial or nonsense task.

We have so far spoken as if our results imply that eye movements and their control processes are themselves the critical factor in our results. However, it is entirely possible that the system controlling visual *attention* is the crucial factor. It is of course typically the case that the focus of attention moves with the eyes, but as Posner, Cohen, and Raffal (1982) have shown, it is possible to separate the focus of visual attention from that of visual gaze. We hope in the near future to separate the effect on visuo-spatial imagery of requiring switches of visual attention from that of voluntary but non-attentional eye movements.

It is perhaps worth pointing out at this point the analogy between the articulatory loop and the VSSP. Both systems appear to take advantage of an essentially passive perceptual input store. In both cases, the problem of coping with rapid decay from the store appears to have been solved by an active control process based on a response system, articulation in the case of the AL and eye movement in the case of the VSSP. These allow the transformation of a passive perceptual store into an active memory system that enables the organism to take information out of the relevant input store and to feed it back, thereby continuously refreshing the trace and minimizing forgetting.

However, despite the attractive analogy between such a model of the VSSP and the articulatory loop, it is important to bear in mind the fact that the evidence for the refreshment of a visual trace by implicit motoric activity is still relatively weak. As Phillips (personal communication) has pointed out, such a process would not seem well adapted to maintaining such visual features as colour and brightness, and if these can be shown to be stored in the VSSP, as Logie's work is beginning to suggest, then some other rehearsal mechanism would seem more plausible. Such a mechanism might involve some form of active maintenance, but on the other hand it could depend on the inhibition of competing excitation, hence minimizing interference. However, although the eye-movement hypothesis may well prove inadequate, it does have the great advantage of being relatively easy to test, and as such certainly merits further exploration.

Imagery and verbal memory

It may be recalled that our first reason for becoming interested in imagery was in connection with the powerful effect that imageability has on the retention of word lists. We proved unable to disrupt this effect and moved on to the more tractable problem of disrupting visuo-spatial immediate memory. Can we now take what we have learned about the VSSP and apply it to verbal memory?

We began by using the pursuit tracking task we had found so effective in previous experiments, and attempting to use it to abolish the effect of imageability on paired-associate learning (Baddeley, Grant, Wight, and Thomson 1975). Tracking was combined with a paired-associate learning task in which subjects were required to associate adjectives with nouns. We created two types of lists, one based on highly imageable pairs such as *bullet-gray* and *strawberry-ripe*, while other lists comprised abstract pairs such as *gratitude-infinite* and *idea-original.* Our subjects attempted to learn and recall these lists either concurrent with pursuit tracking or in a control condition that was free of any secondary task. If the VSSP is essential for the formation and utilization of images, then one might expect the normal advantage to the imageable list to be substantially reduced by concurrent tracking. Our results are shown in Fig. 6.4 from which it is clear that imageability and/or concreteness had its expected massive effect; the concurrent tracking task caused a small but significant

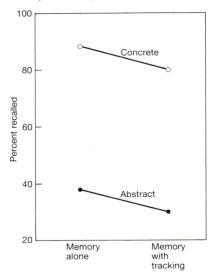

Fig. 6.4. The influence of concurrent tracking on the retention of concrete and abstract word pairs (Baddeley *et al.* 1974).

impairment in performance, but there was no trace of the predicted interaction.

This rather discouraging result left us with a number of possible interpretations. One was that the VSSP was not at all involved in long-term learning. A second was that the VSSP is necessary only when images have to be actively manipulated, something that might not be necessary for the occurrence of the word imageability effect. One way of deciding between these possibilities was to use a visual imagery mnemonic in which the subject was required to manipulate the images evoked by the words that were being learned and recalled. We therefore opted to study the effect of concurrent tracking on the use of a peg-word imagery mnemonic.

The mnemonic we chose was one in which the subject is first taught ten imageable peg-words, each rhyming with one of the numbers from one to ten. Hence he learns that *one* is a *bun*, *two* a *shoe*, a *three* a *tree*, *four* a *door*, etc. The task then involves being given ten unrelated words and imagining the first interacting in some way with *bun*, the second with *shoe*, etc. Hence if the first object were *crocodile*, one might imagine a crocodile with a huge bun between its jaws. If the second item were *pig*, then one might imagine a large shoe (two), with a pig sitting inside and so forth. The recall process involves using the number to cue the rhyming pegword (e.g. *one→bun*) which in turn conjures up the image of the crocodile holding the bun in its jaw.

In our rote learning condition, we prevented the subject from using an imagery mnemonic both by instruction and by presenting the pairs of words rapidly, since there is good evidence to suggest that slow presentation is necessary for the creation and utilization of such imagery mnemonics (Bugelski 1962). In order to ensure that adequate learning occurred, we presented the list of pairs in the rote condition several times, hence equating the total learning time with that operating in the imagery condition. As a further check on our previous result, we had two types of material, one comprising concrete imageable nouns, while the other involved abstract nouns of equal frequency within the language. Recall was tested by presenting the numbers from one to ten in scrambled order, and requiring the subject to provide the word that had been presented with that number. On half the trials, subjects were required to track using the pursuit rotor during both learning and recall while on the remaining trials they were free of any secondary task.

Table 6.2 shows the mean performance of our subjects as a function of learning strategy and concurrent tracking. As expected, the imagery mnemonic was effective. There was also an overall effect of concurrent tracking that was, however, modified by a significant interaction with instruction. As is clear from Table 6.2, tracking disrupts performance on the imagery condition but does not lead to any reliable drop in rote learning performance.

TABLE 6.2
Effect of concurrent tracking on the utilization of a visual imagery pegword mnemonic: per cent correct recall (Baddeley and Lieberman 1980)

Learning strategy	Control	Tracking	Memory decrement from tracking
Rote	50.0	49.5	0.5
Imagery	67.3	57.5	9.8

Insofar as the imageability of the words was concerned, we again found a significant advantage to high imageability words. The effect interacted with learning instructions, being stronger in the imagery than in the rote condition, but as in the previous experiment, there was no suggestion of an interaction between word imageability and concurrent tracking.

The results of this experiment, therefore, suggest that disruption of the operation of the VSSP by a concurrent tracking task will affect long-term learning, provided that learning involves the manipulation of visuo-spatial images. It reinforces the conclusion of the previous experiment in suggesting that the advantage enjoyed by highly imageable words over words of low imageability is unaffected by tracking. The most plausible interpretation of this result is probably to argue that a word's concreteness or imageability reflects certain characteristics of its registration in semantic memory. Such characteristics appear to be directly accessible, and do not need the VSSP in order to allow them to influence performance.

Although the previous experiment clearly supported the view that when there is a need to manipulate images the VSSP plays a role in long-term learning, the effects observed were quite weak compared to those observed using the Brooks spatial matrix task. One possible explanation of this might be that the spatial component in the peg-word mnemonic is considerably less than that in the matrix task. If tracking acts primarily by disrupting the spatial component of memory, then it should be possible to produce a clearer effect if a more spatially based mnemonic is employed. Our next experiment, therefore, studied the influence of concurrent tracking on a location mnemonic.

This study used exactly the same word lists as the previous experiment, but instead of encouraging our subjects to learn the sequence by means of a peg-word mnemonic, we taught them to reproduce a sequence of ten prominent locations on a walk through the University campus. The ten objects in each list could then be remembered by imagining one object at each location. Hence if the first location was the University gates, and the second a letterbox just beyond, then one might imagine that the first object, the crocodile standing guard at the University gates, with the second object, the pig perched on top of the letterbox (perhaps avoiding the crocodile). Recall involves an imaginary walk through the campus, which tends to evoke the image of the relevant object at the appropriate place. As before, recall was serial. The second condition again involved rote learning with several rapid presentations of the list.

The results of this study are shown in Fig. 6.5, and are very clear. The imagery mnemonic was helpful, but only when the subject was unencumbered by tracking, a result that occurred in the case of all 12 subjects tested. In contrast, the rote learning condition was not reliably affected by tracking. On this occasion we observed no significant effect of the abstractness of the material, a result that is consistent with the suggestion of Paivio and Csapo (1969) that serial learning is less sensitive to the effects of imageability than free recall or paired-associate learning. The fact that serial learning *is* amenable to the use of a visuo-spatial mnemonic again reinforces the distinction between visual imagery as a control process or strategy, and the more automatic effects of concreteness or imageability.

So far then, our results are consistent with the view that the VSSP may be used when images need to be manipulated during learning. Unfor-

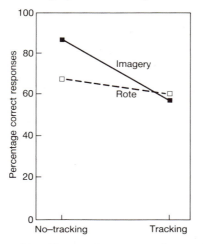

Fig. 6.5. The influence of tracking on the memory for word sequences learnt by rote or by an imagery mnemonic (Baddeley and Lieberman 1980).

tunately, our experiments so far are open to the objection that the condition disrupted by tracking was always that in which the subject was encouraged to use a mnemonic strategy. It is possible that the tracking task would interfere with any organizational strategy, regardless of whether or not visual imagery was involved. In order to test this, we carried out a further experiment in which we studied the influence of concurrent tracking on an alphabetic first-letter strategy which should make no demands on the VSSP, and hence should not be particularly susceptible to disruption by tracking.

The lists of words to be learned comprised ten items from each of eight categories, four comprising concrete items and four abstract. The items were so selected that each of the ten began with a different one of the first letters of the alphabet. The category might be cities and the examples *Amsterdam, Berlin, Chicago, Dublin ... Jerusalem.* In the mnemonic condition, items were presented in alphabetical order, and the subject was informed of this. Under control conditions, order of initial letters was scrambled. Once again, subjects performed the learning task either with or without the concurrent need to perform the pursuit rotor tracking task.

The mnemonic proved to be effective, increasing recall from 66 per cent in the rote condition to 92 per cent. Tracking had a small but significant effect on performance, an effect that did not interact significantly with learning strategy, but was if anything more substantial in the rote condition (reduced to 58 per cent) than in the mnemonic condition (89 per cent). As in the previous experiment, we found no effect of concreteness.

This study demonstrates then that our previous results do not reflect a simple tendency for all mnemonics to be more readily disruptable by tracking than are rote learning strategies. The mnemonic here was of a very similar level of effectiveness to the location mnemonic, and yet it was, if anything, influenced less by concurrent tracking than was rote learning. We therefore seem justified in concluding that it is the visuo-spatial component of imagery mnemonics that makes them susceptible to disruption by concurrent tracking. These results are consistent with the assumption that the VSSP serves as a temporary system within which images are maintained and manipulated during the utilization of visuo-spatial mnemonics.

Two kinds of imagery?

Our results so far seem to indicate that it is the spatial component of imagery that is susceptible to disruption. The location mnemonic gave much clearer disruption effects than the peg word system, while the Brooks matrix mnemonic which would appear to place the greatest emphasis on precise spatial coding seems to be the easiest to disrupt. And yet introspectively at least, images appear to have many components that are not specifically spatial. Pattern and shape do have a spatial component, but precise location is not an important characteristic; brightness and colour appear to have even less of a spatial component. Are these characteristics immune from disruption, or have we simply tended to use spatial disrupting tasks which leave these features of imagery unaffected?

It is conceivable for example that an image with a relatively precise spatial component places peculiarly heavy demands on the VSSP. The Brooks matrix task for instance demands very accurate maintenance and manipulation if the mnemonic is to work, whereas the peg word mnemonic will allow considerable spatial flexibility. In the case of the crocodile and the bun for example it matters little how the two interact, or whether the precise form of interaction is the same during input and retrieval. The question of the non-spatial characteristics of visual imagery remains a puzzling one that awaits a more systematic exploration of the potential interfering effects on imagery of non-spatial tasks.

This point has been explored further by Logie (in press) in a series of experiments in which he attempted to interfere with the use of a pegword mnemonic (selected as not having a particularly high spatial component), by means of visual tasks which also were selected as having a relatively low spatial involvement. In one such study, subjects were required to associate sequences of ten concrete nouns with the numbers 1–10 using the standard one-is-a-bun pegword mnemonic; this was contrasted with learning by verbal rote rehearsal. Logie attempted to devise a task that would provide a visual analogue of articulatory suppression, keeping the visuo-spatial sketch pad continuously occupied by means of a task that was assumed to place minimal demands on the central executive. Two experiments involving the comparison of successive patterns or colours both produced the predicted interaction between learning strategy and interference, with the imagery condition being more substantially disrupted than the rote. However in both of these, rote learning was also significantly impaired. Furthermore the initial level of performance in the imagery condition was substantially higher than in rote learning, so the interaction could be interpreted as due to a floor effect in the rote learning condition.

Logie produced less equivocal results in subsequent experiments in which he tried to produce an analogue of the unattended speech effect. In this, the subject was required to sit in front of a visual display on which a sequence of visual stimuli was presented. Subjects were instructed to keep their eyes open, but not to pay attention to the visual stimuli, concentrating on learning the auditorily presented number–word pairs. By analogy with the effect of unattended speech on visual digit span (Salame and Baddeley 1982), Logie argued that this would disrupt performance, but only in the case where the visuo-spatial sketch pad was being used. In his first study, subjects attempted to learn sequences of ten words using either the pegword mnemonic or rote rehearsal at the same time as patches of colour were presented. The results indicated a significant interaction between the presence of unattended colours and mode of learning, with subjects using the imagery strategy dropping from 69.2 per cent correct to 61.2 per cent, while performance in the rote learning condition showed no such decline, (36.4 to 39.4 per cent correct).

This result was encouraging since there appeared to be no generalized disruption of performance; however the argument could still be made that the rote learners, being at a lower level of performance were for some reason less sensitive to disruption. A second problem stems from the fact that the amount of impairment in the imagery condition is relatively small; it would clearly be desirable to obtain a stronger effect if clear conclusions are to be drawn.

Two further experiments attempted to answer these objections. The first was essentially a replication of the previous study with two modifications. First, an attempt was made to increase the strength of the effect by using more complex unattended material, namely pictures. By analogy with the results of Salame and Baddeley (1982) it was argued that the more similar the unattended material is to those items being processed, the greater the unattended effect should be. It was assumed that pictures of common objects would therefore be likely to cause more disruption of internal imagery representations than was the case with patches of colour. Secondly, in order to decrease the difficulty of the rote task, the number of items was reduced from ten to seven. The results of this study gave clear evidence for the disruption of the imagery condition by the presentation of unattended pictures, while no such disruption occurred in the case of rote learning.

While the results of this last study are impressive, they are still open to the interpretation that the imagery condition is for some reason more susceptible to any form of distraction than the rote learning condition. This hypothesis was tested in a final study using exactly the same procedure as before except that the experimental conditions involved the presentation of unattended speech rather than unattended pictures. The names of the unattended objects depicted previously were spoken at the same rate as the pictures had been presented. The results of this study showed once again that disruption clearly occurs for one condition but not the other; however in this case it is the rote learning that is disrupted, while the imagery condition remains unscathed, suggesting that the effects of both unattended pictures and words are modality specific, and are not attributable to general attentional disruption.

While this line of research is still at an early stage of development, Logie's results are consistent with a concept of the visuo-spatial sketch pad that functions in a way that is analogous to the articulatory loop. His results also argue against the view that disruption will only occur if it has a strong spatial component, suggesting that the difficulty previously observed in demonstrating nonspatial disruption stemmed from the particular memory tasks used. If visual imagery is studied using tasks that rely principally on detailed spatial representation, then they will be most susceptible to spatial disruption. However, a heavy spatial component is apparently not an essential feature of the operation of the visuo-spatial sketch pad.

The VSSP and abacus-derived mental calculation

I would like to conclude the section on the VSSP by describing an intriguing application of the concept of a visuo-spatial sketchpad to the understanding of mental calculation by expert abacus users, a study carried out in Japan by Hatano and Osawa (1983). The abacus is used extensively as a simple but extremely rapid and effective aid to calculation in Japan. Following extensive practice, expert users can dispense with the abacus itself, presumably performing the calculations on some internalized representation.

Hatano and Osawa decided to explore this internal representation, testing three rival potential models. The first of these was the visuo-spatial sketchpad, the second a chunking model, while the third model involved the utilization of LTM. The chunking model assumes that extensive practice allows the experienced user to chunk items hierarchically, hence increasing the amount of information that can be maintained. The LTM transfer model assumes that subjects are able to take advantage of information in LTM in order to recode incoming material more durably. Ericsson, Chase, and Falloon (1980) have shown that their subject, an enthusiastic runner, could extend his digit span to more than 80 items by a recoding strategy, whereby each sequence of digits was coded as a time for running a race of a particular length, and subsequently stored in LTM.

Hatano and Osawa selected three 'grand experts' in abacus-derived mental calculation, all of whom had distinguished themselves in competition. Such competitions involve a mixture of addition and subtraction problems often involving the adding and subtraction of up to 15 numbers, each comprising 5 to 9 digits spoken at a speed of 2.5 digits per second. They decided to test the digit span of their three experts, assuming that they would have substantially greater than normal digit span, and testing a VSSP interpretation whereby the successive digits are encoded in terms of a visuo-spatial internal representation of the abacus. On the basis of this hypothesis they made a number of predictions, including the prediction that forward and reverse recall, being based on a spatial image, would be approximately equally easy, and that performance would be more disrupted by a concurrent visuo-spatial task than by a verbal concurrent task. Finally they predicted that there would be poor long-term retention of the sequence presented, an observation that would allow them to rule out the LTM hypothesis.

Their first experiment compared memory span for digits with span for alphabetic letters and fruit names. It was predicted here that the experts would have supernormal digit span, but would perform normally with both letters and words, since these could not be recoded using their visuo-spatial representation of the abacus. This proved to be the case, with their subjects having a mean digit span of approximately 16 items, while memory span for letters and fruit names was in the region of 5 to 9 items. Not only was span approximately double what one might expect, but there was also very little difference between forward (16 items) and backward span (14 items), a result that was consistent with the suggestion that the experts were able to scan a visuo-spatial image in either direction.

A further study examined the effect of a visuo-spatial or verbal concurrent task on memory for digits and for letters. On the assumption that the enhanced digit span was based on a visuo-spatial representation of the abacus, Hatano and Osawa predicted that performance would be relatively resistant to the effects of a concurrent verbal task, but would be sensitive to a secondary visuo-spatial task. This involved being shown a line drawing of an object, and then being required to point to which of six alternative line drawings was identical to the target. The verbal secondary task involved answering simple questions such as 'Who is the Prime Minister of Japan?' or pronouncing words backwards.

There was a clear tendency for memory for digit sequences to be more disrupted by the visuo-spatial secondary task than the verbal, while memory for letter sequences showed exactly the opposite trend. Such a result is clearly consistent with the assumption that the experts were using a visuo-spatial representation in order to enhance their digit span, a representation that was not available to them in the case of letter span. Such a result is of course entirely consistent with the sketch pad hypothesis, but is not predicted by the chunking hypothesis.

In a final study, Hatano and Osawa tested the LTM hypothesis. Ericsson *et al.* (1980) had shown that their subject relied on LTM for his phenomenal digit span, and was able to recall a good deal of a given sequence even after a delay. This was tested in the case of the abacus experts by first testing them on sequences of 10 digits, each of which had to be retained for 30 seconds, a feat well within the capability of the two experts tested in this part of the study. After 10 such sequences LTM was tested, first by asking for recall and then by recognition memory. This involved representing the 10 sequences as abacus patterns, and presenting these together with 20 new patterns. One subject claimed to have forgotten every digit, while the other was able to recall correctly the last series, but nothing of the preceding ones. Neither subject showed any capacity for correctly recognising the previously retained sequences. It appears then that unlike the subject tested by Ericcson *et al.* (1980), the abacus experts did not utilize long-term memory in order to enhance their digit span.

Hatano and Osawa concluded that their experts were using a visuo-spatial representation of an abacus that appears to be held and manipulated in a system approximating the visuo-spatial sketch pad component of working memory.

Psychophysical approaches to the study of imagery

Anyone reading the present chapter who is unfamiliar with the field might have gained the impression that apart from our own work, and that of Lee Brooks, there has been comparatively little research on imagery over the last decade. In fact, the opposite is the case, with a vast number of papers being published including several books (e.g. Kosslyn 1980; Richardson 1980; Shepard 1980). While I do not propose to review this literature, I think that it is appropriate to describe it briefly and attempt to relate it to my own views.

The theoretical work in this area has been dominated by one question, or pseudo-question, that of whether imagery reflects the operation of an analogical system or is better described in propositional terms. Even if one accepts this as a genuine rather than a pseudo-question, I would suggest that this is not a fruitful question to ask, for two reasons. First, if one assumes that the psychologist is attempting to produce a model of the underlying process, then the distinction between an analogical and propositional representation comes very close to the question of which of two notations is the more convenient. Analogical functions can be simulated using digital systems, and provided the discrete components are fine enough in grain, it will be extremely difficult to distinguish between the two. Since the imagery system is presumably attempting to reflect continuous functions in the real world, then by definition, any system will have to have analogical or quasi-analogical characteristics. At a purely empirical level then, it seems unlikely that demonstrations of the quasi-analogical characteristics of visual imagery of the type that have dominated the study of imagery over the last decade will ever allow us to decide whether the system is basically analogue or propositional.

A second reason for doubting the value of the analogue/propositional question stems from its implicit assumption that imagery represents the operation of a single unitary system. Our own results would be more consistent with the assumption that at least two subsystems are involved, a long-term store that holds our knowledge of the world, and the VSSP, a temporary system for holding and manipulating images. There is no reason to assume that the basic mode of storage is the same in these two; it would for example be entirely plausible to have information in the LTS stored propositionally, as part of a much more extensive and multi-modal representation of knowledge, together with a more analogical system for manipulating those images. My personal view then, is that although the extensive work in this area has shown some interesting phenomena, the actual theoretical progress made has been disappointing.

Empirical research on imagery over the last few years has tended to be dominated by two approaches, one which could perhaps be termed cognitive psychophysics has been developed by Shepard and his associates, while a second approach which might be termed phenomenological psychophysics, has Steven Kosslyn as its most active proponent.

Imagery as cognitive psychophysics

Shepard's work has demonstrated a number of carefully explored and intriguing features of our manipulation of visuo-spatial images. In a classic study, Shepard and Metzler (1971) showed their subjects two shapes on a visual display. Each represented a figure made up from a number of cubes, with one shape tilted relative to the other. The subject's task was to decide whether the two shapes were identical or whether one was the mirror-image of the other, and press a 'same' or 'different' key accordingly. Shepard and Metzler found that the time to make this judgement increased linearly with the difference in angle between the two, just as if the subject were mentally rotating one figure until it matched the other in orientation and then making the decision. Subjects appeared to perform this rotation at a constant linear rate whether in the frontal or depth plane.

Further evidence for the existence of a process somewhat analogous to rotation comes from an elegant study by Cooper (1976). This first involved estimating the rate at which a given subject 'mentally rotated' the relevant stimuli, and then instructing subjects that if a stimulus probe was presented during rotation, they were to judge whether it was the same or a different shape from that being rotated. Cooper then went on to show that if the probe is presented at the hypothetical point reached by the rotated image, then the verification response is very rapid. Hence, if a subject were given two stimuli involving a 90 degree rotation, and this normally took 10 seconds, the presentation of a figure in the 45 degree position after 5 seconds would lead to a very rapid response, just as if it coincided with the orientation of the image in the subject's 'mind's eye'.

Subjects are also able to preset an image in a particular orientation. Hence, if required to judge whether or not the next item will be a capital A, and told that it will be presented at an angle of 60 degrees, subjects appear to be able to form the image and hold it at that angle, thereby obviating the need to rotate the item to be judged, when presented (Cavanagh 1977). While it was initially thought that this could only be done for a specific image, not for the frame of reference in general, Hinton and Parsons (1981) have shown that provided all the items in the rotated set can be conceptualized as facing in the same direction, then the frame of reference can be effectively rotated. (For example the items *F* and *R* tend to be perceived as 'facing' the right, in contrast to *J* and *7* which appear to face left.) Finally and perhaps somewhat surprisingly, the rate of rotation of an image does not appear to depend on its complexity, since complicated images are rotated just as rapidly as simple (Cooper and Podgorny 1976).

There is no doubt that Shepard and his colleagues have produced some elegant demonstrations of the characteristics of the process of mental rotation. The very extensive research in this area has, however, been confined almost entirely to studying a relatively narrow paradigm based almost entirely on the requirement to judge the *handedness* of two stimuli, that is whether they are identical or whether one is a mirror image of the other. As Hinton and Parsons (1981) point out, however, this particular judgement is one that virtually never has to be made in natural situations, being confined to man-made tasks such as reading print. One does not for instance wish to classify a left hand profile of a person and a right hand profile as indicating different people; similarly, object recognition virtually never depends on being able to perceive the handedness of the natural object in question. We know that left–right judgements are very difficult for a wide range of organisms, presumably because there is no good evolutionary reason for making this distinction an easy one. That being so, one cannot escape a suspicion that for all its elegance, recent work on the psychophysics of mental rotation may tell us little about the normal processes of manipulating images.

Nevertheless, the phenomenon certainly does occur and is highly replicable. How could it be fitted into a broader picture of imagery and its function? One possibility is that the visual system of man is designed to cope with a world comprising objects presented in a relatively standard orientation. We *can* perceive and recognize objects while we are hanging upside down, but I suspect the efficiency of this would be rather less than under a normal orientation. On the other hand, the head is continually deviating slightly from the upright, making it desirable to have a system that will take account of this and adjust the frame of reference accordingly. On other occasions, while the perceiver may be upright, a given object may be presented at a slight angle, this time making it desirable that the object rather than the framework be rotated slightly. Whether this process does in fact occur in normal perception, and if so how important it is I do not know. However, I cannot help feeling that if the methodologically elegant theoretically rather narrow work in the Shepard tradition is to develop, that it is important both to explore its ecological relevance more critically, and to attempt to link it with the processes and mechanisms involved in perception, an approach which Hinton and Parsons (1981) have already begun to explore.

Phenomenological psychophysics

A second very active area of research on imagery in recent years could be termed, perhaps slightly unfairly, phenomenological psychophysics. One could caricature this approach by saying that it begins with the hypothesis that imaging is just like seeing, and attempts to collect confirmatory evidence. In one experiment for example, subjects are asked to judge which of two animals is the larger, and it is shown that judgements about animals that are similar in size, for instance a dog and a sheep, take longer than judgements about animals that are very dissimilar, for example a dog and an elephant. The implication here is that the subject forms appropriately scaled images of the two animals and then performs a judgement on the relative size of the two images. Unfortunately, of course, this tendency for similar items to take longer to compare is likely to occur with any judgement, the boringness of books or the injustice of political regimes for example. Although subjects may report using imagery, this itself does not necessarily imply that the image is anything other than an epiphenomenon.

Rather more convincing are attempts to manipulate this effect experimentally. Hence, Paivio (1975) has shown that a subject's judgement can be influenced when the two objects in question are represented by pictures, and the physical size of the pictures is varied. Subjects comparing the size of a sheep and a horse for example tend to be speeded up when the picture of the horse is physically larger than that of the sheep, and slowed down when it is smaller, an effect that does not occur when the pictures are replaced by words written in either large or small print.

By far the most extensive review of work in this area is contained in Kosslyn's (1980) book *Image and mind* which attempts a systematic exploration of the imagery process. Kosslyn carried out a wide range of experiments in which subjects were asked to perform particular tasks using visual images. He might for example instruct his subjects to form an image of a Dalmation dog, focusing on its tail. When asked to see its ears, subjects typically report scanning along the dog's back in order to reach the ears. Furthermore, the time to perform this internal scan appears to be linearly related to the distance scanned. When asked to image an object far away and approach it mentally, Kosslyn's subjects report that the angle subtended by the object gradually increases until eventually it 'overflows' the whole visual field (Kosslyn 1978). Images also seem to show effects of scale that are similar to real scenes. Subjects told to form an image of a duck standing next to an elephant will take longer to report 'seeing' some feature of the duck, such as its eye, than they will if the duck is imagined standing next to a small item like a mouse. The implication here is that the eye takes up a larger proportion of the image in the latter case (Kosslyn 1975). A summary of the work in this tradition is given by Kosslyn and Schwartz (1981).

I must confess to finding work in this vein difficult to evaluate. On the one hand, I do believe that the phenomenology of visual imagery is an interesting and important topic. Furthermore, the fact that latency to perform certain activities behaves in a coherent and consistent way is encouraging. On the other hand, I have a nagging concern that implicitly, much of the experimental work in this field consists of instructing the subject to behave *as if* he were seeing something in the outside world. Given that the imagery system is highly flexible, and that the subject has considerable experience of the world, he is capable of setting up such simulations and producing the desired results. Whether such results in fact tell us how the system works, or indeed tell us much about the phenomenology, I am as yet uncertain.

Once again, my doubts are expressed more eloquently, and indicated more cogently by a demonstration devised by Hinton (1979). Imagine a wire cube placed squarely on a shelf with its base level with your eyes. Imagine taking hold of the bottom corner that is nearest your left hand with your left hand, and the top corner that is furthest from your left hand with your right hand, taking the cube from the shelf and holding it so that your right hand is vertically above your left. What then will be the location of the remaining corners? Most subjects tend to reply that they will form a square along the 'equator' of the cube. In fact the middle edge of the cube is not horizontal but forms a zig zag. Hinton argues that this error occurs because one does not take the image of the cube and rotate it, one rather constructs it according to certain rules. The rules for this type of rotation are relatively complex and what people reproduce instead is a simplified but erroneous construction.

Hinton argues that images are not like pictures, but are much more like constructions generated using the same equipment and rules as are used for perception. Although images may appear to be phenomenologically like pictures, they are very different in the information they contain and of course, in the source of that information. As in the case of Kosslyn's imagined dog, we can fill in plausible information that will make the image resemble a percept in certain specified ways. Much of the information that appears to be there, or perhaps more precisely does not appear to be missing, consists merely of plausible default values, reasonable guesses based on one's knowledge of the situation rather than actual information.

Consider for example the old expression 'to know something like the back of your hand'. You can no doubt form a vivid visual image of the back of your right hand. Imagine it with fingers outstretched. How many major ridges and furrows are there on the knuckle of your little finger? Are there more wrinkles on the knuckle of your ring finger or your middle finger? I suspect you will find that the information you have about the back of your hand in fact concerns your knowledge of the appearance of hands in general. Alternatively, consider the appearance of a penny. Can you form a clear image of a new penny? Now try to 'read off' the detail and check it against an actual penny. Nickerson and Adams (1979) have shown that even an object as familiar as a penny is very hard to remember, though not I suspect, at all difficult to image. In conclusion then, although I have no doubt about the ability of subjects to use images to simulate their perception of the world, I am yet to be convinced that this tells us very much about the underlying processes.

Visual STM

So far this chapter has concentrated exclusively on visuo-spatial imagery, the representation in a quasi-visual mode of material presented, or at least cued verbally. It would seem plausible to assume that such a relatively complex system is based on some form of more direct visual input store. There is no doubt that one or more such stores can be identified, although their relationship to the VSSP is still unclear. The next two sections will be concerned with three clusters of evidence for visual memory. One is concerned with the retention of abstract visual stimuli that are not easily nameable, the second is concerned with retention of pictures of objects, while the third is concerned with visually presented letter sequences. Whatever the relationship of these three clusters of evidence to each other, and to the VSSP, any adequate model of visual working memory must accommodate them.

Memory for patterns

There is considerable evidence of course, for the very brief storage of visual information in one or more sensory or iconic stores. However, such relatively peripheral sensory systems are outside the scope of the current working memory model. There is, however, evidence of a considerably more durable sensory trace. For example Dale (1973) showed that subjects could remember the location of a dot on a one foot square of white paper, but showed forgetting over a matter of seconds. The rate of forgetting was a function of how long the subject was allowed to inspect the dot initially, and of whether or not he was required to perform a demanding number-processing task during the interval.

Phillips and Baddeley (1971) presented their subjects with a four by four matrix of cells of which half were randomly filled and half empty. After an interval ranging from 0.3 to 9 seconds, a second matrix was presented which was either identical, or had one cell changed. The subject's task was to decide whether the change had or had not occurred. As the interval increased, subjects became both slower and less accurate in responding. A subsequent experiment by Phillips (1974) varied the complexity of the stimulus from 4×4 to 8×8 matrices. On immediate test, performance was virtually perfect regardless of complexity, but subsequently, the more complex the stimulus the faster the forgetting.

Phillips went on to carry out a further experiment in which he demonstrated that the initial extremely high level of performance that was independent of complexity only occurred when the presentation and test stimuli were spatially exactly superimposed, with a discrepancy being perceived by the subject as a flicker. When the test stimulus was spatially offset by one cell, complexity had an effect both immediately and throughout the retention interval. This suggests two memory processes, a brief component dependent on exact spatial location and a more durable component based on pattern rather than location.

In a later series of studies, Phillips and Christie (1977a, b) studied the retention of sequences of matrix patterns. They found that recognition performance was unaffected by serial position except for the last item, which showed a much higher level of retention, provided it was tested first. Subjects appeared to be able to maintain the trace of this last item provided they were not required to perform a task involving a heavy information load such as arithmetic. Merely presenting digits without requiring the subject to perform the arithmetic did not cause the last item to be forgotten. This suggests that the cause of forgetting was not masking by another visual stimulus, but diverting processing capacity away from rehearsal.

The issue of whether a visual stimulus can be rehearsed is one that has also cropped up in studies of memory for pictures. The difficulty here, of course, is to ensure that the subject is rehearsing the picture and not a verbal label. While an early study by Shaffer and Shiffrin (1972) found no evidence that subjects rehearsed pictures during unfilled presentation intervals, subsequent studies have indicated that some maintenance rehearsal can occur, given appropriate conditions (e.g. Watkins and Graefe 1981).

Visual memory for letters

Probably the most popular technique for investigating visual rehearsal however, is the letter-matching task devised by Posner and Keele (1967). They had the ingenious idea of taking advantage of the fact that upper and lower case letters may have a different shape, as in the case of the letter *A*. They required their subjects to view a single letter, for example, *A* and then decide as rapidly as possible whether a subsequent letter had the same name or not. The subsequent letter could be either the same case, hence being visually identical (*AA* or *aa*), or could be different in case and hence not physically identical (*Aa* or *aB*), or of course it could be a different letter, (*AB* or *Ab*). Posner and Keele varied the interval between presentation of the two letters and found that provided the second letter was presented within 1.5 seconds of the first, then presenting them both in the same visually identical case led to a faster response. After 1.5 seconds, this was no longer so, either because the visual trace had faded, or else because the subject had changed over to a name code, or of course for both reasons. We know from the work of Phillips and his colleagues that a visual trace can be maintained for considerably more than 1.5 seconds, and Parks *et al.* (1972) have shown that this is also true for the Posner and Keele task. They discouraged their subjects from using verbal coding by requiring them throughout the task to repeat a stream of broken digits. This supplementary shadowing proved successful and they were able to extend the period for which physical identity speeded reaction time up to eight seconds.

The same group of investigators used concurrent shadowing to explore the retention of sequences of letters. Kroll *et al.* (1970) embedded the memory task within a continuous shadowing procedure. In one condition, subjects shadowed letters spoken in a female voice. Embedded within the sequence was a group of letters spoken in a male voice. These also had to be shadowed, but also subsequently recalled. This condition was compared with a visual presentation condition in which the female-spoken shadowing letters continued uninterrupted while the letters to be recalled were presented visually instead of auditorily. When recall was tested immediately after presentation, no difference occurred between visual and auditory letters (96 per cent correct) indicating that both had been perceived adequately. After 25 seconds of shadowing however, recall of auditory digits dropped to 40 per cent while the visual items were substantially better retained at 69 per cent correct.

Further evidence that the encoding of the visually presented letters was not phonological came from a study by Parkinson *et al.* (1971) which again used the shadowing paradigm with the target letters presented either visually or auditorily. They tested for phonological coding by varying the similarity between the target letter and the letters subsequently shadowed. Hence a target letter such as *K* could be followed after varying delays by phonologically similar shadowing letters e.g. *A* and *J*, or by dissimilar letters such as *P* or *C*. With auditory presentation, shadowing phonologically similar letters did impair performance, though only if they occurred within a few seconds. No differential phonological similarity effect was found for the visually presented letters. These and other related experiments by this group are reviewed by Kroll (1975); they demonstrate convincingly the occurrence of non-phonological coding of letters, but with the possible exception of the study by Parks *et al.* using the Posner single letter matching task, do not succeed in establishing whether this alternative code is visual or not. It seems probable that the single letter matching task could be performed using the VSSP, or some equivalent pattern-based store. The work of Phillips and Christie (1977*a*, *b*) however suggests that such a store is capable of holding only one pattern, albeit a very complex one. When a sequence of several letters is presented sequentially, it seems unlikely that such a store could be used for storing them. And yet, there is evidence that non-phonological coding of such sequences does occur and is moderately effective. One possibility is that such results stem from the passive priming of units representing each letter in LTM, rather than the use of a more active visualization process (Kroll and Parks 1978; Walker and Marshall 1982).

Consider first the performance of patients suffering from defective STM, such as K.F. (Shallice and Warrington 1970) and P.V. (Vallar and Baddeley 1984*a*). Such patients show very poor retention of auditorily presented digits, with a span in the region of two items, coupled with much better retention of visually presented digits, with span in the region of 4 or 5. Furthermore, as we saw earlier, the retention of visually presented digits by P.V. was not influenced by phonological similarity (Vallar and Baddeley 1984*a*). This seems to suggest the occurrence of some non-phonological store that is capable of holding about five sequentially presented items. Serial position curves indicate that performance is reasonably good throughout the sequence, and in this respect differ markedly from the evidence from the studies by Phillips and

Christie that suggest that visual STM is based almost entirely on a very high level of performance on the last item presented.

Warrington and Shallice (1972) examined the coding employed by K.F. with visually presented letters, and obtained some evidence for an influence of visual similarity, although the magnitude of the effect was not large and required some relatively detailed and sophisticated analysis in order to reveal it. Furthermore, the sequences used were relatively short, and leave open the possibility that the evidence of visual coding could be based on a contribution from the type of store studied by Phillips and Christie while retention as a whole was based on some other non-visual store.

Another approach to this question is to use normal subjects and standard serial visual presentation techniques, but to avoid phonological coding by means of articulatory suppression. We have just started to explore this line, with some moderately encouraging results. In an as yet unpublished study, Sergio Della Sala and I re-examined the influence of visual similarity on serial recall of letters, a procedure which has previously been tried on a number of occasions with discouraging results. We argued that it might be the case that any effect of visual similarity would simply be swamped by the dominant phonological code. We therefore compared retention of sequences comprising letters that either were visually confusable, as measured by a range of existing studies or were visually relatively discriminable. Subjects either suppressed articulation by counting repeatedly throughout presentation and written recall, or were left free to rehearse in whatever way they wished.

Performance was significantly impaired by articulatory suppression as anticipated. Again, as anticipated, visual similarity had no reliable effect under control conditions. When subjects were prevented from phonological coding by suppression, however, visual similarity had a significant effect, an effect that was small but consistent across the serial position curve. This preliminary result then suggests that visual coding does occur, but is far from substantial. Could it perhaps be due to misperceiving the letters? We carried out a letter copying task, and found that with or without suppression, subjects were virtually perfect at copying, rendering this interpretation unlikely. The fact that the effect is consistent across the curve however suggests that it is probably not based on the system underlying the results of Phillips and his colleagues.

One possible explanation of our result is to argue that the serial recall of letter sequences of this kind relies on some relatively abstract letter code developed in the process of learning to read (c.f. Kroll and Parks 1978). There is for example evidence from studies on the role of eye movements in reading to indicate the presence of some form of letter representation that is insensitive to letter case. The most compelling demonstration of this comes from a computer-based eye movement study by McConkie and Zola (1981) which recorded the location of a subject's fixations in reading text from a visual display unit (VDU). This demonstrated that a subject's behaviour could be influenced by the words appearing on the right periphery of his visual field, that is by sections of text that he is about to fixate. A technique was devised whereby this portion of the text could be changed, and when this happened, the subject's reading was slowed.

The critical experiment was one in which the text was printed in alternating upper and lower case letters. ThIs WoUlD bE aN eXaMpLe Of SuCh TeXt. In the critical condition, the assignment of letters to case was switched between the appearance of a given word in the periphery, and its being fixated. Hence *tExT* would be replaced by *TeXt*. Subjects were quite unaware of this change, and their performance was unaffected. This seems to suggest that the store that is holding the information gleaned from the periphery is at a more abstract level than the shape of a given letter since the shape of upper and lower case letters can be quite different (e.g. *e E*).

Memory for visually presented words

Exploring further the possible link between aspects of visual memory and the processes developed in connection with reading, raises the question of how we remember sequences of visually presented words. Research by Morton and his colleagues (Morton 1979) has presented evidence for what he terms a visual input logogen system. A logogen is a theoretical construct used by Morton to signify a structure specialized for the detection of words. It was initially devised to account for the results of studies of word recognition, but has subsequently been elaborated into a much more complex and ambitious theoretical system (e.g. Morton 1979). The initial concept assumed that a logogen was fed by several different modalities, but more recently evidence from priming studies is accumulating to suggest that it may be necessary to assume a range of different logogen systems, one concerned with visual input, one with auditory input, one with spoken output, and so forth. Since logogens are capable of accumulating and retaining the effects of prior presentation of the item represented by the logogen, they clearly constitute a form of memory system. Since there is evidence that priming the visual logogen system with a cursively written word will prime perception of a visually very different typed presentation of the word (Morton 1979), it seems clear that such systems are not based on simple visual summation. As such they would seem to offer a plausible candidate for a hypothetical abstract visual system. Vivien Lewis and I began to explore this possibility as follows.

We argued that if logogens represent structures developed for the processing of words, then the use of such a system in STM might be avoided by using pronounceable non-words. We therefore carried out an experiment in which subjects attempted to recall visually presented sequences comprising consonant-vowel-consonant words such as *leg, hat* or non-words comprising a reordering of the same letters e.g. *heg* and *lat*. The items were typed on index cards and presented at a 1 second rate, with written recall. To avoid the danger of subjects becoming familiar with the non-words, and possibly starting to grow new logogens, we used different words and non-words on every trial. Subjects were tested on six sequences of each type of material at lengths 1 to 6 items. A total of 16 subjects were tested, with the order of the four conditions (word control, non-word control, word suppression, non-word suppression) determined by Latin Square.

Under normal presentation conditions, we expected immediate memory for the words to be easier, for many different reasons. The critical question however was what would happen under articulatory suppression. We expected, on the basis of our version of the logogen hypothesis that immediate memory for words would be somewhat impaired, but not disastrously so, since we assumed that some form of logogen system could be used to retain the words. There might also be expected to be a semantic component, although with reasonably rapid presentation, we expected this to be small (Baddeley 1966*a*). We assumed that retention of the nonsense syllables on the other hand would be drastically impaired. While a peripheral visual store might be capable of holding as a pattern, three letters, all we know of the system suggests that it would be totally unsuited to retaining successive visual records of three, four or five such trigrams. Since subjects had not experienced any of these trigrams before, one would not expect them to have appropriate logogens to encode them, while since the items were non-words, semantic coding is likely to be minimal.

The results of this study are shown in Fig. 6.6. As expected, under control conditions, subjects found the words easier to recall than the nonsense syllables, and again as expected, articulatory suppression impaired retention of the words to a substantial, though not disastrous extent. What was not expected, however, was the surprisingly good performance on the nonsense syllables under suppression. Performance is indeed impaired by suppression, but as Fig. 6.7 shows, the impairment is no greater for nonsense syllables than for word sequences. How can this be explained? The results of Besner and Davelaar (1982) suggest that articulatory suppression does not prevent lexical and possibly phonological access. One suggestion therefore might be that performance is relying on a phonological code. However, there is of course abundant evidence that articulatory suppression abolishes both phonological similarity and word-length effects for visually presented items, an

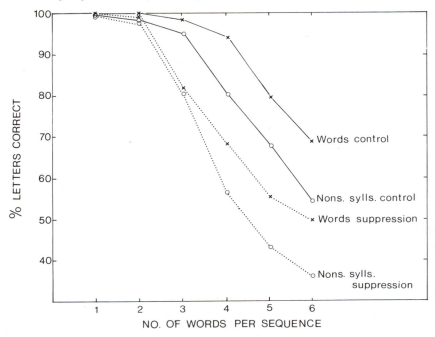

Fig. 6.6. The influence of articulatory suppression on memory for sequences of words and nonsense syllables (Baddeley and Lewis unpublished).

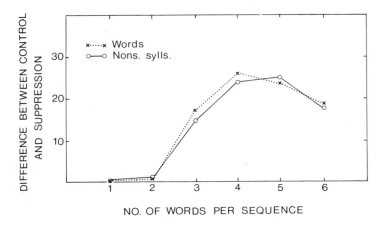

Fig. 6.7. Magnitude of the suppression effect on memory for sequences of words and nonsense syllables as a function of sequence length (Baddeley and Lewis unpublished).

effect replicated by Besner and Davelaar in their study. We would there-fore have to assume a phonologically based memory code that is sufficiently durable to support serial recall, but does not reflect similarity or word-length effects. Such a code may exist, but it is at present supported by little or no evidence. An alternative possibility is that recall in our study was supported by some form of visual store, analogous to the logogen system proposed by Morton, but comprising fragments of words rather than comprising only words.

If one considers the problem of devising a system that will learn to read, then there do appear to be potential advantages in having a system that can store fragments of visually presented orthographic material, possibly at the level of the syllable or letter cluster. Such a system would presumably be specialized for holding sequences of letters, and might possibly develop in a way that would favour those sequences that occur frequently in written language—a lexigen rather than a logogen system. I would doubt however whether such lexigens represent structures, each specialized to receive only one specific letter cluster as seems to be implied by the concept of a logogen. It seems intuitively more likely that the system is equipped to retain varied sequences of letters, probably taking advantage of past learning in order to organize and chunk them, but not mapping onto specific words. It may be recalled that the results of research on the effect of irrelevant speech on memory (Salame and Baddeley 1982) suggests that the phonological store similarly operates at the level of the phoneme or syllable rather than the word (see pp. 90–1).

Conclusions

The study of visual working memory is an area that is as yet only partially explored. We know a good deal about individual sub-regions of the area, but are still far from clear as to how these are connected. There is for example a vast body of work on iconic memory which we have not discussed at all here (see Coltheart 1983, for a recent review). There does appear to be strong evidence for the short term storage of both simple visual stimuli and relatively complex patterns, as evidenced by the work of Dale (1973) and of Phillips and his collaborators. This work implies a system that seems to be specialized for the simultaneous main-tenance of spatial or patterned stimuli, but to be poorly designed for holding temporal sequences of visual items. There also appears to be good evidence for the occurrence of a temporary visuo-spatial store which we have termed the visuo-spatial sketchpad, that is capable of retaining and manipulating images, and is susceptible to disruption by concurrent spatial processing. Preliminary evidence seems to implicate an eye movement or visual attentional control system as playing a role in this type of memory.

The question of whether the VSSP, and the more visual pattern-based system that appears to be implied by the work of Phillips are one and the same remains an open one. Phenomenologically, we do appear to have clear visual images which do not have a very substantial spatial component. We can, for example, form an image of a colour or brightness of indefinite spatial extent and location. Perhaps the simplest hypothesis is to assume that this system, together with that implied by the work of Phillips is all part of a general VSSP. The reason we have not so far succeeded in showing clear disruption of the more pictorial aspects of imagery may simply be that we have yet to discover an appropriate concurrent disrupting task. Logie's recent study supports this view and suggests that this is likely to be an important area for further investigation.

Evidence from visually presented letter sequences seems to indicate the need to assume some form of non-phonological store capable of storing sequences of letters. The most likely assumption here is that the store is lexical in nature and has developed through the process of learning to read. The evidence here is, however, presently very sparse. There is a considerable need to explore both the visual component of this type of storage, and also its capacity for retaining sequences of non-lexical items such as abstract patterns, or symbols from an unfamiliar orthographic system.

In conclusion then, although I believe we know rather less about visual than phonological coding in memory, we already know a good deal, and have available techniques which I believe will make it possible within the next few years to obtain a much more coherent view of the relationship between the clusters of evidence at present available.

7 Passive storage and recency effects

The chapter that follows will principally be concerned with recency effects, the tendency for the most recently presented items to be well recalled. I shall argue that the recency effect reflects the operation of *passive* storage processes whereby information is maintained by the system without the need for active rehearsal by the subject. In this respect they differ from the active processes underlying the operation of the articulatory loop and visuo-spatial sketchpad.

Recency effects are very general, extending across stores with time constants ranging from seconds to months or possibly years. Given this range of operation, to what extent is it sensible to regard recency effects as characteristic of working memory? Recency does appear to provide a potentially important source of mnemonic information, information that is temporary in the sense that the system is continually being updated and modified, with the result that such information is in a constant state of flux and change. In this respect the loss of information resulting from the over-writing of recency resembles the rapid forgetting obtained within the storage systems involved in the articulatory loop and the sketchpad. The recency-based storage process is also of limited capacity, although it is likely that this limitation stems from the overwriting or overloading of earlier cues rather than the fading of a temporary memory trace.

Recency effects differ from maintenance of information by the articulatory loop and sketchpad however in that storage is probably passive and automatic. Hence the insensitivity of the recency effect in free recall to concurrent processing load. Given this degree of automaticity and the fact that such passive storage appears to operate across a wide range of temporal intervals, one might question whether it forms a legitimate component of working memory. I propose to discuss such passive storage here for two reasons; first, because working memory clearly does take advantage of such passive storage, and secondly because the recency effect has played a central role in the development of the concept of short-term and working memory. A model of working memory that can not account for recency effects would rightly be regarded as grossly incomplete.

As noted earlier, the tendency in free recall experiments for the last few items to be well recalled played an important role in the development of theories of memory during the 1960s. The recency effect in free recall is substantial, highly reliable and very coherent in its characteristics, showing an insensitivity to a wide range of variables that are known to influence LTM, coupled with an extreme sensitivity to the interpolation of even one or two items between presentation and test. An extensive review of this literature is given by Glanzer (1972). Any general theory of STM needs to account for this phenomenon.

Explanations of recency tend to fall into three categories, those attributing it to a particular form of coding or rehearsal during input (e.g. Atkinson and Shiffrin 1968; Craik and Lockhart 1972), those which interpret recency as reflecting the output of a single limited capacity but relatively passive input store (Glanzer 1972), and those which attribute the effect to retrieval processes, either coupled with an interference model (Postman and Phillips 1965) or a general model of retrieval (e.g. Tulving 1968). As discussed elsewhere (Baddeley 1976, pp. 131–4) a classical interference theory interpretation of recency does not appear plausible.

Encoding interpretations of the recency effect

Atkinson and Shiffrin (1968) attributed recency to the output of an active rehearsal buffer. They suggest that subjects subvocally rehearse a selection of items, with the probability of an item being within the rehearsal buffer being greater, the more recent the item. Studies by Rundus (1971) in which subjects were encouraged to rehearse out loud during presentation of items for free recall appeared to support this view. Subsequent recall was a function of two factors, number of prior rehearsals and recency of rehearsal. Number of prior rehearsals influenced performance throughout the curve and offered a good explanation of the primacy effect, the tendency for the first one or two items to be well recalled, since these tended to enjoy more rehearsals than later items. In contrast, recall of the last few items appeared to be unrelated to number of rehearsals, but was directly related to recency of rehearsal. Atkinson and Shiffrin assume a limited capacity rehearsal buffer which will tend to drop earlier items as new items come along, hence favouring retention of the most recent items, just as Rundus observed.

A second and related interpretation was presented by Craik and Lockhart (1972) who argued that subjects tend to change their encoding strategy as the end of the list approaches. Earlier items were assumed to be encoded using a relatively deep semantic code since this leads to durable memory traces. In the case of the most recent items, however, such durable coding is unnecessary, and the subject was assumed to rely on a superficial, possibly phonological encoding, thereby presumably allowing more attention to be diverted to maintaining and organizing earlier items. Evidence for this view comes from two sources, the character of intrusion errors and the negative recency effect.

Both Craik (1968*a*) and Shallice (1975) have performed a detailed analysis of errors in free recall. They both report that intrusion errors that are phonologically similar to correct items are relatively infrequent, but do come predominantly from the recency portion of the list. While this is of course consistent with the Craik and Lockhart view, it does not necessarily imply a change in strategy by the subject. It is, for example, quite consistent with the view that subjects encode incoming items both phonologically and semantically throughout the list, but that the phonological code deteriorates more rapidly, as a result of either decay or interference so that no phonological trace of earlier items survives at recall. Conrad (1967) observed exactly this phenomenon in a study using the Peterson short-term forgetting paradigm.

Somewhat more compelling evidence comes from the *negative recency effect*. If, after a series of free recall lists, the subject is unexpectedly asked to recall as many of the words from previous lists as possible, a procedure known as *final free recall*, he will not only show an absence of the previously observed within-list recency effect but may also show a tendency for the last items to be even *less* well recalled than middle items of the list (Craik 1970). Craik explains this negative recency effect on the grounds that the most recent items tend to be encoded phonologically, a strategy that leads to good immediate recall but poor long-term retention. However, the negative recency effect is typically small and is not always reliable. It is furthermore open to a range of alternative interpretations, as Craik himself acknowledges.

One interpretation resembles that of Craik in emphasizing coding factors, but rather than emphasizing learning strategies, concentrates on the nature of the *retrieval* cues used for recency and earlier items. In the case of recency items, it seems likely that the ordinal or temporal retrieval cues used will be very different from those cues, probably semantic, that are used to retrieve items from the earlier part of the curve. Final free recall is much more likely to be able to use the type of cue used for earlier items than it is to benefit from temporal or ordinary recency cues which are likely to have been overwritten by subsequent lists.

Another line of explanation relies on the fact that the process of retrieval itself facilitates subsequent recall. In general, the longer the delay between a given presentation and a successful retrieval, the greater the increment in learning (Landauer and Bjork 1978). Recency items are presented last and typically recalled first, hence minimizing the interval between presentation and test and reducing probability of subsequent delayed recall.

There are, in fact, a number of lines of evidence that argue strongly against an interpretation of recency in terms of phonological coding or verbal rehearsal. First, attempts to demonstrate an association between phonological coding and recency have, as noted earlier, proved somewhat equivocal. Craik and Levy (1970) found that clustering words together on the basis of phonological similarity did enhance their recall, but this effect was present regardless of where the cluster was placed in the list, whether in the recency part or earlier in the list. Furthermore, Glanzer, Gianutsos, and Dubin (1969) found no difference between the disrupting effect on recency of subsequent interpolated items that were phonologically similar to the recency items and those that were phonologically dissimilar.

A final major source of evidence against an interpretation of recency in terms of rehearsal strategy comes from the observation of clear recency effects in incidental learning studies where subjects have no incentive to rehearse (Baddeley and Hitch 1977). In one study, soldiers were required to copy down nonsense syllables in what was described as a study concerning the speed and accuracy with which codes could be copied. Half the subjects were told that they would subsequently have to recall the items and half were not. Both groups showed an equivalent and marked recency effect. In another experiment, subjects heard sequences of first names and were instructed to categorize each as suitable only for a boy (e.g. *John*), only for a girl (e.g. *Jane*), or suitable for either (e.g. *Lee*). Half were warned of a subsequent recall and half were not; both showed clear recency. In conclusion, although specific encoding strategies may indeed influence the recency effect as Shallice (1975) has shown, recency does not seem to be dependent either on phonological coding or on the subject's adopting a specific learning strategy of the type suggested by Atkinson and Shiffrin (1968) or by Craik and Lockhart (1972).

The passive short-term store interpretation of recency

The most careful and detailed exploration of the recency effect has been made by Glanzer (1972) who regards recency as reflecting the contents of a limited capacity short-term store. Glanzer's views do not assume that the subject needs to adopt a particular input strategy, and hence he can explain the incidental memory results just described without difficulty. Glanzer does however assume that the recency effect in immediate free recall reflects a single limited-capacity system. Such a view has difficulty in accounting for the fact that a concurrent memory load of six digits has no effect on the magnitude of recency. It will be recalled that we carried out two experiments in which free recall of unrelated words was accompanied by a concurrent task involving remembering up to six digits. Whether the words were presented visually and the digits auditorily, or the reverse, recency was unimpaired (Baddeley and Hitch 1977). Other studies have shown that recency is not affected by articulatory suppression (Richardson and Baddeley 1975) or by concurrent arithmetic (Silverstein and Glanzer 1971). Glanzer *et al.* (1981) seem reluctant to accept the implications of these results and attempt to explain them in terms of some form of trade-off between the verbal memory and the digit span tasks, with the subject preserving recency by paying less attention to the concurrent digit span task. Such a trade-off is presumably also assumed in the case of his own study (Silverstein and Glanzer 1971) in which memory and arithmetic tasks were performed simultaneously, with no apparent effect on recency.

Glanzer's interpretation of these results is implausible for a number of reasons. First, there is clear evidence from the Baddeley and Hitch delayed recall conditions that the concurrent digit task was impairing long-term learning throughout the list. Given the fragility of the recency effect, which Glanzer himself has shown can be disrupted by merely processing a single subsequent item, I find it difficult to conceive how, on Glanzer's trade-off interpretation, performance could have withstood the effect of the three digit load, let alone the effect of retaining six digits. Glanzer's limited short-term capacity model also seems incapable of explaining the occurrence of long-term recency effects.

Long-term recency

In an experiment carried out in the early 1960s (Baddeley 1963), I required sailors to solve anagrams, providing the solution to the subject if it was not reached within 60 seconds. After he had tackled 12 anagrams, I questioned the subject about his strategies, and then asked him to recall as many of the solution words as possible. I observed a marked recency effect, despite the prolonged activity of subsequent anagram solving and the discussion following the last item. Graham Hitch and I repeated this study under rather more carefully controlled conditions a number of years later with female subjects, and again observed clear recency (Baddeley and Hitch 1977). We had speculated (Baddeley and Hitch 1974) that long-term recency effects would be found extending over lengthy periods, provided the events concerned constituted a sufficiently clearly separable category, and provided items were not easily accessible by other retrieval strategies, such as those based on associations between items. We suggested that recalling instances of personal events such as parties or restaurant meals or visits to London would probably show recency if they could be adequately tested. Unfortunately, of course, it is difficult to check the accuracy of personal recalls of naturally occurring incidents of this sort, and our research budget did not stretch to setting up a sufficiently large number of parties to test the hypothesis experimentally.

We then hit on the idea of questioning rugby players about previous games they had played. Rugby Union has the advantage that it is a game that most players play once a week against a range of other teams that can only loosely be mapped onto any simple retrieval plan or cue such as geographical region. Most games are not part of a league competition, and hence players are unlikely either to rehearse games in connection with their impact on the league, or use league position as a retrieval cue. We therefore asked members of two clubs immediately after a game to participate in our experiment. They were required to write down as many teams they had played against that season as possible in any order they wished. They were subsequently given a fixture list and required to tick off those games they recognized having played. Figure 7.1 shows the mean probability of recalling a game, given that the player recognized having played in it.

There is clearly a marked recency effect. It was fortunately the case that not all players played every week, with most missing some games presumably because of other commitments or injury. This allowed us to separate the effect of elapsed time from that of number of interpolated games. As with the standard short-term recency effect, number of inter-polated items was the crucial variable. Partial correlation indicated a clear association between the probability of recalling a given game and the number of interpolated game played by an individual between a given game and the time of recall, with elapsed time partialed out. When number of interpolated games was partialed out, on the other hand, elapsed time showed no correlation with recall probability.

While studying the recall of rugby games did prove profitable, the degree of experimental control (and indeed subject control) one can exercise in this particular experimental paradigm is somewhat limited.

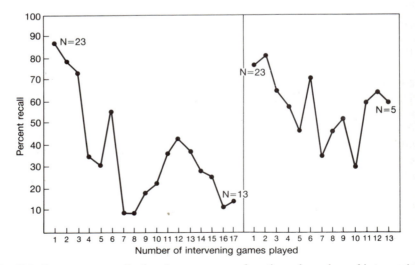

Fig. 7.1. Percentage recall of rugby games as a function of number of intervening games played (data from two rugby clubs) (Baddeley and Hitch 1976).

More recently, Amancio da Costa Pinto and I have explored a rather commoner and more practically useful recency effect, that involved in remembering where you parked your car. We began by carrying out an experiment on our colleagues at the Applied Psychology Unit (APU). For a two-week period, we surreptitiously noted what cars were parked where on each morning and afternoon. We then surprised our colleagues with a request for recall of this information, giving them a map of the Unit parking area with available parking spaces numbered. Figure 7.2 shows the probability of recalling the location correctly as a function of delay. Whether plotted on a strict or a more lax criterion, there was clear evidence of recency. Unlike the rugby players, who missed sufficient games to allow us to separate elapsed time and intervening games, we found (perhaps reassuringly) that APU staff are rather more consistent in their attendance, with the result that delay and number of intervening parking occasions were too highly correlated to allow us to test the decay and interference hypotheses statistically.

We therefore decided to use our subject panel in order to look at this question. We selected a number of occasions when groups of subjects were attending the APU for testing, and noted the location and registration number of their cars. When they were being paid for their services, we checked who had come by car, and subsequently wrote to them

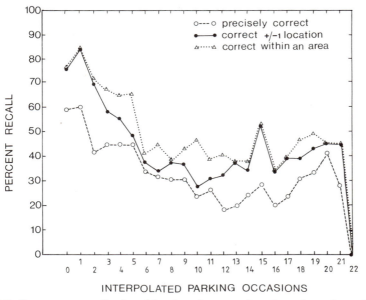

Fig. 7.2. Percentage recall of parking location as a function of number of interpolated parking occasions (Pinto and Baddeley 1984).

enclosing a map of the Unit parking facility and requesting them to try to recall where they had parked. We questioned one group of 26 subjects a week after, one group of 25 subjects a month after, and a further 29 subjects while they were still at the Unit, 2 hours after arriving.

If the results of our previous study had been entirely due to trace decay, then one might expect excellent recall after 2 hours, rather poor recall after 1 week, and abysmally bad recall after 4 weeks. In fact we observed excellent performance in all three groups, with the 2 hour, 1 week and 1 month group recalling the precise location on 72, 73, and 72 per cent of occasions respectively. There was however one difference between the groups. Since parking places are not marked, it is possible for someone to park across two places without being aware of this. For that reason we allowed subjects to specify either a single location or two adjacent locations if they felt they had parked across the two. The number of people parking across two locations was in fact low for all three groups, but the number responding with a double location increased from 4 out of 29 after 2 hours to 8 out of 26 after 1 week and 15 out of 25 after one month, a highly significant difference, ($\chi^2 = 14.0$, $p < 0.01$). This suggests that although the subjects were recalling with a good degree of accuracy, they were less precise or less confident as time elapsed.

Our second experiment seemed to rule out a simple trace decay hypothesis, but left open the question of whether forgetting in interference theory terms was due to retroactive or proactive interference. Since nearly all our subjects had attended the Unit before, a classic PI interpretation seemed unlikely, since this would predict that long delays should lead to more forgetting, despite the absence of interpolated visits. A classic RI interpretation however remained plausible, provided one made the rather strong assumption that parking elsewhere was sufficiently dissimilar from parking at the APU to produce no interference. An interpretation in terms of discriminability among available traces was also a strong candidate.

We therefore carried out an experiment in which we ensured that members of our subject panel came to the APU on two occasions separated by about 2 weeks. One group comprising 30 subjects was contacted 4 weeks after their first visit (the RI group) while the second group of 33 subjects was contacted 4 weeks after their second visit (the PI group). Subjects were sent two envelopes with strict instructions to respond to the contents of one before opening the second. The first envelope asked them to try to recall where they had parked on the visit 4 weeks before. The second asked them where they had parked on the other of the two recent visits. The results of the two questions are shown in Table 7.1 which also includes the results from the previous experiment of the group tested one month after a single visit.

TABLE 7.1

Influence of delay and number of visits on remembering a parking location. Percentage accurate recall (data from Pinto and Baddeley).

Condition	Delay 2 weeks	4 weeks	6 weeks
Single visit		72	
P.I. Group		47	20
R.I. Group	61	39	

It is clear that we did obtain a significant interference effect, with correct recall after a four week delay dropping from 72 to 47 per cent in the PI condition and 39 per cent in the RI condition. While both PI and RI groups were significantly different from the no-interference condition, the tendency for the RI effect to be greater than the PI effect was not significant. Table 7.1 also shows the recall scores of the two groups for their other visit; these do differ, with the 2 week visit of the RI group (61 per cent) being substantially better than the 6 week recall of the PI group (20 per cent).

Interpretation of this second response is of course rather more difficult. There is first of all the question of output interference; has the recall of the other occasion interfered with subsequent recall? Dalezman (1976) and Hitch, Rejman, and Turner (personal communication) have produced evidence to suggest that long-term recency effects are not strongly susceptible to order of recall, and in any case both the PI and RI groups would have an approximately equal amount of output interference, namely one recall. A more serious problem however is raised by the fact that interference and delay are confounded in the case of this second response. Hence the 6 week recall is not only after a longer period than the 2 week, but it has also suffered from RI, whereas the 2 week recall suffers from PI.

Consequently we are left with three possible interpretations: (1) that RI effects are substantially stronger than PI effects in this paradigm; (2) that temporal decay is an important variable, or (3) that time and interference interact, as would be predicted by a temporal discrimination hypothesis. Since we have evidence from the first comparison in this experiment that differences between PI and RI are not particularly large, and from the previous experiment that temporal decay is not of itself a major factor, the data appear to argue by elimination for (3), some form of temporal discrimination hypothesis. When the subject is trying to recall a single distinctive event, performance holds up very well over time, but when he is trying to retrieve one of two similar events separated by an interval, performance declines with time. Evidence from intrusion errors is consistent with such a view. Subjects who were attempting to recall parking occasions 2 and 4 weeks previously showed virtually no errors in which they recalled the correct location but dated it wrongly, whereas subjects recalling parking 4 and 6 weeks before made such errors on approximately 20 per cent of recall attempts.

Before going on to discuss more detailed models of long-term recency, I shall describe one further experiment concerned with the more general theoretical claim made by Hitch and myself. In suggesting that everyday events such as visits to the theatre or parties might each show a recency effect, we were implying that a single person could show several recency effects simultaneously, provided subjects were required to remember categories of events that were sufficiently distinctive. Testing such a hypothesis is dependent on finding a number of situations in which recency can be observed, and this proves to be considerably less straightforward than it might seem. The difficulty is finding sets of items for which other retrieval strategies are not readily available, and this probably requires sets of items which do not have strong inter-item links. This problem was solved in an ingenious study by Watkins and Peynircioglu (1983).

After trying unsuccessfully to obtain simultaneous recency effects by having words spoken by male and female voices, and after attempting to show separate recency effects for different semantic categories, Watkins and Peynircioglu decided to have one last effort in which they selected categories of events that were as distinctive as they could make them. The tasks used included solving riddles, performing simple actions, and stating favourites from specified categories such as singers, painters, etc.

In one condition, subjects were presented with items from three separate categories, the items being interleaved so that the first, fourth, seventh etc. would be from one category, the second, fifth, and eighth etc. from the second category and the third, sixth, ninth, etc., from the third category. After presentation of all items in the single category condition or all items in the triple category case, subjects were cued for recall using the category name as a cue. In the three category case, the categories were used in turn, with order of recall counterbalanced across groups. The results are shown in Fig. 7.3. Not only did each category show a pronounced recency effect, but the magnitude of the effect was virtually as great in the three category case as with a single category. This is particularly striking bearing in mind the fact that each item in the triple list will have three times as many items interpolated between its presentation and recall as in the single category case, even for the category that is cued first. When a category is cued second or third, of course, the number of interpolated recalls between the presentation and recall of an item will make both the number of interpolated events and total time between presentation and recall even greater in the case of the triple list.

In addition to their main finding, Watkins and Peynircioglu noted an

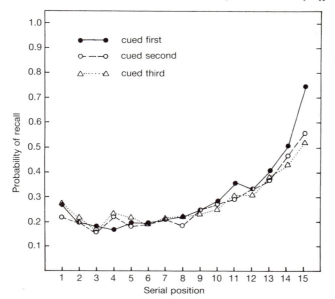

Fig. 7.3. Three simultaneous recency effects. Within-category serial position function for each cueing position (Watkins and Peynircioglu 1983).

overall reduction in mean level of performance with the triple list, an effect that is characteristic of increasing list length in general (Shiffrin 1970). Finally, they did observe over and above their main effect, a slight advantage to the condition that was cued first, an advantage that was particularly marked for the most recent item.

The demonstration of three simultaneous recency effects is clearly incompatible with an interpretation such as that of Glanzer (1972) which assumes recency to reflect the contents of a limited capacity store. I can see no way of defending the Glanzer hypothesis, other than to argue that this is a different kind of recency, and one to which his model does not apply. If an alternative model can be produced that will explain not only the standard recency effect, but also those results that are clearly inconsistent with Glanzer's hypothesis, then such a model should be preferred on the grounds of parsimony.

One way of interpreting recency effects is to liken the recall process to that of discriminating objects at a distance. As Hitch, Rejman, and Turner (1980) point out, this view has been current for many years; they quote the observation of the nineteenth-century British psychologist Sully that 'the time vista of the past is seen to answer pretty closely to a visible perspective'. Crowder elaborates this view as follows:

Items in a memory list presented at a constant rate pass by with the same regularity as do telegraph poles when one is on a moving train. Just as each telegraph

pole in the receding distance becomes less distinctive from its neighbours, like-
wise each item in memory becomes less distinctive as the presentation episode
recedes to the past. (Crowder 1976, p. 462).

This approach to recency has been explored quantitatively by Hitch,
Rejman, and Turner (1980) and by Glenberg, Bradley, Stevenson, Kraus,
Tkachuk, Gretz, Fish, and Turpin (1980). Both groups test a model using
a procedure known as the continuous distractor technique.

The continuous distractor technique

While most of the examples of long-term recency effects described so far
have been based on some aspect of everyday memory, the most common
tool for the theoretical analysis of long-term recency within the laboratory has been the continuous distractor paradigm. Tzeng (1973) and
Bjork and Whitten (1974) independently carried out a modified version
of the standard free recall paradigm. In the critical condition, each item
in the free recall list was separated during presentation by a period of
backward counting. A further period of backward counting intervened
between the last item and recall. Under these conditions a clear recency
effect was observed despite the filled pre-recall delay. This contrasted
with the standard procedure where items were not separated by an interpolated task; under these circumstances recency was abolished by the
brief post-list interval of backward counting.

Hitch *et al.* (1980) and Glenberg *et al.* (1980) both suggest that the
recency effect remains with the continuous distraction procedure simply
because the interpolated counting leads to more temporally distinctive
memory traces than does the more standard massed presentation of
items. The backward counting presumably maintains the temporal
separation by preventing subjects from rehearsing items during the inter-
presentation intervals. To use Crowder's analogy, the telegraph poles were
more widely spaced, and hence more discriminable in the continuous
distraction paradigm.

Both Hitch and Glenberg make the simplifying assumption that such
temporal discriminability will approximately follow Weber's Law, with
the discriminability of individual items being a function of the ratio of the
interval between items (t) to the time elapsed at recall (T). Again following Weber's Law, they assume that this relationship will be logarithmic.
The existence of such a constant ratio rule had been suggested by both
Bjork and Whitten (1974) and Baddeley and Hitch (1977). The hypothesis was elaborated and tested quantitatively by Glenberg *et al.* (1980)
and by Hitch *et al.* (1980) as follows.

Testing the constant ratio rule

In their first experiment, Hitch, Rejman and Turner (1980) test the hypothesis that the discriminability hypothesis and the constant ratio rule can

be fitted to standard immediate free recall, delayed free recall and to the continuous distractor paradigm. If all three can be shown to obey the same function, this substantially strengthens the view that both standard and long-term recency effects have a common origin. They used a separate groups design with 12 subjects being tested on each of the three paradigms. Subjects attempted to recall lists of 15 randomly selected nouns. In the delayed free recall task, subjects were required to cate-gorize 3-digit random numbers as odd or even for a period of 20 seconds between list presentation and recall. In the two standard free recall conditions, words were presented visually for a 2-second period, while in the continuous distractor condition each 2-second word presentation was followed by 12 seconds of distractor task, which again involved categorizing numbers as odd or even.

The predictions generated by the constant ratio hypothesis are illustrated in Fig. 7.4. They are obtained by taking each item presented and calculating the ratio of t (the interval between successive presenta-tions), and T (the time elapsed between presentation of that item and the beginning of free recall). As will be seen from Fig. 7.4, in immediate free recall, the discrimination ratio shows a very marked serial position effect; for delayed free recall the slope is extremely shallow, while an inter-mediate slope is predicted for the continuous distractor technique.

The data obtained are shown in Fig. 7.5 which is replotted in Fig. 7.6 to show the relationship between percent correct recall and log ratio for

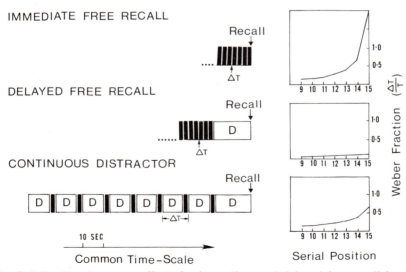

Fig. 7.4. Predicted recency effects for immediate and delayed free recall for the continuous distractor paradigm based on the temporal discrimination hypothesis (Hitch, Rejman, and Turner 1980).

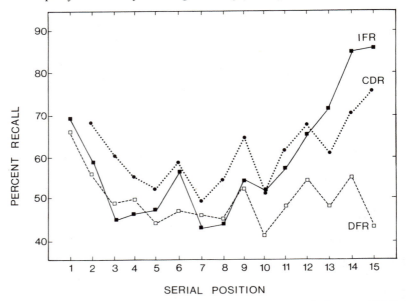

Fig. 7.5. Recency effects obtained by Hitch, Rejman, and Turner (1980) for immediate and delayed free recall and continuous distractor condition.

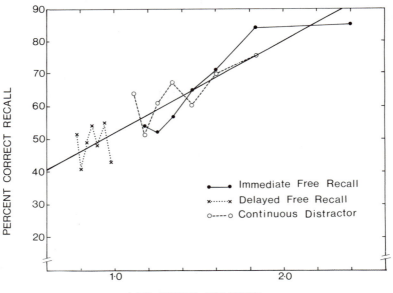

Fig. 7.6. Immediate and delayed free recall and continuous distractor results plotted as a function of the discrimination ratio (Hitch, Rejman, and Turner 1980).

each serial position across the three conditions. The fit is clearly reasonably good, particularly bearing in mind that two potentially important simplifying assumptions were made in computing the ratio. The first of these was that the difficulty of discriminating target traces from non-adjacent traces was negligible: the second was that no allowance was made for changes in temporal discriminability due to elapsed time during the process of recall. Detailed examination of the order of item recall across the three conditions suggested that recent items tended to be recalled early in the standard immediate free recall condition, but not in either of the delayed conditions. Such a strategy is sensible, since brief delay at recall is likely to have a much more dramatic effect on the discriminability of recent times in the immediate free recall condition than it is to have in either of the delayed recall conditions.

In a second experiment Hitch *et al.* test a further prediction of the discriminability hypothesis by asking whether the probability of recall is more influenced by the absolute length of the filled delay between presentation and recall, or by the ratio of inter-item interval to delay, as the constant ratio rule would predict. Four conditions were compared, two in which items were separated by two number classifications, presented at a paced rate of 1.5 seconds per classification, and two with eight classifications. Two filled recall delays were used, involving 15 and 60 interpolated distractors respectively. In one condition a 2-distractor inter-item interval was coupled with a 3-distractor recall delay (2:3), and in a second, an 8-distractor interval was coupled with a 15-distractor delay (8:15). In both these cases the discrimination ratio is high for the last item, and declines rapidly with serial position. These two conditions should therefore give clear recency effects. In contrast, the other two conditions, involving a 2-distractor inter-item interval followed by a 15-distractor delay (2:15), and an 8-distractor interval with a 60-distractor delay (8:60), gave a discrimination ratio for the last item that is low, and hence much less recency should be observed. On the other hand, if the crucial factor is simply delay between presentation and recall, there should be no difference in recency between the two conditions involving a 15-distractor delay, both of which should show less recency than the 3-distractor delay condition.

Again a separate groups design was used with subjects attempting to recall lists of 15 words. Once again the interpolated task involved judging whether random numbers were odd or even. The results were consistent with the discrimination hypothesis, with the 2:3 and 8:15 conditions showing pronounced recency, and the 2:15 and 8:60 conditions showing minimal recency.

Figure 7.7 shows the relationship between percent recall and log ratio for the two Hitch *et al.* experiments. In both cases the data do appear to follow a broadly similar function. Absolute level is different, probably

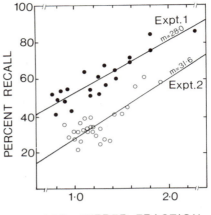

Fig. 7.7. Results of Experiments 1 and 2 of Hitch, Rejman, and Turner (1980) plotted as a function of discrimination ratio.

partly because the second experiment involved a briefer presentation of material and tested a sample from the APU subject panel rather than Cambridge undergraduates who were on average likely to be younger and more intelligent than subject panel members. In general, the discrimination hypothesis does appear to be able to account for data from both standard immediate and delayed free recall as well as long-term recency effects based on the continuous recognition paradigm.

A similar conclusion is reached by Glenberg *et al.* (1980). Their third experiment tested the ratio rule by factorially varying the length of the filled interval between items, and the length of the filled delay between list presentation and recall. They make a number of predictions on the basis of the constant ratio rule, all of which are confirmed by their results. They further show that the recency effect is not influenced by intention to learn, confirming our own observation that deliberate strategy is not an important factor (Baddeley and Hitch 1977). Furthermore, they find no influence of the difficulty of the interpolated task, suggesting that subjects are not surreptitiously processing items during the filled intervals. Both these variables on the other hand do influence the primacy effect, and support the view that primacy is dependent on the cumulative rehearsal of the first few items. In a subsequent experiment Bradley, Glenberg, and Kraus (personal communication) explore the generality of the constant ratio rule across temporal intervals ranging from 4 seconds to 7 days and conclude that it holds throughout this range.

Recency: what is the underlying mechanism?

As Hitch *et al.* point out, although they have produced a good descriptive model of recency in terms of a plausible discrimination process, their results give no clear indication as to what is being discriminated. More specifically temporal and ordinal cues are entirely confounded in all the studies so far described. Whereas Hitch leaves this as a currently unsolved problem, Glenberg advocates a contextual cueing hypothesis.

Glenberg *et al.* (1980) suggest that the constant ratio rule reflects the use of background context as a retrieval cue; 'For this hypothesis, whether the items appear to be well-ordered depends on the degree of detail of the background context that can be reinstated at the test. If enough contextual detail could be retrieved so that the recency items appear against different aspects of the context, then recency is found, and, incidentally, the items appear well-ordered.' (Glenberg *et al.* 1980, p. 368). They cite evidence in support of their hypothesis including for example an experiment contrasting recency in lists of 9 and 36 items presented over the same time period. Unfortunately this and all the other evidence they cite in fact manipulates *temporal* discriminability and simply assumes on an *ad hoc* basis that greater temporal discriminability will be associated with greater contextual change. Somewhat surprisingly, since Glenberg has elsewhere shown clear effects of context on recall (e.g. Smith, Glenberg, and Bjork 1978), no attempt is made to manipulate contextual and temporal factors independently.

However, although no explicit attempt to separate temporal and contextual cues is described, the first experiment in the Glenberg *et al.* (1980) paper might plausibly be interpreted as having done so. This is an experiment in which the concurrent task is made either hard or easy during both presentation and retention interval. One might plausibly suggest that if the same intervening task is used during presentation and during delay, then the context should be preserved to a greater extent than if a different intervening task is used. One might therefore expect that those conditions in which the difficulty of the intervening task is switched between presentation and delay will lead to less recency than those in which the same task is maintained. No evidence for such an interaction appears in the results depicted.

The contextual hypothesis would also appear to have difficulty in accounting for the Watkins and Peynircioglu (1983) demonstration of three simultaneous recency effects. It would surely be the case that switching across three separate tasks should disrupt the background context substantially more than remaining within one task, and as such should lead to a greatly disrupted recency effect. Finally, the concept of an uninterrupted context seems even less plausible in interpreting the data from the car parking studies described earlier. Why should the prevailing context be approximately the same after 2 hours, 1 week and 1 month when trying to recall a single parking location, but be different between one day and the previous day when trying to recall several such occasions?

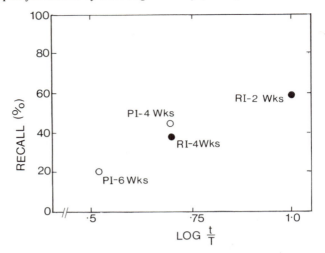

Fig. 7.8. Recall of parking location on two occasions and the constant ratio rule (Pinto and Baddeley 1984).

It might of course be argued by Glenberg that the constant ratio rule does not apply to isolated events such as parking a car, distributed over a matter of days. One can test this by seeing to what extent our earlier parking results obey the constant ratio rule. Figure 7.8 shows the probability of recalling correctly the location of parking for our various conditions, plotted as a function of the discrimination ratio. In the case of those subjects who were only tested after a single visit, it is not possible to calculate an inter-visit interval. However, the other data can be fitted, and as will be seen the observed relationship between delay and interference can be accounted for reasonably well.

If we reject the contextual hypothesis, where does this leave us? The subject appears to be making some kind of temporal or ordinal discrimination. The weakness of this approach is that it assumes that ordinal cues are all-important, but does not specify the nature of such cues. It also leaves unclear the question of what constitutes a category insofar as recency is concerned, and why some categories appear to give rise to robust long-term recency effects while others produce effects that are extremely fragile. Finally, if recency has nothing to do with STM, it is not clear why patients with defective STS functioning should show impaired recency (Shallice and Warrington 1970), while being able to utilize ordinal cues when requested (Vallar personal communication).

A tentative mechanism for recency

I shall begin by suggesting a mechanism that might conceivably provide suitable ordinal cues. The question of what constitutes a category for recency will be considered next, followed by a discussion of why some recency effects should be much more fragile than others. This will be followed by a brief discussion of the neuropsychological evidence.

Let us begin by assuming a range of memory systems. Any given system will contain a number of units; these might be nodes in a network (Collins and Loftus 1975), logogens (Morton 1979), or possibly favoured patterns of excitation (Hinton 1981). For the purpose of making the hypothesis reasonably concrete, I will suggest that each of these units is analogous to a small light bulb, attached to some relatively complex prior processing system, the nature of which varies depending on the particular memory processes involved.

Let us next assume that experiencing an event, whether it be hearing a word or performing one of Watkins and Peynircioglu's activities, or indeed taking part in a rugby game, will involve the illumination of this hypothetical light bulb, and that like most light bulbs, this will generate both light and heat. Let us also begin by assuming that as with a normal light bulb, the heat will dissipate over time. With such a system, a device for homing in on hot areas and triggering off the items so selected would produce a crude recency effect.

There are, of course, problems with such a simple mechanism. First of all, the cooling analogy implies something like temporal decay, while most of the evidence we have cited suggests that the recency effect is much more influenced by interpolated items than by elapsed time.

Another difficulty with this model is that whereas recency has the appearance of being a very automatic process, the mechanism proposed involves making difficult and obscure discriminations. Suppose then that instead of detecting the temperature, our hypothetical system takes advantage of the fact that bulbs that are already warmed will illuminate more readily. On this assumption, if we can feed a current into the array of bulbs that is not sufficient to trigger off a cold lamp but is enough to trigger off a warm one, then we would have the appropriate items 'light up' and hence presumably become available for recall.

This further assumption has the additional advantage of providing a possible reason why not all categories are amenable to having separate recency. This will depend, using our analogy, on the electrical connections among the arrays of bulbs. The fact that different semantic categories within a list of words do not each give rise to a separate recency effect would on this interpretation reflect the fact that we are unable to flood separately these individual categories with excitation. The fact that we can access specific categories in category generation, suggests that the process of flooding with excitation occurs at a different level from that involved in, for example, semantic category cueing. Indeed, the fact that the recency effect is insensitive to such a wide range of characteristics of the words involved argues very strongly for the effect occurring at a non-lexical level.

There are, of course, other advantages to the flooding by excitation occurring at a relatively 'shallow' level since the system would clearly not work if factors such as frequency operated in a similar way. If it did, then the 'flooding' strategy might well produce the most frequent rather than the most recent items. However, while this argument may explain why the categories involved in the recency effect are not taxonomic but occur on some other level, it does not explain what determines that level. Indeed, since it seems likely that this process can operate within a whole range of stores both long and short-term, it seems unlikely that there is a single determining factor that constitutes a usable category.

As discussed above a cooling bulb seems a somewhat implausible analogy for a phenomenon that does not show temporal decay. However a non-decay based analogous process almost certainly could be envisaged, for example within a parallel activation model such as that outlined by Hinton (1981). It is quite conceivable within such a system that the most recently activated pattern of excitation would be the most readily reactivated. The process of discrimination implicit in the constant ratio rule might then apply either to the probability of activation, or to the discrimination of the activated pattern from a noise background.

I do not of course wish to claim that this represents anything but a highly tentative speculation based on a type of simulation model I myself am not competent to set up or test. However, given the robustness of the recency effect, and the ability of the constant ratio rule to give a quantitative account of it across a wide range of situations, I would like to suggest that we have reached a point at which direct modelling is likely to prove fruitful.

Ecological relevance of the recency effect

While the recency effect in free recall has proved to be a robust and theoretically interesting laboratory phenomenon, there has been little speculation as to its relevance outside the laboratory. As we shall see in the chapter on fluent reading, Glanzer and his colleagues have argued for the importance of recency in prose comprehension and reading (Glanzer, Dorfman, and Kaplan 1981). Apart from this however, there has been little speculation as to the ecological validity of the recency effect, partly because it has tended to be conceived within a very narrow verbal learning paradigm. Recency is however, a very pervasive phenomenon, resisting the effects of stressors such as alcohol (e.g. Baddeley 1981), and brain damage from closed head injury (Brooks 1975). It occurs across cultures (Wagner 1978) and indeed across species (Hitch 1984) suggesting that it is a rather fundamental characteristic of memory. What function does it serve? I would like to suggest that it may play a central role in the crucial, but poorly understood process of orienting ourselves in time and space.

If one is to function effectively, it is necessary at any given time to be able to access information about where we are, where we have just come from and where we plan to go. This process operates simultaneously at several different levels. For example I am at present dictating while walking through a clearing in a wood. I know that it is just past noon and that I have spent the morning writing about the recency effect. At a more general level, I know that it is Wednesday, that I have been in Norfolk since Sunday and must leave shortly. At an even more general level I know that it is winter and will soon be Christmas and so forth. In terms of geographical location I can similarly locate myself at various levels. I am retracing my tracks along a path that will I hope eventually lead to a pub and lunch. I am located in a certain part of England which is in Western Europe, etc. etc.

At an even more fundamental level, even having a personal identity depends on being able to access a network of knowledge and autobiographical experience that constitute me as an individual. Not to be able to increment this, as is the case with a densely amnesic patient can be dispiriting, but at least the typical amnesic will have knowledge as to his distant past and his identity. Patients who are disoriented as a result of post-traumatic amnesia following a blow on the head, or as a result of advanced senile dementia may not have even this consolation, leaving them in an even more parlous mental state (Baddeley and Wilson in press).

What is the mechanism whereby we orient ourselves in the world? I would like to speculate that it is by some process analogous to that underlying the recency effect. It is a process that appears to tell us where we have just been and what we have just done, thereby linking us with a continuous web of conscious experience. Indeed one might argue that the creation of this web is the most central and important function of memory.

Part IV

Applications of Working Memory

8 Fluent reading

It should be clear by this point that although the concept of working memory overlaps with the earlier concept of short-term memory, it has a much more functional emphasis. It is concerned with the role of temporary storage in a wide range of information processing skills. As such, an important factor in evaluating any specific model of working memory is its capacity to throw light on such skills. A successful model should not necessarily tell one in advance how people read or write or count, but should provide a framework for studying these cognitive skills in a way that both increases our understanding of the skill in question, and at the same time enriches and develops the model of working memory.

The next two chapters attempt to illustrate this aspect of working memory describing work carried out in connection with the analysis of fluent reading, and of the problem of learning to read. These are both areas that have attracted considerable research in recent years, and a thorough review of either one of them would take up considerably more space than the whole of the rest of the book. This would clearly be both impracticable and inappropriate, hence once again I will concentrate primarily on work done by my colleagues and myself explicitly within a working memory framework, describing related work only when it bears directly upon our own research. Although this strategy severely limits the scope of the discussion, it does have the advantage of making the link between reading and working memory more explicit.

Fluent reading and WMG

Before attempting to apply a more detailed WMS model to the study of reading, it is clearly desirable to establish the existence of at least a broad involvement of WMG in the overall process of fluent reading. Fortunately, although none of our earlier studies was directly aimed at the analysis of reading, several of them do bear directly on this issue. We have for example, investigated the influence of a concurrent memory load on a range of tasks requiring language comprehension.

The assumption that working memory plays an important role in reading is made by a number of current models (e.g. Just and Carpenter 1980; Kintsch and van Dijk 1978), and has recently been tested by Glanzer and his colleagues. In one series of experiments, Glanzer, Dorfman, and Kaplan (1981) showed that interposing a filler task between successive sentences of prose led to slower reading of the

169

sentence that followed the break, although no effect was detected on comprehension accuracy.

In the case of our own earlier studies, it may be recalled that comprehending a spoken or written prose passage was reliably impaired by a concurrent digit load of six items. One might reasonably object to drawing strong conclusions from this result however, on the grounds that our comprehension measure had a substantial long-term memory component to it and it might be this memory component that was disrupted by the concurrent task rather than comprehension *per se*. While reading and comprehension do involve memory, long-term episodic memory is not essential to reading since grossly amnesic patients can typically read and comprehend very adequately, although they may well not be able to recall what they have read after a brief delay.

Such a criticism can not be made of those studies in which we required subjects to read sentences and decide whether they were true or false. In some cases the judgement involved knowledge of the world, in order to verify sentences such as *Robins have red breasts*, while in others, the requirement was to evaluate the sentence as a description of the order of two letters e.g. *A is followed by B—BA*. As Figs 4.1 (p. 58) and 4.5 (p. 67) showed, even a relatively modest concurrent digit load was enough to slow down performance, while a larger load of six or more digits significantly increased the error rate on the semantic verification task. One might, however, object that in neither of these cases were we studying typical reading; one task involved a relatively complex grammatical reasoning procedure with minimal semantic content, while the other was primarily concerned with sheer speed of access to semantic memory. Syntactic and semantic analysis are of course crucial to the process of reading, but one might argue that these conditions of testing, based as they are on speed of response to very short simple sentences, are highly atypical. We therefore decided to explore the role of WMG in reading connected text, extending a study by Daneman and Carpenter (1980) which investigated individual differences in adult reading skill within a WMG framework (Baddeley, Logie, Nimmo-Smith, and Brereton 1985).

Individual differences in fluent reading

Most approaches to the study of fluent reading have attempted to break down performance in some way, either by presenting the stimuli very briefly, by accompanying reading by some distracting secondary task, or by taking advantage of the disruption of reading that sometimes occurs following brain damage. All of these offer a valuable means of gaining insight into the process of fluent reading, but all are open to the objection that what is studied is some impaired or disrupted form of reading which may or may not give results that are directly applicable to fluent reading.

It is clearly important to try to relate the conclusions drawn from such studies to the performance of readers when they are reading normal text and are unencumbered by any supplementary task or disability.

One possible way of studying reading without disruption is to take advantage of the individual differences that occur in reading ability across subjects. Subjects can then be given a range of other tasks, and a correlational approach is used to identify which components of cognitive processing appear to be associated most closely with capacity to read fluently. While correlational studies are inevitably limited, and do not allow one to draw firm causal links between components, they nevertheless offer a potentially useful tool for studying the mature fluent reader.

Using this approach, Daneman and Carpenter (1980) attempted to test the hypothesis that reading depends upon WMG. Earlier studies (e.g. Perfetti and Lesgold 1977) had attempted to explore this question using standard digit span measures, and had found only a weak relationship between digit span and reading skill. Daneman and Carpenter, however, argued that the digit span measure was not a good indicator of WM capacity. They argued that the essence of WM is that it divides its capacity between storage and processing. Digit span might be a reasonable measure of a certain type of storage, but requires little in the way of simultaneous storage and processing. They devised instead a task which they refer to as working memory span, and which requires both processing and storage.

In their first study, Daneman and Carpenter measured WM span by requiring their subjects to read a sequence of sentences, and subsequently recall the last word of each sentence. Span was defined as the maximum number of sentences which the subject could read while correctly remembering the final words. They tested a range of college students on this and on a task involving the reading of passages of prose about which they had subsequently to answer questions. There proved to be a highly significant correlation between working memory span and the reading score they devised ($r = 0.72$, $p < 0.01$) and a healthy correlation of 0.59 with performance on a more general test of comprehension, the scholastic aptitude test. While these were encouragingly high correlations, it could, of course, be argued that Daneman and Carpenter were merely predicting one reading score from another. They therefore carried out a further experiment in which WM span was measured using auditory presentation. Once again, the correlation between span and their reading performance measure was impressively high ($r = 0.81$).

One weakness of the Daneman and Carpenter approach to reading is that it is open to the objection that their working memory span test is itself a highly complex task involving not only the storage and retrieval of verbal material, but also comprehension. At one level this is a strength, since they can claim to have developed a brief and sensitive measure of comprehension. It seems highly plausible that the very success of this measure stems from the fact that it taps such a wide range of different subprocesses. In this respect, it resembles the Stanford-Binet test of intelligence, which comprises a range of subtasks of many different types. While no individual test would claim to be an adequate indicator of general intellectual ability, the composite measure does provide a very useful indicator of general intelligence. Looked at from an analytic viewpoint however, it would clearly be desirable to have a more detailed breakdown of the subcomponents contributing to reading than is provided by the Daneman and Carpenter WM span measure.

There have been a number of attempts to tackle this problem. For example, Hunt and his colleagues have attempted to use some of the paradigms and techniques developed within the psychology laboratory during the 1960s and 1970s to study individual differences in cognitive performance. Within the domain of reading, Hunt, Frost, and Lunneborg (1973) have suggested that an important component of reading is the ability to access a phonological code on the basis of a visual stimulus. They suggest that this capacity can be measured using two tasks devised by Posner and his colleagues, both of which involved deciding whether two letters of the alphabet are or are not the same (Posner, Boies, Eichelman, and Taylor 1969). In one of these, the two letters are always of the same case, e.g. AA (yes) or bb (yes), vs AB (no), ba (no). Under these circumstances, 'yes' items always involve presenting two *physically identical* stimuli, while 'no' items always involve physically different letters. This may be contrasted with the second condition in which the subject is required to decide whether two letters share the same *name* or not, but where the two are always of a different case, for example Aa (yes), Bb (yes) vs Ab (no), Ba (no). In order to perform this latter task, it is suggested that the subject accesses the names of the letters and performs his comparison on these. Some of Hunt's earlier results seem to suggest that the difference in time to make a physical match and a name match provided a good measure of a subject's speed of accessing phonological codes, which in turn predicted his general intelligence and reading ability (Hunt *et al.* 1973).

Further support for this view seemed to come from studies by Jackson and McClelland (1979) who attempted to predict the reading scores of college students on the basis of a range of cognitive tasks, including the Posner physical and name matching test. They conclude from their studies that reading is dependent on two main factors, general comprehension ability and 'speed of accessing overlearned memory codes for visually presented letters' (Jackson and McClelland 1979, p. 151). A detailed examination of their results, however, indicates that the bulk of the variance in their reading measure is accounted for by a test of auditory comprehension, with the Posner name-matching task being only one of a range of reaction-time tasks, all of which are intercorrelated, and are related relatively weakly to reading performance. The reading performance score itself is based on multiplying speed and accuracy scores. Hence it is not implausible to assume that the relationship between reading and the speed with which visual stimuli can be used to access verbal codes, may merely be a reflection of a given subject's general capacity to perform laboratory reaction time tasks rapidly.

Finally, both Jackson and McClelland and Daneman and Carpenter limited their study to college students, who obviously represent a very narrow range of both age and ability. We therefore decided to attempt to replicate the results of both Daneman and Carpenter and Jackson and McClelland using a much wider range of subjects (Baddeley, Logie, Nimmo-Smith, and Brereton 1985).

We tested in our first study a total of 51 members of the APU subject panel ranging in age from 18 to 60 with a mean of 40. We opted to use the standard Nelson-Denny reading test which involves presenting the subject with passages or prose. The subjects' task is to answer questions about the passage as quickly and accurately as possible using whatever strategy they wish.

We used a modified version of the working memory span task in which subjects were presented auditorily with a series of sentences, each of which described a subject performing some action on an object. Each sentence could be either meaningful e.g. *The sailor bought the parrot,* or meaningless e.g. *The banker kicked the idea.* Subjects were required to categorize each sentence as sensible or nonsense, and were subsequently cued to recall either the subjects or the objects. Hence if the previous two sentences had been presented, the correct response should be 'sensible' and 'nonsense' respectively, and if cued for *subjects,* the response should be 'sailor, banker'.

Other tasks included the Mill Hill recognition vocabulary test, the Posner physical and name match tasks and a further task involving lexical decision in which subjects decided whether letter sequences comprised words or nonwords. We included this for two reasons. First, we felt that it would give us an indication of the speed with which subjects could access the mental lexicon in which words are represented. Secondly, it provided a further measure of phonological coding, as follows. In one test sequence, all the nonwords were phonologically quite different from real words, while in another sequence, nonwords were all homophones of real words, such as *brane* and *frute.* Rubenstein, Lewis, and Rubenstein (1971) have shown that subjects take longer to reject such nonword homophones in a lexical decision task than they do to reject nonwords that do not sound like real words, such as *brone* and *fruke.* This implies some form of automatic access to a phonological code. We hoped that the inclusion of this task would tell us whether good readers were more likely to have such an automatic phonological access, and hence to be slowed down more by nonword homophones.

Our subjects were tested in groups under considerably less carefully controlled conditions than were present with either the Daneman and Carpenter or the Jackson and McClelland studies, and consequently we felt our study would test the robustness of their results, but would not necessarily give rise to such high correlations.

The results we obtained are shown in Table 8.1 which shows the correlation between the various measures included in our study. In general, our results replicated those of Daneman and Carpenter, showing a reasonable correlation of 0.46 between comprehension and working memory span. The more detailed measures of information processing were rather less successful, with the exception of lexical decision, which is of course a task that directly involves reading. The various tasks which supposedly measure distinctly different cognitive processes are highly intercorrelated. When combined with the working memory score, these measures added relatively little to our ability to predict fluent reading. Stepwise multiple regression suggested that WM span accounts for 21.4 per cent of the variance, lexical decision with non-homophonous items adds a further 15.8 per cent and vocabulary a further 7.1 per cent. Additional variables do not add significantly to the accounted variance.

It might, of course, be objected that we ran our test under such poorly controlled conditions, that we were not entitled to expect any impressive correlations from the more complex laboratory-based tasks. However, our measures certainly produced the standard effects of slower processing of nonword homophones, and in the Posner task, consistently slower performance on the name match than on the physical match. Furthermore, the fact that our various information processing tasks correlated with each other suggests that the noisiness of the data is not the major problem. It is however likely that derived measures such as those cited are likely to show greater variance than the primary measures on which they are based. None-the-less it is hard to escape the conviction that differences based on time to match physical codes, name codes or make lexical decisions do not provide good predictors of fluent reading performance.

A second study correlated the reading comprehension of a further sample of 107 subjects with WM span, vocabulary and a counting span task devised by Case, Kurland, and Goldberg (1982). (See pp. 193–6 for further details of this task.) Again WM span accounted for a significant 19.5 per cent of the variance in comprehension scores, and vocabulary for a further 23.2 per cent. Considered alone, the Case *et al.* counting measure accounted for 7.8 per cent, but whereas WM span and vocabulary were virtually uncorrelated, the counting span variance could be entirely attributed to its correlation with WM span.

TABLE 8.1
Correlations among measures used to predict reading comprehension by Baddeley, Logie, Nimmo-Smith and Brereton (1985)

	Working memory span	Rate	Vocabulary	Lexical decision			Letter matching		
				Standard	Homophone	S–H difference	Physical	Name	P–N difference
Comprehension	0.463‡	0.135	0.329†	0.511‡	0.254	0.334*	0.260	0.401†	−0.015
Working memory span		0.026	0.330*	0.298*	0.023	0.337*	0.403†	0.438†	−0.306*
Reading rate			0.127	−0.091	0.060	−0.189	0.073	0.300*	−0.295*
Vocabulary				−0.074	−0.275*	0.227	−0.230	−0.034	−0.075
Lexical decision (standard)					0.740‡	0.118	0.647‡	0.509‡	−0.042
Lexical decision (homophone)						−0.506‡	0.473‡	0.454‡	0.035
Difference							0.076	−0.072	0.130
Physical–letter matching								0.620‡	−0.249
Name–letter matching									−0.557‡

*$p < 0.05$; †$p < 0.01$; ‡$p < 0.001$.

In conclusion, there does appear to be good evidence for the involvement of WMG in fluent reading comprehension. In the remainder of this chapter, we will be concerned with the attempt to use our specific model of working memory to understand some of the subcomponents of reading.

Phonological coding and fluent reading

There is no doubt that the origins of reading lie in speech, both historically and developmentally (Conrad 1972). Davies (1973) suggests that silent reading was rare in both classical and Medieval times, and there is an apochryphal story regarding Saint Augustine, that when he was observed reading silently, it was regarded as evidence of some magical power. Similarly, children in our culture are almost invariably trained to read aloud, and only subsequently begin to read silently. A question that has concerned those studying reading for the last century at least is that of the role played by speech coding in fluent adult reading.

The case for the importance of some form of inner speech in reading, is perhaps made most eloquently in the following frequently quoted section from Huey's classic text on reading: 'The carrying range of inner speech is considerably larger than that of vision. . . . The initial subvocalization seems to help hold the word in consciousness until enough others are given to combine with it in touching off the unitary utterance of a sentence which they form. . . . It is of the greatest service to the reader or listener that at each moment a considerable amount of what is being read should hang suspended in the primary memory of the inner speech. It is doubtless true that without something of this there could be no comprehension of speech at all.' (Huey 1908).

There is, of course, no doubt that reading *can* proceed on the basis of phonological coding. For example it is possible to understand sentences made up of nonwords, provided that when these nonwords are pronounced they sound like real words. For example: *Iff yew kan sowned owt thiss sentunns, ewe wil komprihenned itt.* This indicates that comprehension *can* be based on phonological coding, it does not of course imply that such coding necessarily or typically occurs in normal fluent reading. A great deal of research over the last fifty years has aimed at exploring just this question. We shall begin by assessing the evidence for articulatory coding in reading, and then proceed to the question of acoustic and subsequently visual coding.

Articulatory coding and reading

One of the most direct and obvious ways of exploring the role of articulation in reading is to use electromyographic measures of the movement of the muscles of a subject's lips or larynx. Using this approach, Hardyk and Petrinovitch (1970) studied the ability of their subjects to read prose passages of varying levels of difficulty. They found that subjects could be trained to read easy passages with no apparent electromyographic activity, but that difficult passages did tend to induce some articulatory subvocalization.

There are however at least two problems with this approach. First, it is conceivable that any electromyographic activity may be purely incidental to the process of reading. Kinsbourne (1974) for example has suggested that any demanding cognitive task may give rise to excitation in areas of the brain surrounding that involved in performing the task. This may show up in such manifestations as a deviation of the gaze in one direction or another, or an interference with verbal processing. Such manifestations however, are essentially the result of an overflow of cortical excitation rather than a direct component of the task itself. One might therefore argue that the articulatory activity shown by Hardyk and Petrinovitch's subjects while reading the difficult passages might merely reflect an overflow of excitation within the general language area of the brain rather than a specific use of subvocal coding in reading.

A second possible objection to this approach to subvocal coding stems from the fact that it is concerned with a very peripheral manifestation of the articulatory process; it may be that the important component is a relatively deep set of speech motor programmes which might conceivably be run independent of the external speech musculature. Evidence for such a view comes from the dysarthric patient G.B. discussed in Chapter 5 (Baddeley and Wilson 1985). It may be recalled that although G.B. had no control whatsoever over his speech muscles, he nevertheless showed clear evidence of the phonological coding of written material as indicated by the influence of both word length and phonological similarity on his memory span, and by his ability to make accurate rhyme judgments on written words and nonwords with both regular and irregular spelling patterns (see pp. 105–6). In conclusion, although electromyographic measures may sometimes provide an additional source of information, it seems unwise to regard them as providing an adequate measure of phonological coding in reading.

A second approach to phonological coding in reading is to use the task of *lexical decision* in which the subject is instructed to detect non-words embedded within a sequence of normal English words. By varying the nature of the non-words, evidence can be produced of the type of coding involved. In this task, there is clear evidence that performance is slowed down when the non-words are homophones of real words. Hence *brane* would take longer to reject than *brone* (Rubenstein, Lewis, and Rubenstein 1971). However, as Coltheart, Davelaar, Jonasson, and Besner (1977) have pointed out, this effect influences the rate of processing of the non-words only. As such it implies the phonological coding of non-words, but not necessarily of words, and hence does not speak directly to the question of phonological coding in the fluent reading of English text.

A closer approximation to normal reading occurs in a study by Baron (1973) in which the subject was required to judge whether each of a series of short phrases was or was not meaningful. The phrase always comprised a triplet of real English words, but in some cases the words made sense, e.g. *tie the knot*, whereas in others they were phonologically equivalent to meaningful phrases but were not in fact meaningful, e.g. *tie the not*. In order to control for visual similarity, sequences were presented in which a sensible word was replaced by one which was visually similar to the correct item but was not a homophone (e.g. *I am ill* and *I am kill*). Baron observed that processing time was not slowed down in the case of the homophone nonsense phrases, but that the probability of error did increase, implying that phonological coding was playing some role in the task. This technique does not indicate whether such coding is articulatory, acoustic or both.

Baddeley and Hitch (1974) used a related approach to study the role of phonemic similarity in reading by presenting subjects with sentences largely comprising phonologically similar words, and comparing the speed and accuracy with which they processed such sentences with their performance on dissimilar control sentences. It was argued that if comprehension depended on some form of phonologically encoded representation of the sentence, then the similarity among the words should impair performance, just as it did in the case of immediate memory span.

The subject's task was to read sentences such as *Rude Jude chewed his crude stewed food*, or semantically equivalent but phonemically dissimilar control sentences such as *Rough curt Jude ate his plain boiled meal*. He was required to decide whether each sentence was or was not correct. Incorrect sentences were produced by transposing the order of two adjacent words. Subjects were consistently slower at processing the similar sentences, although this effect was unfortunately not consistent across all the sentences sampled. In view of this we decided that we should replicate the effect before drawing any conclusions.

In this study 10 further subjects classified a total of 20 semantically permissible and 20 anomalous sentences. Again the order of presentation of sentences was random, and again half the sentences contained a large number of phonemically similar words while half were semantically equivalent but phonemically dissimilar sentences.

The results showed an overall tendency for similarity to slow down performance when analysed across subjects, and on this occasion we observed a significant interaction between similarity and sentence type reflecting the absence of the similarity effect in the case of semantically permissible sentences. When analysed across sentences however neither the interaction nor the main similarity effect was significant.

A further replication was therefore performed; it included two types of anomalous sentence. The first simply involved permuting the order of two words (e.g. *Rude chewed Jude crude stewed food*), while the second type was obtained by substituting for the target word a semantically anomalous word (e.g. *Rude Jude queued crude stewed food*). Since we have previously suggested that the articulatory loop is particularly concerned with processing order information, it seemed possible that phonemic similarity might impair detection of anomalies of word *order*, while leaving the subject able to detect semantic anomalies.

A total of 17 members of the Applied Psychology Unit subject panel classified 80 sentences. These comprised 40 semantically appropriate sentences, 20 sentences with anomalous word order and 20 with anomalous word substitution. The results showed a significant effect of similarity whether the data were analysed by subject or by sentence. Subjects were reliably faster at detecting transposition errors than they were at detecting impossible substitutions or classifying sentences as semantically acceptable. There was a mean overall error rate of 14.5 per cent, but this was not significantly affected by similarity.

While we were gratified to have replicated our main result, and to have obtained an effect which held across sentences as well as subjects, we were slightly surprised to observe no interaction between the type of sentence and similarity. More specifically, we had expected to find the largest effect for transpositions and little or no effect in the case of substitution. Similarity again had no effect on errors whether analysed across subjects or sentences.

In conclusion, it appears that our similarity effect is not dependent on requiring the subject to detect order errors. There were however some worrying features to our results; the effect is consistently significant for subjects but not always for sentences. Furthermore, we found no effect of similarity on errors. This is puzzling since the phonological similarity effect in short-term memory shows up primarily in errors which stem from difficulty in maintaining order information (Wickelgren 1965). We shall return to this point after exploring further the effect of articulatory suppression on reading.

Articulatory suppression and reading

A third approach to the role of phonologial coding in reading utilizes the technique of articulatory suppression, in which the subject is continually required to repeat subvocally an irrelevant item, such as the word 'the' or the digits '1, 2, 3, 4, 5, 6'. Levy (1977, 1978, 1981) and Slowiaczek and Clifton (1980) have used this technique in a series of studies in which the subject is presented with a sequence of sentences which he must read. His comprehension is then tested by requiring him to respond to a subsequent sentence. When this technique is used, articulatory suppression typically causes clear performance decrements when the material is read, in contrast to a control condition where presentation is auditory.

Unfortunately, however, it is difficult to know whether these results stem from the process of reading comprehension *per se*, or from the method of testing comprehension. There is clear evidence that articulatory suppression impairs both immediate memory (e.g. Baddeley, Thomson, and Buchanan 1975) and delayed recall (e.g. Richardson and Baddeley 1975), particularly with visual presentation. It is therefore difficult to know whether Levy's results demonstrate the general importance of articulatory coding in reading, or are simply further demonstrations of the role of articulation in verbal memory.

It seems clear then, that if one wishes to use articulatory suppression to study the role of phonological coding in reading *per se*, then it is wise to avoid assessing the subject's comprehension by means of a memory test. Kleiman (1975) ran a series of studies in which the role of phonological coding in reading was studied under conditions which appear to make considerably less demand on the subject's memory than was the case in Levy's studies. He attempted to suppress articulation by requiring his subject to repeat a stream of random digits while reading material of various types. He found that this shadowing task impaired the subject's ability to detect a rhyme within a sentence (e.g. is there a word rhyming with *cream* in the sentence *He awakened from the dream*?: is there a word rhyming with *soul* in the sentence *The referee called a foul*?).

The effect of shadowing was much less when the subject had to make judgements of graphemic similarity such as whether there is a word graphemically similar to *bury* in the sentence *Yesterday the grand jury adjourned*, or in the case of category judgements where the subject had to decide, for example, whether a game was mentioned in the sentence *Everyone at home played Monopoly*. One could, however, argue that all these conditions involve an implicit memory task since they require the subject to hold the target word in memory while he processes the sentence. One might further argue that a subject about to make a phonological judgement would be most likely to maintain the word phonologically, whereas the graphemic and semantic judgements might be more likely to be supported by visual and semantic representations. In short, one could argue that the effects here came from the interference between the shadowing task and phonologically maintaining the target word, not between shadowing and reading.

Kleiman included one other condition which is not open to this objection. His subjects were required to judge the semantic acceptability of sentences, half of which were meaningful (e.g. *Noisy parties disturb sleeping neighbours*) and half of which were semantically anomalous (e.g. *Pizzas have been eating Jerry*). Performance on this task was impaired by shadowing. Unfortunately, however, even this result is not unequivocal.

The concurrent task selected by Kleiman was shadowing, in which the subject was required to listen to and repeat back a sequence of random digits. There is considerable evidence to show that this is a relatively demanding cognitive task which would not only act as an articulatory suppressor, but would also place a considerable cognitive load on the subject's working memory. It is possible, therefore, that the decrement observed by Kleiman stems from information overload rather than suppression of articulatory coding.

Evidence for such an interpretation comes from Baddeley (1979, Tables 1 and 2) who required his subjects to verify sentences under conditions involving either articulatory suppression (continually repeating the digits 1 to 6), a concurrent cognitive load (remembering a sequence of six digits) or a control condition with no supplementary task. The reading task involved classifying sentences such as *Wasps have legs* or *Canaries have gills* as true or false. Two studies were carried out and gave consistent results: there was no difference in processing time between suppression and control, whereas a concurrent digit load produced a clear increase in verification time.

However, while these results seemed clear-cut, they were open to the criticism that the very simple sentences used were atypical of normal prose. Furthermore, the error rate was very low, possibly leading to the masking by a floor effect of any effect of suppression on accuracy. We therefore decided to replicate using more complex material (Baddeley and Lewis 1981).

Subjects were presented with a total of 96 sentences of which 64 were semantically meaningful while 32 contained an anomalous word. The semantically anomalous word was in fact related to the word it supplanted in one of several ways, being either visually similar, phonemically similar, both visually and phonemically similar or dissimilar on both counts. Unfortunately it proved very difficult to generate sets which balanced the various types of similarity in an entirely satisfactory way, particularly since visual and phonemic similarity tend to be closely associated, and for that reason we shall not discuss the effects of similarity further.

The sentences were considerably more complex than those used in the previous study, examples being *She doesn't mind going to the dentist to have fillings, but doesn't like the pain (rent) when he gives her the injection at the beginning,* or *After the football match, the goalkeeper had some pain (rain) in his left leg which he got from being hit hard by the centre forward.* The words in brackets are examples of the semantically anomalous words substituted for the preceding word in order to make the sentence in question anomalous. A test sequence comprised 32 anomalous sentences, 32 control sentences, created using the same criteria, and serving as the basis for anomalous sentences for other subjects, and 32 filler sentences. The filler sentences were included to reduce the overall probability of anomaly, thereby it was hoped making the task somewhat more like normal reading. All subjects verified half the sentences under control conditions and half under articulatory suppression; this involved the subject in repeatedly counting from one to six, with the sentence being exposed halfway through his first counting sequence. Subjects were monitored and encouraged to keep their rate of counting at one of about four digits per second. A total of 32 members of the APU subject panel were tested, half beginning with the suppression and half with the control condition.

Figures 8.1 and 8.2 show the effect of articulatory suppression on the speed and accuracy of sentence verification. We found a clear effect of articulatory suppression on accuracy, whether analysed across subjects or across sentences. There was also a significant effect of whether the sentence was semantically permissible or not and a highly significant interaction between suppression and semantic anomaly, largely due to a very high error rate when subjects are required to read semantically anomalous sentences while suppressing. In contrast to its clear effects on accuracy, suppression of articulation had no effect on speed of sentence verification.

We seemed therefore to have shown that suppression *can* have an effect on the accuracy with which a reading task is performed. However, our results are open to at least two objections. First, it could be argued

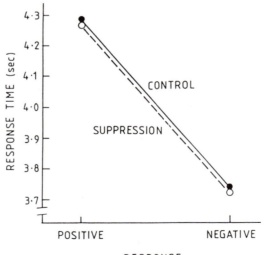

Fig. 8.1. The influence of articulatory suppression on speed of classifying sentences as meaningful (positive) or meaningless (negative) (Baddeley, Eldridge, and Lewis 1981).

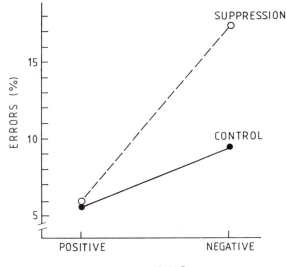

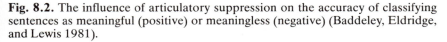

Fig. 8.2. The influence of articulatory suppression on the accuracy of classifying sentences as meaningful (positive) or meaningless (negative) (Baddeley, Eldridge, and Lewis 1981).

that our material is highly artificial. Secondly, and more seriously, it could be argued that suppression influences performance by acting as a general distractor, not through its specific effect on the articulatory loop.

We therefore carried out a further study in which we required our subjects to read silently passages of prose taken from a travel book (Baddeley, Eldridge, and Lewis 1981). Their task was to detect occasional errors, an error being the reversal of the order of two words hence *he was very rich* might be transformed to *he very was rich*. In one condition, subvocal articulation was suppressed by requiring the subject to repeat the word *the* at a rate of about 3–4 per second. Performance was compared with a control condition in which subjects were free to indulge in whatever subvocal activity they wished. Finally, in order to control for the possibility that performing *any* supplementary task will impair performance, we included a tapping condition in which the subject was required to tap with a pencil, again at a rate of 3–4 times per second. It was assumed that this would provide a level of distraction approximately equivalent to that of uttering the word 'the' at the same rate.

The results of this experiment are shown in Table 8.2, from which it is clear that suppressing articulation substantially impaired detection performance ($p < 0.01$) while tapping led to no significant decrement ($p > 0.10$). In contrast to the clear effects of suppression on errors however, we obtained no effect on speed. Our previous results indicated that

TABLE 8.2

Influence of articulatory suppression and tapping on the detection of errors in prose

	Control	Suppression	Tapping
Misses (out of 5)	1.54	2.40	1.64
False alarms	0.09	0.08	0.14
Time/passage (s)	68.03	69.19	68.44

articulatory suppression had no detectable influence on the processing of brief and simple sentences for which the error rate was universally low, but had a marked effect on the accuracy but not the speed of performing more complex comprehension tasks. This suggests that being free to subvocalize may be important for complex comprehension tasks. Furthermore, since speed of processing is unaffected by suppression, our results suggest that subvocalization operates in parallel with other aspects of comprehension, providing a supplementary backup, probably one that is particularly useful when it is important to process order information accurately.

Suppression and phonemic similarity combined

The experiments we have described so far could be accounted for by making the simple and plausible assumption that phonemic coding is necessary for verifying complex but not simple sentences. There remain however a number of worrying secondary features to our results. Why, for example, does phonemic similarity produce an impairment in speed while having no effect on errors, in contrast to articulatory suppression which appears to leave speed unaffected while causing a clear decrease in accuracy? We were also worried by the failure of the phonemic similarity effect to be consistently significant when tested across sentences, although it came through clearly enough when tested across subjects. We decided therefore to explore the situation further by testing the stronger prediction from the short-term memory analogy, namely that the phonemic similarity effect should disappear when combined with articulatory suppression.

Our next experiment was therefore based on our first Rude Jude replication study with the exception that the additional variable of articulatory suppression was introduced. The same 20 sentences were used in both the similar and dissimilar form and both transposition and substitution errors were inserted. Of the 16 APU panel members tested, 8 began with the control condition and then performed the task under articulatory suppression, which once again involved counting repeatedly from one to six, while the remaining 8 performed in the opposite order.

The effects of similarity on verification time for the various types of sentence are shown in Table 8.3. When analysed across subjects there proved to be a significant effect of similarity, although the effect interacted with type of sentence. Somewhat paradoxically, the effect appears to be greater for the semantically acceptable sentences than for either of the anomalous sentences, exactly the opposite pattern to that obtained in a previous experiment. When analysed across sentences however the similarity effect failed to reach significance. There was no effect of articulatory suppression on processing speed, indeed there was a non-significant tendency for subjects to process faster while suppressing.

TABLE 8.3

The effect of phonemic similarity and articulatory suppression on speed of sentence verification (secs per sentence) (Baddeley and Lewis 1981).

	Similarity		
	Possible	Impossible	
		Substitution	Transposition
Similar	2.78	2.69	2.57
Dissimilar	2.63	2.68	2.46
Similarity effect	0.15	0.01	0.11

	Suppression		
	Possible	Impossible	
		Substitution	Transposition
Control	2.75	2.77	2.52
Suppression	2.66	2.59	2.51
Suppression effect	0.09	0.18	0.01

The distribution of errors for the various conditions is shown in Table 8.4. There is no effect of similarity on error rate for either subjects or sentences. There is a clear tendency for suppression to increase error rate whether measured across subjects or across sentences. In addition, there is a highly significant effect of sentence type across both subjects and sentences, and this in turn interacts with suppression. As is clear from Table 8.4 the effect occurs because the transpositions are harder to detect than substitutions, and furthermore are much more subject to disruption by articulatory suppression. Indeed, a number of subjects were virtually at chance level when attempting to detect transpositions under suppression.

The pattern of errors under conditions of suppression are very much what one might expect on the assumption that the articulatory loop is involved in verifying these more complex sentences. Order information is

TABLE 8.4

The effect of phonemic similarity and articulatory suppression on mean percentage of errors in sentence verification (Baddeley and Lewis 1981).

	Similarity		
	Possible	Impossible	
		Substitution	Transposition
Similar	9.4	14.1	23.8
Dissimilar	5.3	10.9	27.8
Similarity effect	4.1	3.2	−4.0

	Suppression		
	Possible	Impossible	
		Substitution	Transposition
Control	5.0	9.4	15.9
Suppression	9.7	15.9	35.6
Suppression effect	4.7	6.5	19.7

particularly vulnerable just as one might expect from the short-term memory literature. In short, we are producing clear evidence for an effect of articulatory suppression on performance.

Two features of this result should be noted however. First, note that the effect is on errors only; preventing subjects from using the articulatory loop may make them less accurate but it certainly does not slow them down. The second feature of interest is that the effects of articulatory suppression are completely at variance with those of similarity. The similarity effect has no effect on errors, and shows no evidence at all of the predicted interaction with suppression. In view of the consistency and magnitude of this interaction in the short-term memory literature (Levy 1971; Murray 1968; Peterson and Johnson 1971), the absence of such an interaction is striking. It clearly suggests that the similarity effect in comprehension can not be attributed to the articulatory loop. How then should it be explained?

An alternative explanation of the Rude Jude effect is in terms of visual similarity. Words that are similar in sound are typically also visually similar. This is not, however, always the case, as became clear when we examined closely the material we had used. We therefore decided to attempt to measure the degree of visual similarity within our sentences, and correlate mean verification time with similarity across a range of studies in which we had used these sentences. Our measure of similarity was based on number of repeated pairs of letters, hence a sentence like *The lone crone was shown the phone thrown on the stone* would have a high visual similarity score since it contains a large number of repeated

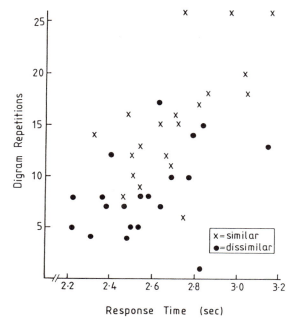

Fig. 8.3. The mean time to verify phonologically similar and dissimilar sentences as a function of visual similarity. Visual similarity is measured in terms of number of repeated letter diagrams (Baddeley and Lewis 1981).

letter patterns, whereas a sentence like *I sigh and cry as the sly guy dies* has a relatively low visually similarity score, despite being made up of phonologically similar words.

Figure 8.3 shows the relationship between visual similarity scored in this way and mean verification latency. There is a highly significant correlation ($r=0.60$, $p<0.001$). Although this may be partially due to the highly correlated variable of phonological similarity, inspection of the scatter plot suggests that this is probably not the only factor. Across the middle portion of the graph for which there are a reasonable number of examples from both the phonologically similar and control sets, there is no evidence to indicate that phonologically similar items take longer to verify than dissimilar items of approximately equivalent visual similarity. It would clearly be desirable to separate these two variables, but unfortunately so far, the task of producing a reasonable sample of sentences made up from words that are visually similar but phonologically dissimilar has been too much for us.

Reading and the visuo-spatial sketchpad

While I myself have done no work on the role of the VSSP in reading there are two sources of evidence that the sketchpad may be important in reading. Kennedy (1983) has pointed out the importance of maintaining an accurate spatial orientation with regard to the lines of text that are being scanned in normal text reading. Maintaining spatial orientation on the page is likely to be particularly demanding when the eyes move back to re-read a word or phrase, or when the eyes move from the end of one line of text to the beginning of the next. Logically, this would seem to demand a visuo-spatial system capable of storing information about the location of the text on the page. The sketchpad would seem to offer a possible system for achieving this.

A second source of evidence for the involvement of a visual imagery system such as the VSSP in reading comes from two studies on the comprehension of sentences of high and low imageability.

In the first of these studies, Glass, Eddy, and Schwanenflugel (1980) presented subjects with a complex visual pattern which they were required to retain while verifying sentences that were either highly imageable such as *The star of David has six points*, or were abstract and non-imageable such as *There are seven days in a week*. Retention of the pattern was impaired more by the imageable than by the abstract sentences. The effect was not, however, symmetrical, since concurrently holding a pattern did not slow down the verification of imageable sentences any more than it did the verification of abstract sentences. This asymmetry is reminiscent of some of our own results using the preload technique, and may be due to the fact that the subject regards the sentence verification tasks as primary and is prepared to stop attempting to maintain the pattern in VSSP if this interferes with verification.

A second study by Eddy and Glass (1981) attempted to obtain more direct evidence for an influence of imageability on language processing. They selected sets of abstract or imageable sentences which were matched for verification speed when presented auditorily. They then compared verification time when subjects were required to read the sentences, the argument being that reading, being a visual task would interfere with the utilization of imagery.

The first experiment showed a clear tendency for the high imagery sentences to take longer to read and verify than low imagery, whether presented as a single sentence, or produced gradually, one word at a time on a visual display. Two subsequent experiments showed that this was also the case when subjects had merely to decide whether a sentence was meaningful or semantically anomalous. For example *A book opens at the right side* would be a meaningful high imagery sentence, while *A book opens on the right wheel* would be a semantically anomalous high imagery sentence. Again, sentences that were comprehended at the same rate when presented auditorily differed when read, with high imagery sentences taking significantly longer to verify than low imagery sentences.

A final experiment attempted to establish that the crucial feature was comprehending the semantics of the sentence. Eddy and Glass argue that if a sentence can be rejected on purely grammatical grounds, a subject will have no need to involve imagery, and no differential effect will be found. In this instance, sentences were made anomalous by substituting a syntactically inappropriate word. Hence, the example just given would be changed to *A book opens on the right high*, with the subject required to decide whether the sentence in question is grammatical.

Unfortunately, in addition to changing the nature of the verification task, Eddy and Glass also changed the manner of presentation, using the rapid serial visual presentation (RSVP) technique whereby the words are presented rapidly and successively on the same location of the visual display. They observed no difference between the high and low imagery sentences in verification time, a result they attributed to requiring a grammatical rather than a semantic judgement, the implication being that only semantic processing involves imagery. This result is however equally open to an explanation in terms of the possible disruption of imagery by eye-movements. This is the only experiment using the RSVP procedure, and hence the only one in which the eyes were not required to move in order to perform the reading task. A further experiment is clearly needed to decide between these two interpretations. Whichever result emerges, this does seem to be a promising line offering scope for applying techniques devised to study the VSSP to understanding the role of imagery in comprehension.

Reading and recency

As long ago as 1967, Jacqueline Sachs showed that the verbatim recall of printed text was accurate only if tested immediately, and deteriorated substantially when even one sentence was interpolated between presentation and test. Subsequent work by Jarvella (1971) using a running memory span technique suggests that subjects maintain accurate verbal memory for only a single clause, apparently tending to 'dump' the verbatim representation of all but the last clause. More recently, Glanzer *et al.* (1981) have used a cueing technique to study recency in the retention of text read by their subjects. The critical portion of the text comprised simple sentences, and they observed in agreement with Jarvella's results, that only the last was remembered virtually perfectly. They did however also note that the recency effect was not limited to the last sentence, but produced enhanced recall of at least the last two sentences. They attribute their results to STM. While there is no doubt that a recency effect does occur for sentence memory, this does not of course imply that the underlying process is necessarily one of STM (see Chapter 7).

It is almost certainly the case however, that recency does play an important role in text comprehension, and Perfetti and Goldman (1976) have suggested that one difference between good and poor readers is their capacity for carrying information across from one sentence to the next. They tested this using a modification of Jarvella's technique in which their subjects were required to read passages of prose extending over many pages. From time to time, on turning a page, subjects would find instead of text, a question requiring recall of what they had read. If the query concerned a sentence that was still incomplete, then both good and poor readers were roughly equivalent in their ability to answer. On the other hand, if it concerned an earlier sentence, then the performance of good readers was better than that of the poor readers.

A subsequent study by Daneman and Carpenter (1983) explored this aspect of the role of working memory in comprehension in rather more detail. They suggest that the process of integrating information lies at the heart of comprehension, and approached the problem by studying the capacity of subjects with low, medium or high working memory capacity to resolve apparent inconsistencies in prose passages. The following is an example of one of their passages.

There was a strange noise emanating from the dark house. Bob had to venture in to find out what was there. He was terrified; rumour had it that the house was haunted. He would feel more secure with a stick to defend himself and so he went and looked among his baseball equipment. He found a bat that was very large and brown and was flying back and forth in the gloomy room. Now he didn't need to be afraid any longer.

Most readers start by interpreting the ambiguous word 'bat' as 'baseball bat' because of the prior context. Only when it is described as 'flying about' does the second interpretation that it is a creature not an object become clear. Drawing such an inference requires the integration of the occurrence of the ambiguous word 'bat' with the disambiguating further information that the bat was flying. In some passages, the ambiguous noun and the disambiguating information occurred in the same sentence while in others the two occurred in separate sentences. Such 'garden path' sentences can be contrasted with unambiguous sentences such as 'He found a bird that was very large and brown and was flying back and forth in the gloomy room'. Since 'bird' has only one plausible interpretation here, no ambiguity occurs.

The text was presented on a computer visual display unit one word at a time, with the subject pressing a key to move on from one word to the next. Subjects then answered questions about the passages, the results of which are shown in Fig. 8.4. It is clear that working memory capacity had a marked effect on the accuracy with which subjects interpreted the text, an effect that was particularly striking in the case of ambiguous words

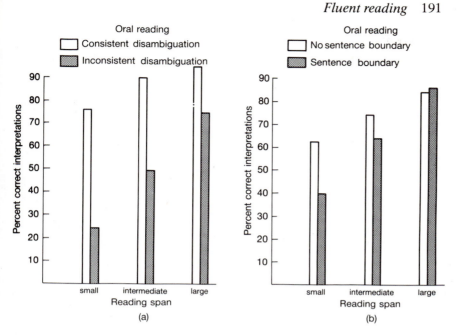

Fig. 8.4(a). The percentage of correct answers to probe questions in oral reading as a function of reading span and the consistency of the disambiguating phrase (Daneman and Carpenter 1983). **(b).** The percentage of correct answers to probe questions in oral reading as a function of reading span and sentence boundaries (Daneman and Carpenter 1983).

such as bat, where subjects with low working memory span were quite likely to report that Bob had found a baseball bat, rather than a flying bat. As the second part of Fig. 8.4 shows, subjects with a small working memory capacity found it particularly difficult to cope with such ambiguities when the process of disambiguation involved carrying information across from one sentence to the next. Hence they would find it particularly hard to cope if the information were presented as 'He found a bat. It was very large and brown and was flying back and forth in the gloomy room'. In contrast, subjects with large working memory spans were unaffected by whether the disambiguating information was presented in two adjacent sentences, or in only one, suggesting that a larger working memory capacity increases the ability to integrate information across sentences within a written passage, a result that is entirely consistent with the study by Perfetti and Goldman (1976) described earlier.

A related area in which memory is clearly implicated in reading is that of anaphoric reference. This occurs when an item that has appeared earlier in the text is referred to without being explicitly repeated. An instance would be the sailor in the following: *The drunken sailor fell down the stairs. The stairs were rickety but fortunately not very high. He picked himself up and rubbed his head.* In order to understand such a passage, one must remember that 'he' refers to the sailor. The probability of doing this is likely to be greater if the anaphoric reference is to something relatively recent; if a whole paragraph had intervened before the reference to he, then subjects would have considerably more difficulty comprehending the passage.

There has been a good deal of interest in this phenomena (see Sanford and Garrod 1981). McKoon and Ratcliffe (1980*a*, *b*) for example offer a three component model of the processing of anaphora. They suggest that the occurrence of the pronoun referent which in our example could be *he* requires first a search in LTM for an appropriate concept, (in this case *sailor*). The second stage involves making the concept available in working memory, and this in turn allows the third stage, namely that of integrating the concept with those concepts already in working memory as a result of processing the current sentence.

McKoon and Ratcliffe have explored their model using a range of techniques. One of these involves probing by presenting a word and requiring the subject to decide whether or not that word has previously appeared in the passage. Using this technique, they show that the occurrence of a pronoun reference such as *he* in our passage leads to consistently faster subsequent identification of the word that was its referent, which in our case was *sailor*, supporting their contention that the pronoun makes the relevant concept available in WM.

Such results support the view that an important function of WM is to maintain earlier information and to integrate it with the new information that is fed into WM as reading proceeds. Subjects with a large WM capacity are better able to perform the integration of information across successive sentences that is essential for the comprehension of passages of complex prose.

Conclusion

Working memory does not offer, or attempt to offer a complete model of reading. A plausible model of working memory should however contribute to the understanding of the complex skills displayed by the fluent reader. I would claim that the techniques and concepts developed in the study of working memory have already shown promise and are likely to continue to prove fruitful as both fields of study develop.

9 Developmental applications of working memory

Development of memory span

There is a very clear and consistent tendency for memory span to increase systematically throughout childhood. There has in recent years been considerable controversy within developmental psychology about the appropriate interpretation of such changes in short-term memory performance. Some theorists argue for a gradual increase in capacity of a hypothetical short-term memory system (e.g. Pascual-Leone 1970; Halford and Wilson 1980). Others argue that the development of span is based not on a growth in capacity, but in the development of more sophisticated control processes and strategies which are thus able to use the available capacity more effectively. Chi (1978) takes this view. An intermediate view is taken by Case, Kurland, and Goldberg (1982) who agree with Chi in arguing that the total capacity of STM does not change with age, and furthermore concede that subjects do become more sophisticated and are able to use more enterprising strategies. However they argue that the primary cause for increase in memory span stems not from a change in strategy adopted, but rather from an increased efficiency in carrying out the relevant control processes. They assume that the limit to memory span performance is set by the total available attentional capacity. Control processes use up some of this capacity, but as the child develops, processing becomes more practised and demands less attention, hence allowing more items to be stored.

A characteristic of all these approaches is that they essentially assume a unitary short-term memory system. The system is of course assumed to use a range of strategies and control processes, but all of these seem to operate within a unitary system not dissimilar to the modal model of the late 1960s. The chapter that follows explores the possibility of applying the concept of working memory within the area of developmental psychology, first considering the interpretation of the development of memory span, then moving on to the role of working memory in learning to read.

As in earlier chapters, my view will be somewhat egocentric, concerned with those areas that seem at present to bear most closely on working memory. Unlike the previous chapters however, the bulk of the work described has been carried out by others, frequently not explicitly

within a working memory framework. While I have attempted to represent the work accurately and fairly, the reader should perhaps bear in
mind my probable bias and comparative lack of experience in this area.
However, the concepts and techniques of working memory do appear to
be able to make sense of a good deal of the developmental literature. If
this proves to be the case, then it clearly adds substantially to the scope,
credibility and usefulness of the working memory model. In this respect
one might hope that developmental psychology might play a similar role
in the understanding of adult cognition to that played by neuropsychology, a role that has proved mutually beneficial (Baddeley 1982c).

The M space hypothesis

I will begin with the study that prompted Case *et al.* to propose their
compromise solution to the question of how memory span develops.
Their study comprises four experiments, two concerned with the development of memory span, and two with the development of 'M space'. M
space is a term used to refer to a hypothetical system concerned with
performing transformations on a series of inputs and storing these, a
concept not unlike that of working memory capacity. Their first study
was concerned with the relationship between digit span and the speed
with which their subjects could process digits. This was measured by
presenting a series of digits auditorily, and requiring the subject to repeat
back each digit as he or she heard it, with the latency of repetition used
as a measure of processing efficiency. Case *et al.* observed that both these
measures increased systematically with age, and were highly correlated
($r=-0.74$, $p<0.001$). When age was partialled out, the correlation
remained significant ($r=-0.35$, $p<0.02$).

Case *et al.* interpret their result as follows; as children develop, their
language skills become more efficient. This allows them to perform
operations such as rehearsal more easily making fewer demands on the
limited attentional capacity, and hence allowing more items to be stored.
However, as they point out, such correlational evidence is inevitably
ambiguous. It might for example be the case that an increased general
processing capacity allows both tasks to be performed more efficiently.
Or alternatively, it may be that repetition speed does increase as the child
matures. As he matures he will also be able to use more ambitious
strategies however, and it may be this that leads to his increased memory
span. In short, the two phenomena may be unrelated, except in that they
are both produced by a third process of general maturation.

In an attempt to break out of this impasse, Case *et al.* carried out a
second experiment in which they took adults, and set up conditions
whereby their item identification speed was likely to be equivalent to that
of a six year old child. If processing speed is the crucial factor, then
memory span under these conditions should also resemble that of a

child. They slowed down their adult subjects by using nonsense words such as *brup* and *zarch* instead of familiar digits. As in the first experiment, memory span for the material was measured, as was repetition latency. As predicted, both memory span and repetition speed were much slower for this novel material. More importantly, the degree of impairment on the two tasks was related as would be predicted from their developmental study, with the subject's span and latency both approximating that of a six year old child dealing with normal digits.

A third and fourth experiment applied the same logic to the development of M space. They measured M space using the dot counting task described in the last chapter. This involves presenting a series of slides each containing dots of two colours. Subjects are instructed to count the dots of a specified colour, and then retain that total while counting the number of dots on subsequent slides. After the last slide, the subject is required to report the number of dots on each slide, his capacity being measured by the total number of slides he can accurately report. On this occasion, processing speed was measured in terms of the rate at which the subject could count dots when not required to retain the results of previous countings.

Both counting span and counting rate were found to increase linearly with age, and to be highly intercorrelated ($r=-0.69$, $p<0.001$). When age was partialled out, the relationship was smaller, but still statistically significant ($r=-0.35$, $p<0.001$).

In their final experiment, Case *et al.* attempted to limit the processing speed of adults by requiring them to count using invented number names, hence *one, two, three* became *rab, slif, dak*. As in the case of the memory span studies, this operation reduced both the counting speed and the counting span to a point at which the adults' performance fell very close to the function relating speed and span in children.

While other theories might well predict that performance of adults in the two studies would be impaired, only a theory that related the impairment in the two tasks to the same process would explain why the relationship between the two tasks should remain the same, and tie in so neatly with the performance of the children tested. A single experiment in which this predicted relationship was observed could reasonably be argued as due to a fortunate chance, but its observation in two studies using very different material and tasks makes such an interpretation unlikely.

Could the working memory model handle these results? It could in fact do so in either of two ways. The interpretation put forward by Case and his colleagues could be rephrased as follows: Both memory span and counting span are dependent on the limited capacity central executive. The executive will use processes such as the articulatory loop system to store information, thereby freeing capacity for storing more items, either directly within the central executive, or indirectly by the more efficient use of control processes. As a child develops, the articulatory speech programmes will become more and more efficient, and as such require progressively less monitoring by the central executive. When an adult is required to articulate unfamiliar material, this too will require more attention from the central executive, hence reducing the amount of capacity remaining for storing subsequent items. This is essentially a translation of the explanation presented by Case, with the additional stipulation that the control process is one of articulation.

A second interpretation however might be to argue that the effects could be explained entirely in terms of the articulatory loop, without recourse to further assumptions about the central executive. Such a view has the advantage of parsimony, and as such merits exploring more fully before accepting the more complex compromise model advocated by Case. Fortunately, such a view of the development of span has been explored recently by three research groups in Britain.

The articulatory loop hypothesis

The possibility that the increase in memory span with age might be entirely attributable to increased rate of articulation was suggested by an intriguing study by Nicolson (1981) which explored the influence of word length on the memory span of adults and of children ranging in age from 8 to 12 years. The children were familiarized with words ranging from one to four syllables after which both memory span and articulation rate was measured for words of each length. Nicolson's results were remarkably clear-cut with data from all subjects and all word lengths falling on a single straight line. This means of course that given the rate at which a subject can articulate, one can accurately predict his memory span.

Nicolson's results are however open to the objection that his articulation condition involved presenting the words visually, introducing differences in reading ability as an obvious potential confounding factor. A subsequent study by Hulme, Thomson, Muir, and Lawrence (1984) avoided this latter problem by using auditory presentation for both the memory span and the rehearsal speed task. Their results are shown in Fig. 9.1. Like Nicolson, they observed a very clear relationship between articulation rate and span that holds across word lengths and extends to children as young as four years old. Their function suggests that a child or adult can remember as many items as he can articulate in 1.5 seconds; the younger the child, the slower his articulation and the smaller his span. The longer the word, the slower the articulation and the smaller the span. There appears to be no need to assume anything more complex than this in order to account for the data.

Needless to say, the situation does prove more complex, as is shown by

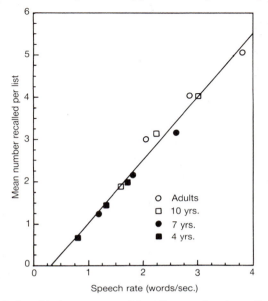

Fig. 9.1. The relationship between word length, speech rate, and memory span as a function of age (Hulme *et al.* 1984).

a series of experiments by Hitch and Halliday (1983). Some years before, Conrad (1971) had developed a technique for studying memory coding in children who were not yet able to read by requiring them to remember sequences of readily nameable pictures. One set comprised pictures with phonologically similar names (e.g. *bat, hat, cat*) while the other set were phonologically dissimilar (e.g. *ball, dog, clown*). He observed that very young children were unaffected by the nature of the picture names, but began to be susceptible around the age of 5. This suggested that the very young children were not using phonological coding when remembering pictures, possibly relying on a visual code but that a phonological encoding strategy gradually developed as they grew older.

Hitch and Halliday used the Conrad technique to study the word-length effect, requiring their children to remember sequences of pictures having names comprising one syllable (e.g. *chair*), two syllables (e.g. *window*) or three syllables (e.g. *elephant*). In order to check that any effects were indeed due to name length, and not to other variables, they included a condition involving articulatory suppression in which the subject was required continually to utter the word *butterfly* while performing the task. This is of course known to abolish the word-length effect in adults (Baddeley, Thomson, and Buchanan 1975). In their initial study they tested a group of six-year old children, observing an overall effect of articulatory suppression, but no consistent word-length effect

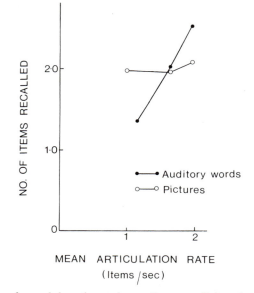

Fig. 9.2. Effect of word length on immediate recall by six-year olds. Items presented auditorily as words, or visually as pictures, and plotted as a function of the mean time to articulate the relevant name. (Data from Hitch, Halliday, and Dodd in press).

either with or without suppression. Since Hulme *et al.* had observed a word-length effect with children as young as four, this was somewhat unexpected. The crucial difference between this and the Hulme *et al.* study however lay in the mode of presentation, and a second study explored this interpretation.

This second experiment also used six-year old children, and items with names comprising one, two or three syllables. On half the trials, the material was presented visually as pictures, as in their first experiment. On the other half, the names were presented auditorily. On this occasion, no articulatory suppression condition was included. Results are shown in Fig. 9.2, analysis showed a significant effect of length ($p < 0.01$), no effect of mode, but a significant mode of presentation by length inter-action ($p < 0.01$). When the two modes were analysed separately, there was a very clear effect of word length with auditory presentation ($p < 0.01$), but no effect with visual presentation. It appears therefore that six-year old children do show evidence of a word-length effect, indicating some form of a subvocal rehearsal, but only when material is presented auditorily.

Schiano and Watkins (1981) have shown that adults do show a word-length effect in remembering sequences of pictures. It therefore seems likely that older children will develop a verbal coding technique for picture recall, as suggested by Conrad (1971). This was examined in a third experiment by Hitch and Halliday that was essentially a replication of their second experiment using three age groups, six-year olds, eight-year olds and ten-year olds. They also included a post-test in which the items were presented visually, but the subject required to name them. Articulation rate was also measured by requiring the subject repeatedly to utter pairs of words of different lengths.

The results were clear-cut. As in the previous study, the six-year olds showed word-length effects with auditory, but not visual presentation, with a significant interaction between mode of presentation and word length. The eight-year olds again showed a clear effect of word length with auditory presentation together with a nonsignificant tendency for items with longer names to be harder with visual presentation and no significant interaction between mode and word length. The ten-year olds showed significant word-length effects for both visual and auditory presentation, and no trace of an interaction between mode and word length. When considered across all subjects, articulation rate was highly significantly correlated with recall of auditory material ($r = 0.937$, $p < 0.01$). The overall effect was not significant for visual presentation, the only group showing a significant effect being the ten year olds.

If we take the word-length effect to be an indicator of subvocal rehearsal, then these results suggest that children as young as six years old will rehearse auditorily-presented material in a memory span situation, but do not spontaneously rehearse visually presented items until they are approaching ten years old. Is this failure simply due to not recoding the material?

The post-test condition examined this by requiring subjects actively to name the pictures as they were presented. If verbal recoding guarantees rehearsal, then this should produce word-length effects for all ages tested. In actual fact, naming had no effect other than to cause a slight impairment in performance in the case of the ten-year old children. It appears therefore that requiring a child to name does not guarantee that he will rehearse. It would incidentally be interesting to see what happens in this context to the phonological similarity effect. This is of course assumed to reflect registration in the phonological store, in contrast to the word-length effect which indicates active verbal rehearsal. It is thus entirely possible that the young children in the post-test naming condition might have been using phonological information from the names to aid recall, but not subvocally rehearsing them, in which case they would be expected to show a phonological similarity effect despite the absence of an effect of word length. Alternatively they could have been ignoring the phonological store in this condition and relying entirely on a visual code.

So far then, evidence from the word-length effect in children seems to support the articulatory loop hypothesis rather than the approach advocated by Case and his colleagues. However, as Dempster (1981) points out, it is possible to reverse the argument and explain the word-length effect itself by suggesting that longer words take longer to identify, hence using up more of the available M-space. Hitch, Halliday, and Littler (1984) set out to test this interpretation directly. They tested the memory span of two groups of children, eight-year olds and eleven-year olds across sequences of words comprising one, two or three syllables, with and without articulatory suppression. They then measured the articulation and reading rates together with the word identification time of their subjects for each type of material.

What would the two models predict? Consider first the articulatory loop hypothesis: this would suggest that a word-length effect would occur for both the young and the older children, and that the data from both age levels and all three lengths would fit a straight line function. The hypothesis would also predict an interaction between suppression and word length, with the word-length effect being abolished by suppression. Finally, if the only factor in distinguishing the memory span of young from older children is in the operation of the articulatory loop, one would predict that the age difference would be abolished by suppression.

The identification-time hypothesis would also predict a relationship between word length and performance, but in this case identification time should be a better predictor of performance than articulation time across age groups and word lengths. On this hypothesis, however, there is no reason to predict that articulatory suppression will abolish the word-length effect, nor that it will reduce the difference in performance level between younger and older subjects, since identification is presumably a critical factor with or without articulatory suppression.

Table 9.1 shows the mean memory span for the two groups of subjects

TABLE 9.1
Memory span as a function of word length, age, and articulatory suppression. (Data from Hitch, Halliday, and Littler 1984).

	Word length		
	One syllable	Two syllables	Three syllables
11-year olds			
Control	4.67	4.09	3.87
Suppression	2.78	3.00	2.70
8-year olds			
Control	3.83	3.55	3.24
Suppression	2.45	2.25	2.12

as a function of word length under control conditions and under conditions whereby the subject suppressed by repeatedly counting from 1 to 5. It is clear first of all that a word-length effect is present under control conditions, and that it is largely abolished by suppression, as indicated by a significant interaction between suppression and word length. In this respect, the results support the articulatory-loop rather than the identification hypothesis. It is clear however that the difference between eleven-year olds and eight-year olds is not completely removed by articulatory suppression. This can be interpreted in two ways, either by arguing that the task of suppression is more demanding for the young, and hence absorbs more of the central executive's available capacity, or secondly by arguing that the articulatory loop component is responsible for some, but not all of the differences in performance due to age.

The clearest separation between the item identification and the articulatory loop hypotheses is provided by the correlation data. Fig. 9.3(a) plots the relationship between memory span and articulation rate for the two age groups and three word-length sets. The data fall on a straight line ($r(4)=0.974$, $p<0.001$) indicating that articulation rate is an excellent predictor of mean memory span. This result was further checked by examining the data from individual subjects. The small number of data points meant that the reliability of individual correlations could not be calculated, but a broad indication of the consistency of the effects was obtained by recording the proportion of subjects in whom the relationship was in the predicted direction. This proved to be significant on a sign test for both eight-year olds ($p<0.05$) and the eleven-year olds ($p<0.005$). When reading rate rather than articulation rate was used as a predictor of performance, essentially the same picture obtained.

Figure 9.3(b) shows the correlation between identification time and span. In this case, the data points offer a poor fit to a straight line ($r(4)=-0.723$, $p>0.05$). They appear instead to fall into two separate clusters, one for each age group. When individual data were examined, there was no significant tendency for the relationship to be consistently in the same direction across subjects. In short, the results suggest that articulation rate is a much more satisfactory predictor of performance than identification time. An essentially similar picture obtains when the equivalent study is run using auditory presentation of the material for recall (Hitch personal communication).

To what extent then can we explain the development of memory span purely on the basis of the articulatory loop? With auditory presentation the picture still seems very straightforward; as children become older, their articulatory skills improve, either as a result of practice, maturation of the central nervous system or both. This allows them to rehearse subvocally at a faster rate, and hence maintain more items in the phonological store. While such an interpretation may eventually prove over-

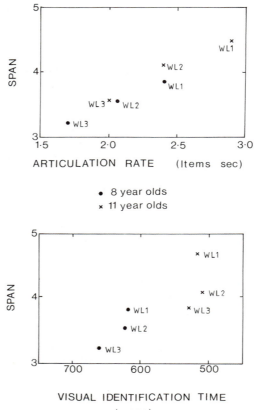

Fig. 9.3. Immediate memory span and word length in eight- and eleven-year-olds. (a) Plots span as a function or articulation rate. (b) Plots span as a function of visual identification time. It is clear that articulation rate gives the better fit. (Hitch, Halliday, and Littler 1984).

simplified, it does appear to account for the evidence remarkably well, and as such is to be preferred on grounds of parsimony to more complex interpretations.

In the case of visually presented material, we need to assume a second strategic factor since young children simply do not appear to adopt a strategy of subvocal rehearsal, even though the results with auditory presentation suggest that such a strategy is open to them under certain conditions. The data from Conrad (1971) suggest that very young children do not spontaneously encode and use picture names in a memory test; furthermore, the post-test carried out by Hitch and Halliday indicates that even when children are required to name the pictures, this does not induce them to use subvocal rehearsal. Why should that be? Let us consider first of all why they do appear to be able to rehearse auditory material. There is as we have discussed earlier, evidence to suggest that the repetition of auditory material is a very compatible response. It appears to require minimal attention (McLeod and Posner 1984) and is insensitive to Hick's Law, again implying a highly compatible response (Davis, Moray, and Treisman 1961). It seems plausible to assume that repetition of heard responses is indeed an important mechanism in helping a child learn to speak; if so, one would expect it to be present from an early age. It is therefore plausible to suggest that the subvocal rehearsal of auditory material is a highly compatible strategy placing minimal demands on the subject, and one that is present in very young children.

In the case of the rehearsal of visually presented material, two further stages are required. The first of these is the naming of the material, itself a comparatively slow and demanding task for young children, together with a second stage of repeating an internally generated name. In the Hitch and Halliday post-test condition, where external vocalization was required, it seems likely that this would make fluent internal rehearsal even harder since the child would have to coordinate the continuous and presumably cumulative internal rehearsal with the overt articulation of each successive presented item.

I would argue therefore that we can at present account for the development of memory span in children purely in terms of the articulatory loop. In the case of auditory presentation, older children talk faster, rehearse more effectively and hence remember more. In the case of visual presentation, the process of naming and rehearsing is probably considerably more demanding and hence may not be used until a much later age. Whether this is because the young child is unable to use this technique until his naming and articulation skills reach a certain point, or whether he chooses not to do so at the articulation rates he can achieve, because the cost exceeds the benefit is at present unclear. In conclusion, although it seems intuitively unlikely that such a simple hypothesis should be completely adequate, I do not at present see any reason to invoke other factors in order to explain the development of memory span.

Although the data do seem to fit a simple articulatory loop hypothesis remarkably well however, I would still feel that a note of caution is advisable. The study by Hitch, Halliday, and Littler (1984) indicated that suppression did not completely remove the influence of age on performance, as a straightforward articulation hypothesis might predict. While this could be attributed to the relatively greater demands of articulation as a secondary task on younger children, such an interpretation does have an air of special pleading about it. Furthermore, the developmental literature in general appears to suggest that rehearsal is a skill that must be learned, and certainly does not spontaneously occur for five-year olds as the word-length data would suggest. However, even though it may seem intuitively unlikely that the only difference in performance beween younger and older children is the rate at which they articulate, this simple hypothesis does fit the data remarkably well. Given a conflict between a simple model and consistent data on the one hand, and an intuition that "life must be more complicated than this!", the sensible thing seems to be to favour the simple hypothesis — at least until further data show it to be inadequate.

Working memory and learning to read

Although memory span is one of the oldest and most widely used techniques in psychology, one might argue that it is a somewhat artificial procedure of doubtful relevance to performance outside the laboratory. If it is merely an intellectual toy for the amusement of psychologists, then one might reasonably suggest that explaining its development is of little significance. Fortunately, it does appear to have ecological validity, which one hopes is why it is used so widely in educational and clinical psychology. Perhaps its most obvious relevance is in relationship to learning the complex but important skill of reading.

Developmental dyslexia and the articulatory loop

Reading is an essential skill for full participation in most western cultures. It is however a much more artificial skill than for example speaking or comprehending language (see Liberman in press for an excellent discussion of this). It forms perhaps the major component of much early education, and in the case of most children is acquired relatively painlessly. There does however appear to be a substantial minority of children who find great difficulty in learning to read. While some of these have problems because of lack of general intelligence, or from attentional, emotional, or motivational difficulties, there is in addition a sizeable number of children who appear to have a specific difficulty in acquiring reading and spelling skills, despite normal, or sometimes substantially above normal intelligence.

While such children indubitably exist, there is considerable controversy over whether they form an identifiable separate group, and particularly over what this group should be called. I myself tend to use the term developmental dyslexia, dyslexia implying a language problem which I believe the evidence strongly supports. Other terms include specific reading disability, (which I do not favour since the disability is not specific to reading but as we shall see below, occurs in other functions and other areas), and learning disability. The term learning disability is common in the United States, but has the drawback that it is far too general, since children with developmental dyslexia may show excellent abilities in learning non-phonologically based skills. Also common in American work is the classification of children into good and poor readers. This categorization also has the drawback of being both too general in implicitly including children whose poor reading is attributable to low intelligence or social or emotional deprivation, and too specific in suggesting that the problem is limited to reading. However, in actual research practice, it is often the case that good and poor readers are matched for intelligence, and that a substantial difference in reading ability is required in order to categorize a subject as a poor reader. Since subjects in some of the studies we describe would not be regarded as sufficiently severely retarded in reading to be classified as dyslexic, we will use the rather more general term good and poor readers.

It should however be borne in mind that there may be qualitative differences as a function of severity, and on the basis of aetiology. For example Boder (1973) has claimed that three subgroups of reading disabled child are found, one in which the difficulty stems from phonological processing difficulties, a second based on visual processing problems, and a third group with both. It has also been suggested that some of the subtypes of acquired dyslexia that occur in previously normal adults as a result of focal brain damage may also occur developmentally in children without apparent focal lesions (e.g. Temple and Marshall 1984). However, although it seems intuitively probable that reading difficulties would stem from a range of different causes, our own attempt to categorize dyslexic children into different groups has proved disappointing (Baddeley, Logie, and Ellis in preparation), with subjects tending to show a very similar pattern of difficulties, associated largely with phonological and articulatory processing. While it seems likely that at least some children will have specific neurological problems leading to a range of potential reading difficulties (Temple and Marshall 1983), the available evidence does not at present force us to assume more than one kind of reading disability, and therefore I shall adopt the more parsimonious approach of treating dyslexia or reading disability as if it were a unitary category, meanwhile being alert to the very real possibility that varieties of developmental reading disability may in due course be identified.

Phonological coding and learning to read

In an influential paper Conrad (1971) looked at the development of memory span using the previously described technique of presenting a series of pictures of nameable objects and requiring subsequent recall. As described previously, half the pictures had phonologically confusable names while the other half were phonologically dissimilar. The presence of a phonological similarity effect was used as an indicator that the child was using speech coding in performing the task. Conrad observed that the onset of speech coding occurred at about the time that children were learning to read and suggested that the use of speech code was a necessary precursor of learning to read.

The possibility has been explored extensively by a group at the Haskins Laboratory in New Haven. In one study Shankweiler and Liberman (1976) studied the immediate memory performance of good and poor readers by auditorily presenting sequences of consonants selected from either a phonologically similar set (e.g. *b c v t*) or a dissimilar set (e.g. *k w r y*). They found that the good readers were superior to the poor readers with the dissimilar set, but were much more handicapped by the introduction of phonological similarity, with the result that the two groups did not differ in retention of the similar consonants. They argued that the young readers were not affected by phonological similarity because they were not using a phonological code, and suggested that this absence of phonological coding might be crucial to their reading difficulty.

In a subsequent experiment, Liberman, Shankweiler, Liberman, Fowler, and Fischer (1977) showed a similar pattern of results using visually presented consonant sequences, while Mann, Liberman, and Shankweiler (1980) showed that memory for sentences showed a similar pattern, with good readers remembering more than poor readers with dissimilar material, but being substantially impaired in performance by the introduction of phonological similarity. In general, the effect of phonological similarity was more marked when recall followed an unfilled 15-second delay, suggesting that the use of subvocal rehearsal during the delay by the good readers may have exaggerated the effects of phonological coding (Liberman *et al.* 1977; Shankweiler and Liberman 1976).

Further evidence of the importance of phonological coding came from a long-term memory study by Mark, Shankweiler, and Liberman (1977) in which the subjects read out 28 words. In an incidental learning procedure, subjects were then asked to recognize the words they had read from a list of 56 words, half of which were repeats of the original words and half of which were distractors. Some of the distractors were phonologically but not visually similar to the items presented. Good readers were much more likely to select these phonological lures than were poor readers, suggesting more extensive phonological coding in this group. Additional evidence that the difference between the good and poor readers was specific to verbal material came from another long-term memory study by Liberman, Mann, Shankweiler, and Werfelman (1982) using a repeated item recognition task. This involved presenting subjects with a stream of items and requiring them on each occasion to judge whether they have seen that item before. Good and poor readers were tested using nonsense designs, faces and nonsense syllables. The poor readers were significantly poorer at remembering the nonsense syllables, but were equivalent to the good readers with the visual material.

Evidence that the specific decrement by poor readers is limited to processing linguistic material, or material that can be labelled is very extensive (see Ellis and Miles 1981; Hulme 1981; Vellutino 1979 for reviews). Ellis and Miles (1978) showed that dyslexic children have unimpaired short-term visual memory, together with clearly impaired digit span. In one study they used the Posner letter matching task, observing that dyslexic children are impaired when a name-match is required, but not when the task involved a visually based physical match. There is then a very substantial body of evidence suggesting that children with difficulties in learning to read also show impaired or absent phono- logical coding in memory tasks. I was prompted on the basis of this to suggest that one component of reading impairment might be a direct result of the failure to use the articulatory loop (Baddeley 1979).

I proposed that the articulatory loop provides an extremely effective backup for the difficult problem of attacking and decoding an unfamiliar word. A child who did not use the articulatory loop was assumed to have the difficult task of simultaneously retaining the sound of the letters he has already decoded while attempting to decode the remaining letters, hence overloading the central executive. The strategy of using the articu- latory loop to store those letters that had been decoded was assumed to help by leaving the central executive free to deal with later letters and other decoding processes.

In order to test this hypothesis, Nick Ellis and I studied the immediate memory performance of a group of dyslexic boys, using the phonological similarity effect, the word length effect and articulatory suppression as indicators of whether our subjects were making use of the articulatory loop. We predicted that we, like Liberman *et al.*, would find no evidence of subvocal rehearsal in our poor readers. We tested a sample of boys who were attending a school that specializes in teaching children with dyslexia, and compared their performance with a group of boys of similar age, intelligence, and background from a nonspecialist private school. The results of our study are shown in Table 9.2.

The pattern of performance across our two groups is very straight- forward. The dyslexic boys show a consistent impairment of perform- ance across all conditions, but no evidence of failure to use subvocal rehearsal. They show a phonological similarity effect, a word-length effect, and an effect of suppression that is just as marked as that shown by the normal controls. We appeared therefore to have failed completely to replicate the results of Liberman and the Haskins group.

Unfortunately our own failure to replicate the findings of Liberman and her colleagues is by no means an isolated case. For example, Hall, Wilson, Humphreys, Tinzmann, and Bowyer (1983) carried out a series

TABLE 9.2

Memory span of dyslexic and control subjects as a function of type of material (Data from Ellis, Baddeley, and Miles, unpublished study.)

Condition	Dyslexic group	Age-matched control group
Digit span	5.37	6.70
Digit span with suppression	3.70	5.17
Short word span	3.88	4.28
Long word span	3.33	3.65
Similar word span	3.23	3.42
Dissimilar word span	4.25	4.70

of four experiments in which good and poor readers of equivalent general achievement were required to recall sequences of similar or dissimilar consonants. They found clear evidence of a decrement due to phonological similarity in all groups. They suggest that the results of Liberman and others who have found an attenuation of the phonological similarity effect in poor readers may be due to a tendency for the similarity effect to disappear when the level of difficulty of the task exceeds a certain level. In most studies of poor readers, the poor readers have a smaller overall span than the good readers, a finding that was not a strong characteristic of the groups studied by Hall *et al.* This in turn may stem from their selection of control subjects who were matched with the poor readers in scholastic achievement. While most experimental studies of good and poor readers match the groups on intelligence, they are by no means always matched on scholastic achievement. It may be the case that poor readers who are otherwise high in scholastic achievement are an atypical group.

Such selection restrictions were not however applied in other studies which have failed to replicate the Shankweiler result. For example Johnston (1982) studied nine to fourteen year old children with reading disabilities, and found clear evidence of a phonological similarity effect in both groups. However both Johnston's and our own subjects were somewhat older than those typically studied by Liberman *et al.* This point was further explored by Siegel and Linder (1984) who studied the visual and auditory span for similar and dissimilar consonants in children ranging in age from seven to thirteen years. They found clear evidence for phonological similarity effects in the nine to thirteen year olds, but no reliable effect for the seven to eight year olds. These results could be interpreted in terms of the claim by Hall *et al.* that memory span becomes insensitive to the effects of phonological similarity when difficulty level rises beyond a certain point. The youngest children who are poorest readers may be finding the task the most difficult. Siegel and

Linder themselves interpret their results in terms of a developmental lag model which suggests that an association occurs between poor reading and the late development of the utilization of phonological coding.

However, as they point out if developmental delay were the only problem, one might expect the difficulty of poor readers to disappear, once the articulatory loop was available to supplement their reading skills. This is clearly not the case since differences continue to occur in span performance between good and poor readers even though both are clearly using the articulatory loop, as our data and that of Siegel and Linder demonstrate. It also appears to be the case that severely dyslexic individuals continue to show impaired span coupled with difficulty, particularly in spelling, long after they have become adult. In short, they appear to be using the articulatory loop system normally, although the system in question may typically be of reduced capacity.

In conclusion, the relationship between the phonological similarity effect, age and reading disability remains obscure. There is enough evidence from many studies by Liberman and her colleagues, and from other laboratories (e.g. Byrne and Shea 1979; Torgeson *et al.* 1985) to suggest that there is a genuine effect here. Unfortunately its replication and interpretation continue to present problems, suggesting that we still have a very imperfect understanding of the phenomenon.

The available evidence therefore suggests that the failure to use the articulatory loop occurs only with young children with reading disability. They subsequently appear to show every sign of phonological coding, but nonetheless remain impaired in their overall memory span performance, and indeed in their reading skills. Follow-up studies of dyslexic children many years later suggest that those who have severe problems, although they may learn to cope very adequately nevertheless do not typically achieve normal levels of reading and spelling (Zangwill personal communication). It is however probably the case that the root cause of such disabilities provides a particular handicap during the demanding early stages of reading, probably becoming much less acute as the skill develops and other less phonologically-based skills become increasingly important to reading comprehension.

The evidence however seems to suggest that poor readers lag in their use of phonological coding and the articulatory loop, not that the loop is permanently absent. This rules out the simple interpretation that the failure to use phonological coding causes reading disability, suggesting instead that poor readers may have an articulatory loop system that functions normally, but is more limited in capacity. This in turn raises the further question of where such a limitation might occur, whether in the capacity of the phonological store or in the process of articulation, or possibly in the mapping of one on to the other. This question is explored in the next section.

Reading and rate of articulation

In testing our group of dyslexic boys for evidence of phonological coding, we also included a range of other tasks that we hoped might tap functions that were related to their underlying disability. These included auditory digit span, visual span with and without articulatory suppression, span for phonologically similar and dissimilar words, rate of picture naming, and rate of counting from 1 to 10.

The results of this study are shown in Table 9.3, which gives the correlation between performance on the various tasks. For present purposes the crucial row is that relating performance on the various tests to reading ability. Note that the best predictors are counting rate and immediate memory for visually presented digits. It is arguable that what these have in common is the involvement of articulation. In the case of counting, the involvement of articulation is obvious, but why should articulation be crucial to the retention of visually presented digits? Presumably this occurs because adequate retention is dependent on turning the visually presented digits into a phonological code and maintaining this by rehearsal. Consistent with such an interpretation is the fact that the correlation between span and reading is virtually abolished when such recoding is prevented by measuring span under articulatory suppression. The much weaker correlation observed in the case of memory for auditorily presented digits presumably reflects the fact that articulatory encoding and rehearsal in this condition is much less demanding. Our results are consistent with a study carried out by Latham (1983) in which she correlated visual and auditory digit span with the reading achievement of 48 seven-year-olds. Using the Neale test of reading, she found a correlation of 0.55 ($p < 0.001$) between reading quotient and visual span, together with a nonsignificant correlation ($r = 0.18, p > 0.05$) with auditory span. This visual auditory difference may well explain the lack of unanimity in the literature on the question of whether memory span and reading correlate noted by Perfetti and Lesgold (1977). It is notable for example that Perfetti and Goldman (1976) who failed to note any relationship between digit probe performance and reading used auditory presentation.

The possibility that articulatory coding might be the crucial variable limiting the reading performance of poor readers was suggested by Spring and Capps (1974) in a study where good and poor readers were required to name digits and pictures as rapidly as possible. There was a clear tendency for the poor readers to be slow in producing a naming response. This was explored further in a recent study that Spring and Perry (personal communication) carried out on 3rd–5th grade children who were either good or poor readers. The subjects in the first experiment were required to read ten groups of five random digits as rapidly as possible, and were then tested on their memory span for sequences of

TABLE 9.3

Correlations among measures of non-reading skills and single-word reading performance in dyslexic boys. (Data from an unpublished study by Ellis, Logie and Baddeley). N=32.

	Count	Pictures	Suppression	Similarity	Auditory span	Visual span	Visual span with suppression
Error totals in reading	0.40	0.07	−0.32	−0.25	−0.27	−0.43	−0.15
Counting		0.16	−0.10	−0.08	−0.24	−0.10	0.00
Picture naming			0.01	−0.20	−0.05	0.17	0.20
Articulatory suppression				0.36	0.41	0.65	−0.59
Phonemic similarity					0.78	0.42	0.06
Auditory span						0.48	0.11

$r = 0.349$; $p < 0.05$: $r = 0.409$; $p < 0.01$.

pictures having phonologically similar or dissimilar names. The good readers read the digits significantly more rapidly than the poor readers (2.29 versus 1.59 digits per second). Their memory study replicated the results of Liberman *et al.* in showing a clear advantage to the good readers in recalling pictures with dissimilar names, but no significant advantage when the names were phonologically confusable. Furthermore, in the case of the dissimilar items, there was a highly significant correlation between articulation rate and memory performance ($r=0.57$, $p<0.001$) but no significant relationship in the case of phonologically similar pictures for which subvocal rehearsal would of course be much less helpful.

Spring and Perry go on to estimate the relative success of their two tasks in predicting whether a child will be a good or poor reader. They find that speed of digit naming is capable of accounting for 68 per cent of the variance, and memory 28 per cent. However, all but 2 per cent of this 28 per cent is common to both the digit naming and the memory scores, whereas the digit naming task contributes 34 per cent of the variance over and above that which is shared with the memory task. Whatever is responsible for the difference between the two groups therefore appears to be much more closely related to digit naming speed than to the evidence for phonological coding derived from the memory task.

A second study attempts to isolate the articulatory component by using a repeated counting task and comparing it with the previously described digit naming task. Unlike digit naming, the counting task has no visual component, virtually no stimulus processing and a highly redundant response comprising a set of very overlearned motor programmes. Counting therefore removes a large number of components which might plausibly be assumed to contribute to the complex skill of reading. If nevertheless it proves to be a powerful predictor, then this strongly suggests that articulation *per se* is an important factor.

Spring and Perry tested a further 30 children from grades two to five, again divided into good and poor readers. The good readers performed the digit naming task at a rate of 2.00 digits per second, compared to a rate of 1.11 digits per second in the poor readers. The counting rate for good readers was 5.0 digits per second compared to 4.05 digits per second in the poor readers; the differences on both these tasks between good and poor readers was highly significant. Performance on the two tasks was highly correlated ($r=0.67$, $p<0.001$). Once again digit naming proved to be a good predictor of reading disability accounting for 61 per cent of the variance. However the bulk of this (41 per cent) was also contributed by the counting task, with the further 20 per cent presumably added by all the additional stimulus input, recoding and response selection processes that are involved in digit naming but not in counting. Spring and Perry conclude that sheer speed of articulation is the main feature that distinguishes the two groups who are matched for general ability, but differ in reading achievement.

There is then a good deal of evidence to suggest a relationship between the operation of the articulatory loop and the process of learning to read. Children who have difficulty in learning to read despite normal intelligence tend to be later in showing evidence of the phonological similarity effect in memory tasks, to have impaired memory spans, and to be slower in naming numbers or pictures and in articulating than good readers. While this pattern of evidence is broadly coherent, it does tend to be piecemeal, with different procedures and different samples of subjects used by different investigators. For that reason, it is particularly interesting to consider an extensive series of experiments carried out by Torgesen and his collaborators. This starts by specifying a particular subject group, namely learning disabled children with normal intelligence but impaired digit span. It then systematically explores across a series of seventeen experiments what the implications are of this deficit. As such it provides an extremely valuable set of converging operations, focusing on the same problems as those described in the last section, but from a different viewpoint and with a carefully specified subject group.

Torgesen's LD-S studies

Torgesen's approach begins with the assumption that children with learning disabilities (LD children) are heterogeneous, and that any attempt to understand their problems must be preceded by careful selection of appropriately homogeneous subgroups. He selected children with short-term memory deficits on the grounds that this deficit would be likely to create considerable difficulties for children attempting to learn. Furthermore, earlier experiments on a heterogeneous sample of LD children using a range of memory tasks had suggested that their problems might stem from using inappropriate mnemonic strategies. When appropriate strategies were taught, they no longer compared poorly with normal children (Torgesen and Goldman 1977). As we saw earlier, there are a number of investigators who have suggested that the development of short-term memory in children represents a development of more sophisticated strategies, and if this did prove to be the case then such an investigation would have obvious implications for helping such children by teaching them strategies.

Torgesen therefore selected three subgroups of children, all of average intelligence and without severe behavioural problems. One group comprised children who were classified by their schools as learning disabled, and who in addition showed consistently low performance in immediate recall of sequences of digits, failing to recall more than five items in the standard WISC digit span subtest. A second group were also classified as learning disabled, showing academic difficulties across a range of subjects, but had normal digit spans. The third group comprised children of equivalent age and intelligence whose academic performance was normal. The investigation so far has included some seventeen experiments described in a series of papers (Torgesen and Houck 1980, in press; Torgeson, Rashotte, and Greenstein 1985; Torgeson, Greenstein, Houck, and Portes 1985).

Torgesen and Houck began by establishing that the differences in digit span across the groups were stable and consistent; they found this to be the case, with no change over six successive sessions. They went on to check that the differences were not due to lack of motivation in the group having low digit span (the LD-S group) by offering rewards and incentives for improved performance. The differences remained suggesting that motivational factors were unlikely to be responsible. A third study examined the effect of rate of presentation on performance, with presentation rates ranging from four per second to one every two seconds. The LD-S group was inferior at all rates of presentation, a result that Torgesen and Houck interpret as suggesting that rehearsal is not critical, since rates of four per second are clearly too fast to allow rehearsal during presentation. However, the possibility remains that rehearsal does occur between presentation and recall, particularly with auditory presentation such as was used in this study; a better way of ruling out rehearsal would have been to require articulatory suppression during both input and recall (c.f. Baddeley, Lewis, and Vallar 1984).

The next study by Torgesen and Houck explored the possibility that the LD-S group were simply not chunking or clustering the items as well as the other two subject groups. They therefore introduced temporal grouping by inserting a brief delay between successive clusters of digits. This enhanced recall for all three groups to an approximately equal extent, suggesting that grouping was unlikely to be the source of the difference between the groups. The attentional capacity of the LD-S group was investigated next in a study where the subjects were required to listen to a stream of digits and pick out certain prespecified targets. The LD-S group proved quite capable of performing this task at rates of presentation typical of those used in the memory studies.

The first sign of a difference between the groups occurred in a memory study where subjects were required to articulate the name of each digit as it was presented. This impaired performance on the two control groups but had no effect on LD-S subjects. Presumably the requirement to articulate each digit on arrival interfered with the concurrent rehearsal process; the absence of an effect for LD-S subjects therefore implied a possible absence of subvocal rehearsal. Torgesen and Houck followed this up in a further experiment which was based on the assumption that rehearsal would be more rapid and more efficient for familiar than for unfamiliar material. They therefore measured memory span for highly familiar material, namely digits, for rather less familiar words and for totally unfamiliar consonant–vowel–consonant nonsense syllables. The performance of the LD-S group was substantially worse than the control groups on digits, somewhat worse on words, but not significantly different with CVCs.

A final experiment in this series attempted to look at articulation speed more directly using a naming task in which subjects from the three groups were required to name digits and pictures of animals. There was a significant tendency for the LD-S group to respond more slowly than the LD-N (learning disabled with normal span) or the N (normal) groups. When mean digit naming speed was correlated with digit span across the groups the relationship proved to be significant ($r=0.55$, $p<0.01$), a result that replicates those of Spring and his collaborators described in the previous section. At this point then, Torgesen and Houck had successfully ruled out a wide range of possible interpretations of the specific defect of the LD-S group, and had produced evidence for the importance of some form of phonological or articulatory factor.

This line of investigation was pursued further by Torgesen, Greenstein, Houck, and Portes (1985). They began by comparing their three groups across a range of memory tasks to investigate the generality of the impairment shown by their LD-S group. The LD-S group proved to be quite normal on memory for abstract forms, as Liberman *et al.* (1982), and others have found. They were also quite unimpaired in performance on a task that involved sorting pictures and then unexpectedly being asked to recall the content of the pictures. Recognition memory for words was also normal, whether tested by re-presenting the words or by presenting pictures (e.g. present the word *cat*, test with a picture of a cat). The LD-S group clearly then does not have a general memory difficulty since their ability to recall or recognize material encoded visually or semantically appears to be normal.

What then is impaired? Not surprisingly, reversed digit span was lower in the LD-S group. Again as expected, recalling sequences of words by ordering sequences of pictures was impaired; this is similar to the task investigated by Conrad (1971) (see previous section). Digit span was impaired whether tested visually or auditorily, as was sentence span. In short, the LD-S group did not show a general memory impairment but were impaired on tasks that might reasonably be expected to depend on phonological or articulatory coding.

Most of the tasks that were performed poorly by the LD-S group involved order information, however a subsequent experiment indicated that this was not critical. They were required to remember sequences of phonologically dissimilar consonants, with the requirement being to recall the items only in one condition, and items plus order of presentation in the next. The LD-S group was impaired on both these tasks. The next experiment manipulated the phonological similarity of the material to be recalled and essentially replicated the results of Liberman *et al.* (1977) with the LD-S group performing substantially more poorly than the LD-N or N groups when the consonants were dissimilar. With similar sequences however the performance of the two control groups was much more dramatically impaired, leaving them approximately equal in performance to the LD-S group.

The next phase of the investigation by Torgesen, Rashotte, and Greenstein (1985) was concerned with the possible classroom implications of the specific memory deficit shown by the LD-S group. They speculated that such children might have great difficulty following classroom instruction and tested this initially by using a task that closely resembles the Token Test of de Renzi. In this, the child was given a number of painted wooden shapes and required to follow instructions regarding their manipulation. The commands could either be non-ordered, for example *Pick up the blue triangle, the red square and the white circle* or ordered, for example *Make a pile with a triangle on the bottom, a red square next and then a white circle.* The LD-S group performed significantly more poorly than the two control groups (LD-N and N), which did not differ; all groups found the ordered instructions harder, but there was no interaction between ordering and subject group. Presumably the subjects needed to store these non-redundant commands while interpreting and carrying them out. I have suggested elsewhere (Baddeley 1979) that the articulatory loop may be required for performing the Token Test, but may be much less crucial for the comprehension of normal text for which there is considerable built-in redundancy. Torgesen *et al.* investigated this possibility in their next experiment.

Their three groups of subjects were all required to perform both a comprehension and a memory task involving passages of prose. The comprehension test involved the cloze procedure in which after four to six sentences, a word would be omitted and the subject required to guess it. The assumption here is that it is necessary to comprehend the prior context in order to guess sensibly. The memory task involved a probe procedure whereby a word from within the passage was presented and the subject required to remember what word had followed it in the passage. In this study, a fourth group of children was included. These comprised younger normal children who were matched with the LD-S group on memory span. The results of this study demonstrate that there were no differences between the LD-N and the normal group, who were both superior to the young normals on both memory and comprehension. Interestingly, the low memory span LD-S group resembled the younger children in their memory performance but showed approximately equivalent comprehension to their normal and LD-N contemporaries. This suggests that they are unlikely to have difficulties in comprehension, except with the highly non-redundant material such as is presented in the Token Test.

Since the issue of comprehension was clearly a very important one from a practical viewpoint, Torgesen *et al.* decided to explore it further, this time using a technique whereby the child hears a story and then is required to retell it. In recalling stories, normal subjects tend to be much more likely to remember important features than unimportant. Torgesen *et al.* argue that a failure to understand the story should lead to a distortion of this pattern, with overall amount recalled probably being reduced, and the tendency to remember important features also being disturbed. All three groups listened to two Japanese folk tales, both approximately 400 words long and comprising some 50 or more separate idea units, varying in importance as rated by independent judges. The children then retold the story in their own words, and recall was plotted as a function of rated importance of the constituent units. All three groups were approximately equal in amount recalled, and all showed a similar pattern with the most important units being much better recalled than the less important. On this measure also then, the LD-S children appeared to show normal comprehension.

If comprehension is normal, then what aspects of the child's performance are impaired? Bearing in mind the previous section, it is hardly surprising that Torgesen and Houck (in press) found that the LD-S children were significantly poorer than the LD-N on reading performance, whereas on maths the two groups were equivalent. On both reading and maths however the two groups were inferior to the normal group, perhaps an unsurprising result since they were selected as being learning disabled in the first place. Reading performance was explored in more detail, and showed that the capacity of the LD-S group to read normal words was poorer than that of the LD-N which in turn was poorer than the normal group. There was an even greater difference between the LD-S and LD-N groups when the children were required to read pronounceable non-words. Torgesen *et al.* go on to test the suggestion (Baddeley 1979) that the reading difficulty might stem from the problem LD-S children have in maintaining phonetically coded items during the process of decoding and blending the letters in an unfamiliar word. They examined the performance of the three groups on a sound-blending task taken from the Illinois Test of Psycholinguistic Abilities. Both real and nonsense words are broken into smaller sound segments that are presented at a rate of two segments per second, with a break between successive sounds, for instance, the word 'babies' is presented 'buh-eh-buh-ih-ss'. The subject's task is to speak the word after it has been presented in segments. The mean score obtained by the LD-S group for this task was 8.1, while the LD-N group averaged 14.7 and the N group 13.9. Sound blending obviously presents a substantial problem for the

LD-S group, but not for the LD-N subjects, exactly what one might predict on the assumption that LD-S subjects have an impairment to the functioning of the articulatory loop making it difficult to retain the sequence of sounds. Furthermore, such an impairment is clearly likely to prove a substantial handicap in the process of learning to read.

Learning to read and the articulatory loop

We have now surveyed two parallel sources of evidence on the relationship between learning to read and the type of phonological and articulatory coding involved in the articulatory loop. The first of these began with normal children and suggested that the capacity for phonologically encoding visual stimuli is one that develops at about the time that children learn to read. The second line of evidence suggests that children who have difficulty in learning to read typically show impaired memory span, a later development of the use of phonological coding and slower rates of articulation. The third line of argument began with children who had impaired digit span with normal intelligence, and showed that such children show evidence of poorer phonological coding, defective sound blending and impaired reading. Such a pattern of results is clearly consistent with the hypothesis that specific reading disability is associated with impaired functioning of the articulatory loop. Why should this be so?

As Liberman (in press) has cogently argued, the task of decoding an alphabetically written language such as English depends first of all on an ability to segment the continuous flow of spoken language into a series of constituent phonemes. These can then be mapped onto the letters representing that sound in the written word. The capacity to segment spoken words into constituent phonemes is by no means fully developed in many children of kindergarten age.

Bradley and Bryant (1983) have suggested that the awareness of rhyme and alliteration may be an important precursor to learning to read. Their study is methodologically one of the most sophisticated in the field in that it attempts to combine a cross-sectional approach based on a large sample of subjects with an intervention study. They argue that while correlations can be important indicators of possible relationships, they can not demonstrate causality, whereas experimental intervention provides a much more powerful means of testing specific causal hypotheses.

Bradley and Bryant tested the performance of 118 four-year old and 285 five-year old children in categorizing sounds. The crucial task involved presenting the child with a sequence of spoken words, all of which had a given sound in common except for one. The child's task was to pick out the word that did not fit. The four-year old children heard sequences of three words (e.g. *hill* pig pin, or cot pot *hat*), while the five-year olds heard sequences of four words (e.g. bud bun bus *rug*); in each case the italicized word is the odd one out. Intelligence was measured using the English picture-vocabulary test.

Subsequently, at the age of approximately eight years and six months, all the subjects were tested on reading (Schonell and Neale tests), spelling (Schonell), IQ (WISC/R) and mathematics (MATB-NFER).

There proved to be significant correlations between the reading and spelling scores of both the four- and five-year old group and sound categorization (correlations ranged from 0.44 to 0.57), intelligence as measured by the picture-vocabulary test (correlations ranging from 0.31 to 0.52), and word span performance (correlations ranging from 0.20 to 0.40). The combination of these variables was able to account for approximately 50 per cent of the variance in the reading scores for the four-year olds, and approximately 30 per cent for the five-year olds; of this, the sound categorization task accounted for approximately 7.5 per cent of the variance for the four-year olds and 4.25 per cent for the five-year olds ($p < 0.001$ in each case), when IQ, picture vocabulary score, chronological age and memory were statistically controlled.

The second part of the study involved training matched subgroups of children for 40 individual sessions spread over a 2-year period. One group was trained in categorizing sounds, a second both categorized sounds and were taught, with the help of plastic letters, how each common sound was represented by a letter of the alphabet. A third group acted as a baseline control and receiving no training, while a fourth group received training in categorizing words semantically but not phonologically. It was predicted that the first two groups, who practiced sound categorization, would show better performance on reading than the second two. The predictions were broadly born out, with the group trained on both sound and letters showing the best performance (mean Schonell reading age 96.96 months), the sound only group showing the next best performance (mean reading age 92.23 months), the semantic categorization group being somewhat poorer (88.48 months) and the baseline control performing most poorly (84.46 months).

While these results are encouraging for the Bradley and Bryant hypothesis, they are at this stage far from compelling. Consider first the correlation study. Since Bradley and Bryant's sound categorization task relies on a combination of storage and processing, it could be argued that the crucial factor was working memory span (Daneman and Carpenter 1980) rather than capacity for phonological analysis. Bradley and Bryant clearly hoped to deal with the problem of short-term memory by showing that their memory span measure correlates less highly with performance than their rhyme categorization test. However, as we saw in the previous chapter, simple memory span in adults predicts reading much less effectively than working memory measures in which memory and processing are required simultaneously. The rhyme task is just such a measure. The correlational data therefore are still somewhat equivocal.

The training component of the study is potentially important, but unfortunately the data are simply not strong enough to draw clear conclusions. First, the size of group is unfortunately rather small ($n=13$) for all except the semantic categorization group which contained 26 subjects. Of the various conditions, that involving practice on rhymes together with familiarization of letters and their sounds could be regarded as so close to reading as to represent additional reading lessons, rather than simply practice in phonological categorization. The no-treatment control is a useful baseline, but the crucial control group is that in which children are given an equivalent amount of attention but no phonological coding practice, namely the semantic categorization group. The acid test of the hypothesis then resides in a comparison between the group given practice in categorization of sounds only, and that given practice in semantic categorization. Unfortunately this difference fails to reach significance. In conclusion then, the Bradley and Bryant study is methodologically an important development, but as yet does not provide compelling evidence for their view.

Mann and Liberman (in press) tested the ability of kindergarten children to perform a syllable segmentation task in which the child was required to tap on the table with a dowel rod once for each syllable in a spoken word. Memory span for spoken words was also tested. Substantial individual differences among the kindergarten children occurred for both these measures. Reading training does not occur in kindergarten, but it was possible to obtain reading scores for these children in first grade one year later. There proved to be a significant correlation between reading performance and performance one year before on both syllable counting ($r=0.40$, $p<0.01$) and memory for words ($r=0.39$, $p<0.01$).

This is an important finding since it bears on the question of the causal relationship between impaired memory and impaired reading. A correlation between the two can be interpreted either in terms of the reading influencing memory, memory influencing reading, or both being influenced by a third factor. In the present instance, the memory and counting performance was carried out before the child had learnt to read, allowing one to rule out the suggestion that the memory performance is a direct result of the child's reading capacity. By the first grade, all the children were able to perform the syllable counting task virtually perfectly, but of course still varied in their level of performance on the memory span task. They were tested on both phonologically similar and dissimilar words. The correlation between reading and memory performance was significant for both types of material (for similar $r=0.52$, $p<0.01$, for dissimilar, $r=0.65$, $p<0.001$). When split into three subgroups, good, average and poor readers, only the poor readers failed to show a phonological similarity effect. Finally, all subjects were also given a test of spatial memory span, the Corsi Blocks test. This proved to be unrelated to reading performance.

A similar involvement of segmentation in early reading was observed by Fox and Routh (1983). They studied two groups of first grade children who were matched for intelligence, but differed in their reading capacity at this early stage. They measured the segmentation ability of the two groups for sentences, disyllabic words and syllables within words. They did so by speaking the material to be segmented and asking the child to say it 'a little bit at a time'. They found that the poor readers in the first grade were impaired on ability (1) to segment sentences, implying poorer knowledge of word boundaries, (2) to segment words into syllables and (3) to segment syllables into their constituent phonemes.

Some three years later they re-examined the same children. By this time, all the children were able to perform the segmentation tasks, but nevertheless the difference in reading had persisted with the result that the good readers in the first grade were now at a mean grade level of 4.9, whereas the poor readers were at a grade level of 2.5, a year and a half behind the expected norm. The poor readers also tended to make more 'bizarre' spelling errors in which at least two sounds were misplaced.

I would like to suggest that the performance of a segmentation task involves holding the item to be segmented in the phonological store while the task of decomposing it into its components is carried out. The child who has severely limited articulatory loop capacity would be expected to have difficulty in performing this task.

However, as the work of Fox and Routh shows, children are still impaired even when they have reached the point at which they can apparently segment quite adequately. Why should this be? Possibly because such children are still penalized by having a poorly developed articulatory loop system. Consider the task of a child who is attempting to read a word which is not in his sight vocabulary, for example the word *mad*. If one listens to the child one will often hear him operate roughly as follows. The initial letter is decoded into its relevant speech sound. Unfortunately since consonants are virtually impossible to pronounce in isolation, children typically add a redundant *uh* sound, so that *m* will become *muh*. This must be remembered while the second letter is decoded *a*, and the third, *duh*. The child will then frequently say the three letters rapidly and attempt to blend them into a single unit, at the same time trying to map this blended sound onto a plausible real word.

In the case of a word like *mad*, the *uh* sounds are likely to be something of a nuisance in performing the blending. Note also however that the addition of the same redundant vowel sound to every consonant produces what is effectively a phonologically similar string of items, with all consonant names ending in the same *uh* sound. Hence a word like *string* would become *suh, tuh, ruh, ī nuh, guh.* Such a phonologically similar sequence is maximally difficult and particularly liable to disruption of order information (Wickelgren 1965). Once one gets beyond three or four letters then, the child is likely to have quite a substantial memory task with far from ideal material.

So far we have considered only regular words such as *mad.* However what of a word such as *made*? In this case, the child who is proceeding sequentially from left to right has the further complication of reaching the last letter and, if he knows the rule, having to retrace his steps and revise his pronunciation of the vowel. This again is likely to be a difficult memory task. Once again then it is hardly surprising that a child whose articulatory loop is impaired will have particular difficulty in this task. Finally, as Torgesen *et al.* showed, even when the child is given the necessary speech sounds and required merely to blend them, impaired span will substantially limit performance, presumably because the component letter sounds in a long word may be forgotten before the letter decoding is complete.

Are there ways in which such a limitation can be circumvented? It seems unlikely that learning to read without the involvement of the phonological system will prove advisable for anything other than a very limited sight vocabulary (for an extensive discussion of this see Liberman, in press). What one can do however it to attempt to encourage the use of strategies that minimize the demands placed on the articulatory loop. The first of these might be to encourage the child to scan the word before he begins to decode the individual letters. This will allow him to spot features such as double vowels or terminal *e*'s that affect the way in which earlier items should be pronounced. Having noted this, he can then go ahead without the disruptive complication of needing to backtrack.

A second way of minimizing the memory load is to avoid the strategy of decoding individual consonants. If instead of decoding consonants one at a time, the child processes consonant–vowel pairs, this will have two advantages. First of all, it will obviate the need to add the redundant *uh* sound to each consonant, hence both reducing the total length of material to be recalled and minimizing the phonological similarity of the string of items he needs to hold in memory. Secondly, by combining a consonant and vowel into a single item, he will be producing fewer, and more speech-compatible chunks than would otherwise be the case. Such a strategy should substantially increase the amount of material the child can hold in his articulatory loop. I realise that neither of these strategies is completely novel, and both are no doubt used by experienced teachers of reading. However, so far as I know they tend not to be emphasised, nor is the reason for their value generally acknowledged.

Conclusion

The working memory model was not created with a view to explaining data from developmental psychology. It does however aim to provide a model of some generality. Hence its ability to account for developmental data and its fruitfulness in linking basic concepts to important applied developmental problems have an obvious bearing on the scope, robustness, and productiveness as an explanatory model.

So far, it has proved far more successful than I would have dared to predict. Its account of the development of memory span is simpler, more precisely specified and at least as successful as concepts such as M Space that were explicitly devised to deal with developmental data. While the role of working memory in learning to read is far from fully understood, the articulatory loop concept does offer a coherent account of the substantial body of evidence pointing to the importance of speech coded memory in the process of learning to read. Finally, the concept of an articulatory loop appears to offer a promising theoretical tool for understanding the important problem of developmental dyslexia.

10 The central executive and its malfunctions

As its name suggests, the central executive is a crucial component of working memory, a component that logically perhaps should have been tackled first. And yet, very little has been said about it; until recently I was not even sure that I could write anything worthwhile on the topic. Over the years, my strategy has been to concentrate on the apparently more tractable slave systems, perpetually intending to start to work on the central executive, but somehow never quite starting. Over the last month or two this has finally changed for a number of rather different reasons. First, writing this book has forced me at least to attempt to come to terms with the problem of tackling the central executive. An account of working memory that emphasizes principally the articulatory loop is like a critical analysis of *Hamlet* that centres its attention on Polonius and completely ignores the prince.

A second reason stems from collaborative neuropsychological research on patients who at first sight at least, appeared to have defective functioning of the central executive as a major component of their deficit. In connection with this, I have come to study more carefully a recent attentional model developed by Norman and Shallice (1980), and applied to the analysis of performance deficits in patients suffering from frontal lobe damage (Shallice 1982). The Norman and Shallice model seems to fit very neatly within a working memory framework, and as an unexpected bonus appeared to offer an explanation of results that I had obtained over 20 years ago, but had been unable to relate to conventional information processing models. Consequently, over the past two weeks I have become very enthusiastic about the possibility of analysing the central executive. Inevitably my current views being so newly formed are still inadequately worked out, and may quite possibly have changed substantially by the time this chapter appears in print. However, it is perhaps not inappropriate for a final theoretical chapter to be somewhat speculative both in its conceptualization, and in its attempt to apply these relatively untried concepts to specific problems.

The central executive: ragbag or supervisor?

Throughout all the previous chapters of this book, the concept of the central executive has served two separate and quite different purposes. On the one hand, it has served as a conceptual ragbag; any process which was regarded as part of working memory, but outside the specific system being studied has tended to be referred to as operating within the central executive. Indeed at times I have described the central executive as the area of residual ignorance within the working memory system. Such a strategy has been heuristically very useful in allowing us to concentrate on the details of one part of the system without feeling obliged to speculate in detail about the rest of the system. It has however created potential confusion with the second and more specific use of the term central executive.

The second use of the term implies some type of supervisor or scheduler, capable of selecting strategies and integrating information from several different sources. I have tended to suggest that this more specific function was probably related to the control of attention, and possibly to the function of consciousness, always leaving the issue suitably vague. Conscious of the evasion, I have for at least ten years been resolving to try to integrate the concepts of working memory with those of attention. However, until my recent enthusiasm for the Norman and Shallice model, this has never happened. With a view to making one final attempt, I took advantage of an extremely useful recent review by Broadbent (1982) of the theoretical issues that have concerned the study of attention from the 1950s to the 1980s.

Models of attention and the central executive

Reading Broadbent's review was in one sense reassuring. The issues discussed were all reasonably familiar, not in detail but at least in the sense that I had heard and read papers on virtually all of them at one time or another. It also made it clear why I had not rushed over to the attention literature in order to gain suitable insights for understanding the central executive. Had I done so I would almost certainly have returned empty-handed. This is not because the field has stood still, but rather because it has been dominated by the role of attention in perception, whereas my own concerns are with the control of memory and action.

Even within the perceptual area, the study of attention seems to have become fragmented into a number of rather separable approaches, with each approach typically concentrating rather narrowly on one or two paradigms. To quote Broadbent, 'One can distinguish traditions drawn from psychophysics (Eriksen), from skilled performance (Posner), from learning and mathematical psychology (Shiffrin), and from higher mental processes or artificial intelligence (Neisser), with communication across traditions being inferior to that within each' (Broadbent 1982, p. 281).

The traditions appear to share common questions, and in particular the question of wherein lies the limitation in attentional capacity. To an

outsider this seems a strange question to ask, given the variety of paradigms studied and the probable complexity of the underlying processes.
As a general question this seems analogous to a city planner asking the
question 'What limits travel through London?', and not specifying
whether he is referring to people walking through London, using the
tube, the bus, changing flights in London, or driving. Just as each of these
different methods of travelling through London is likely to have different
limitations occurring at different points, so the limitations of attention
seem likely to differ according to the particular demands of the specific
task. To attempt to answer such a question in a general sense without
considering the underlying processes is surely unlikely to be very profitable. While those working within the field of attention are no doubt well
aware of this diversity, it was not obvious to an outside observer like
myself, that the use of common terms did not necessarily imply common
concepts and assumptions.

I am not of course claiming that work in these various traditions has
not been extremely fruitful. Work in the area of visual attention by Posner
and by Treisman for example is arguably among the most elegant work
that cognitive psychology has produced. What appears to be less successful however is the attempt to provide a broad overview. The reason may
be due at least in part to the fact that the various topics included within
the term *attention* are too diverse to incorporate within a single framework. In that respect, the concept of attention resembles that of memory
which tends to be applied to an enormous range of phenomena from
iconic memory to autobiographical recollection and semantic memory.
Perhaps the study of attention needs its STM-LTM controversy to help
point up the various distinctions for those of us who are not active in the
field.

Attention to action: the Norman and Shallice model

Norman and Shallice (1980) put forward a model that is concerned
primarily with the attentional control of action. As such, it provides a
suitable 'off-the-shelf' model for the central executive, and I decided to
try to fit it into the working memory framework, and if successful, to
attempt to use it to give an account of the memory problems of the
elderly. I shall begin by giving a brief outline of the model. Figure 10.1
shows a simplified representation of the model taken from Shallice
(1982). It assumes that most actions are controlled by schemata, collec-
tions of actions that are run off automatically, given the appropriate
triggering. Such schemata can operate at a range of different levels from
the simple barely conscious brushing of a fly off one's arm through the
operation of such overlearned skills as walking, to more complex
patterns such as are involved in driving a car or tying a shoelace. At any
given time, several such schemata may be operating. For example at

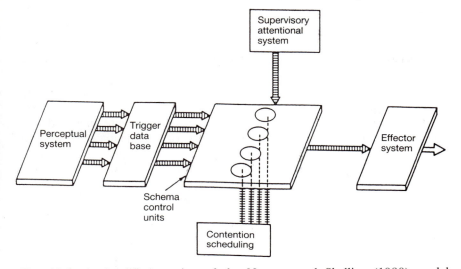

Fig. 10.1. A simplified version of the Norman and Shallice (1980) model representing the flow of control information. The lines with arrows represent activating input, the crossed lines represent the primarily mutually inhibitory function of contention scheduling. The term 'effector system' refers to special-purpose processing units involved in schema operation for both action and thought schemas. In the latter case schema operation involves placing information in short-term stores that can activate the trigger data base (Shallice 1982).

present I am walking and talking into a tape recorder. Both these activities proceed with minimal attentional control, while my attention is concentrated primarily on planning how to express the next concept.

If left to their own devices, such schemata would be likely to conflict from time to time, leading to a disruption of behaviour. This is avoided in the Norman and Shallice model by an automatic conflict resolution process. This selects one of the conflicting schemata according to priorities and environmental cues and gives it precedence at any given moment. Such a procedure is common in many artificial intelligence programs, in particular those using the production system approach of Newell and Simon (1972).

In addition to this semi-automatic conflict resolution process there is an overall controller, the supervisory attentional system. Within the model shown in Fig. 10.1 the schemata are represented by horizontal threads, and the supervisory control by vertical threads. The latter can be used to bias the activation of schemata, favouring one over its rivals. Such conscious attentional control is used to override other influences on the conflict resolution system when this is necessary because of external factors. For example I stopped both walking and talking when the path I was on met a main road, where I needed to take out a map to see where I should go next.

The supervisory attentional system, or SAS as Shallice terms it, is assumed to have limited capacity. This is called upon under a range of circumstances including: (a) tasks that involve planning or decision making: (b) situations in which the automatic processes appear to be running into difficulties and some form of trouble-shooting is necessary: (c) where novel or poorly learned sequences of acts are involved: (d) where the situation is judged to be dangerous or technically difficult: and (e) where some strong habitual response or temptation is involved. Norman and Shallice identify this process with the will, backing up their claim with some plausible anecdotal evidence.

They apply their model to a number of phenomena, for instance, those situations in which subjects are able to perform two apparently demanding tasks simultaneously. An example is the demonstration by Allport, Antonis, and Reynolds (1972) of the ability of highly skilled pianists to sight-read and play music at the same time as shadowing auditory speech. It is suggested that both of these involve the running off of highly practiced schemata, where much of the coordination can be carried out through the low level conflict resolution procedures, without overloading the SAS system.

The model can also handle many of the slips of action reported by Reason (1979). For example Reason describes an incident where his respondent went to his garage to drive to work and found that he had 'stopped to put on my wellington boots and gardening jacket as if to work in the garden' (Reason 1979). It is suggested that this represents a 'capture error' in which the SAS system is occupied by yet another task, allowing the triggering of a schema that is appropriate for the environmental context, but inconsistent with the longer term plan.

In conclusion then, the model assumes that action is controlled at two levels. First via conflict resolution between horizontal threads or schemata; this avoids the production of incompatible responses or the overloading of subcomponents of the system. Secondly, overall supervisory control is exercised by the SAS system (for a more detailed account, see Norman and Shallice 1980 and Shallice 1982).

Suppose we equate the central executive with the SAS system, what does this gain us? One immediate and quite unexpected bonus was a possible explanation of a series of results I had collected more than 20 years before, results that were remarkably coherent and consistent, and yet did not appear to fit into any current theory of information processing. After 20 years of trying to understand the results in a theoretically coherent way totally without success, I was delighted to find that the Norman and Shallice model provided a simple and plausible interpretation. The task in question was that of random generation and it stemmed from an attempt to separate out the informational demands of stimulus selection from those of response initiation in a reaction time task. I will describe this before going on to relate the Norman and Shallice model to working memory.

Random generation and the central executive

One of the major sources of theoretical ideas in the 1950s was information theory. W. E. Hick (1952) showed that time to react to a stimulus was linearly related to amount of information conveyed by that stimulus. With a range of equiprobable stimuli, the information value of each is given by the logarithm of the number of alternatives from which the stimulus was selected. To use the 1950s terminology, the rate of gain of information was constant, a relationship that has subsequently become known as Hick's Law. There was considerable interest at the time in attempting to explain Hick's Law. In that connection I wanted to separate out the demands imposed by the need to discriminate between the potential stimuli on the one hand, and those of selecting among the appropriate responses on the other. In an attempt to isolate the response selection process from that of stimulus processing, I devised a task in which my subjects were required to select an item at random from a given ensemble, the 26 letters of the alphabet, at rates ranging from two per second to one every four seconds (Baddeley 1966c).

In order to get some idea as to what is involved in this rather curious task it is perhaps worth trying it yourself by attempting to produce a random stream of letters at a rate of one per second. Most people find this surprisingly difficult after the first 15 or 20, and tend either to omit responses or to utter a disproportionate number of stereotyped sequences. Common stereotypes include those following the alphabetic sequence (e.g. *ABC, QR, XY*), and frequent initials such as TV, VD and BBC.

A person's success in performing this task can be measured in a number of ways. One is simply to count the frequency with which each letter is emitted; the more biased the distribution, the more redundant the output. A similar measure can in theory be used for the output of digrams or letter pairs, although it is rarely possible to collect sufficient responses to allow a conventional information measure to be applied validly. Instead I used an approximation that involved scoring the number of different digrams generated in a hundred responses. A third measure used was that of number of stereotyped digrams, pairs of letters such as *AB, TU,* and *XY* that follow the alphabetic sequence. Figure 10.2 shows the performance of 12 subjects who were attempting to generate sequences of one hundred random letters at each of four rates.

All three measures gave the same picture, namely that the randomness, and hence the amount of information generated increased with the time

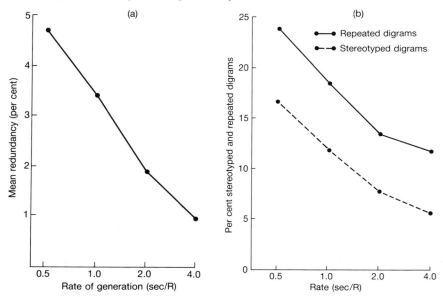

Fig. 10.2(a). Random generation of letters; first order redundancy as a function of rate of generation (Baddeley 1966c). **(b).** Random generation of letters. Number of stereotyped and repeated digrams as a function of rate of generation (Baddeley 1966c).

allowed per response. Furthermore, the relationship was linear when plotted on a $\log_2$ scale, exactly what one might expect by analogy with Hick's Law.

The results were all that I might have hoped, and yet how should one explain them? Clearly there seems to be some sort of selection process that behaves very lawfully and has limited capacity, but what else? How is such a mechanism involved in more standard processes? The results were not implausible, they simply did not seem to fit into any available model of underlying mechanisms.

Suppose we think of this process in terms of the Norman and Shallice model. Presumably the supervisory system is attempting to control a set of retrieval processes. The retrieval processes might be expected to be relatively automatic (see Chapter 3), but will tend to produce items that are strongly associated, such as alphabetic sequences and common initials. Indeed the very process of retrieval is likely to strengthen such associations producing an increasingly stereotyped output. Since the subject is expressly attempting to avoid this, he is likely to have a difficult task, perpetually intervening to break up developing patterns and to favour weak schemata, a task which in itself requires him to monitor the occurrence of prior responses and to attempt to maintain some kind of long-term strategy. It is then a situation in which the Norman and Shallice supervisor is being pitted against the underlying schemata. At slow rates, the SAS is able to perform very effectively, approximating a random distribution of responses. As the pacing increases however the capacity of the supervisor to cope is overloaded and the randomness of the output steadily declines.

Before describing two more experiments in this series it is perhaps worth considering some alternative explanations. I discovered that I was by no means the only person to have looked at random generation as a task (see Tune 1964 for a review). However, most of the earlier studies used binary generation, a situation that has the advantage of providing large numbers of observations in individual and digram cells, but of placing a very small informational load on the subject. Deviations from randomness do occur, but tend to show up only when patterns comprising three, four or five responses are analysed. Such results are often interpreted in terms of either a subject's forgetting what he has generated, or as resulting from a faulty concept of randomness.

While these interpretations are plausible as an explanation of the high order redundancy involved in the two-alternative case they do not offer a good explanation of my own results. If subjects were simply reflecting a faulty concept of randomness, then there is no reason to assume that their concept should become systematically more appropriate as they slow down, reaching an entirely appropriate concept at four seconds per item. The forgetting interpretation similarly has problems in explaining why subjects should apparently remember perfectly at the slow rate, nor why at rapid rates they should be particularly likely to produce alphabetic stereotypes. However, the most convincing evidence on both these points is to try the task yourself under rapid paced conditions. Unfortunately however, the combination of use of two-choice situations together with a preoccupation with the subject's concept of randomness has tended to create a good deal of confusion in this field, while the absence of good models has limited its theoretical development.

To return to the Norman and Shallice model; let us suppose that the amount of information generated does give an indication of the available capacity of the supervisor. Then we should be able to show that absorbing some of this capacity by a secondary task will reduce the amount of information generated in the randomisation task. This was explored in a second study (Baddeley 1966c) in which I combined choice reaction time and random generation. The subject's primary task was to sort playing cards into 1, 2, 4, or 8 categories. He was required to make one response every two seconds, a rate that allowed perfect performance even in the most demanding 8 choice condition. However, the more difficult the sorting response, the more of his available supervisory capacity

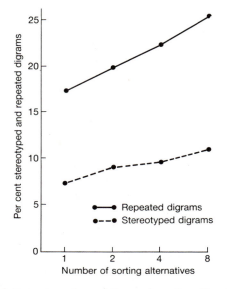

Fig. 10.3. Random-letter generation while card sorting. Number of stereotyped and repeated diagrams as a function of number of sorting alternatives (Baddeley 1966*c*).

should be absorbed, given that the card sorting task was not highly over-learned, and the less random his output of letters should become. The results of this study are shown in Fig. 10.3. As predicted, the amount of information generated declines systematically as the demands of the sorting task increase. In all except the individual item frequency measure, the relationship is linear, as would be expected from the analogy with Hick's Law.

A third study investigated the effect of the size of the generation set on speed of generating in a self-paced situation. Subjects were given sets of either letters or two-digit numbers ranging in size from 2 to 26. Subjects were instructed to imagine they were drawing the items from a hat, writing each item down, throwing it back and shaking the hat again before drawing another response. They were instructed to work as quickly as they could without deviating from randomness. In one condition they were allowed to set their own pace while in a second, they were instructed to try to keep up with a metronome beating at a rate of 1 per second. All subjects were given three successive two-minute test runs. In order to avoid carry-over between conditions, we used a large number of subjects (437), each of whom generated using only one type of item and one set size. The results are shown in Fig. 10.4, from which it is clear that although speed increased across the three runs, the general pattern of

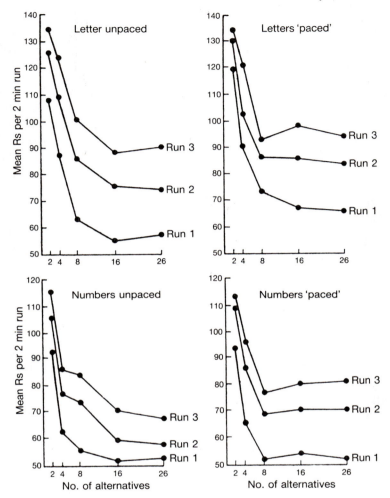

Fig. 10.4. Rate of random generation of numbers and letters as a function of number of alternatives (Baddeley 1966c).

performance remained constant. Rate of generation decreased with set size up to a limit of about 8 items, and then levelled off. The pattern was virtually the same for letters and numbers and for unpaced subjects and those who were attempting (unsuccessfully) to keep up a 1 per second rate. The particular measures I was using made it very difficult to compare redundancy across different vocabulary sizes. I did however analyse one condition in some detail and found that subjects were relatively successful in all conditions in approximating a random output, suggesting that they had obeyed the randomization instruction across conditions, maintaining randomness by slowing down their performance as set size increased.

One might expect by simple analogy with Hick's Law that the rate of generation should continue to increase logarithmically with set size up to the maximum size used. Having obtained this discontinuity I began to scan the literature for comparable reaction time data. Most of the classic studies limit the number of alternatives to 8 or 10, largely I suspect because most subjects have a maximum of 10 fingers. With larger set sizes, problems of discrimination occur, and the degree of learning of individual items tends to be less. I could find only two studies in which large sets had been used and well practiced. In one of these, Seibel (1963) had studied a chord keyboard in which a large number of responses could be produced by pressing two or more keys simultaneously. He suggests that his results indicate 'a function which increases from 1 to approximately 3 bits (from 2 to 8 alternatives), and shows little further increase from 3 to almost 10 bits (from 8 to almost 1024 alternatives)' (Seibel 1963, p. 222). The other relevant study, Schmidtke (1961) reports a simple linear relationship between reaction time and number of alternatives during the early stages of learning, which changed with practice to give a discontinuous relationship with reaction time increasing up to 10 alternatives and from then being roughly constant. Both these and our results are of course broadly consistent with Miller's Magic Number Seven Plus or Minus Two. It is tempting to suggest that this limit represents the maximum number of sources that the SAS system can monitor simultaneously.

Before departing from random generation, it is perhaps worth mentioning one further result. This was an unpublished study in which a total of 17 postmen were required to generate two successive sequences of 100 responses at a rate of one per second. The postmen were also given a general intelligence test, Alice Heim's AH4. There proved to be a significant correlation between intelligence and both the number of cells occupied, and measure of digram redundancy ($\tau = 0.43$, $p < 0.01$) and number of stereotype responses ($\tau = 0.46$, $p < 0.01$). Redundancy due to individual letters was unfortunately not calculated. If random generation does indeed represent the capacity of the supervisor, then it is reasonable to expect that it should correlate with general intelligence, as indeed proved to be the case.

The supervisor and WMG

The Norman and Shallice model may provide a good account of random generation, but how does it fare with the results of our experiments exploring the evidence for a general working memory? Consider first the major overall findings. We found that performing a concurrent digit span task did impair performance on learning, comprehension and reasoning tasks, but not nearly as dramatically as might be expected by the modal model. This pattern of results is consistent with the assumption that the secondary digit span task and/or the primary task could be performed at least partly by existing schemata. Such an interpretation is no better and no worse than that offered by other limited capacity models. The Norman and Shallice model perhaps fares slightly better when one looks at details.

Take for example the question of a trade-off between performance on reasoning and concurrent memory span. It may be recalled that the relationship proved to be positive, with errors on the memory task being associated with slow reasoning, not rapid as would be predicted on the assumption that the subject was trading-off performance on one task against performance on the other. I speculated that the interference might come primarily from the demands of coping with a breakdown in performance on the digit span task. This is consistent with Norman and Shallice's suggestion that troubleshooting is likely to make heavy demands on the supervisor.

An area in which we found much less interference than anticipated was that of retrieval. It might be argued that the actual process of retrieval involves the running off of schemata rather than directly involving the supervisor; such an assumption would be broadly consistent with our own findings. When latency rather than accuracy of retrieval was measured, we found that a concurrent task did influence performance; this is exactly what one would expect from two largely automatic processes operating simultaneously, with potential conflicts resolved via the conflict resolution process.

The one task in which concurrent load very clearly affected performance was that of category generation. This is a situation in which one might reasonably expect the supervisor to play a major role, since there are no built-in programmes for producing sequences of items from a specified category as rapidly as possible while avoiding repetitions. It is perhaps significant that this task is one of the most sensitive measures of damage to the frontal lobes (Milner 1964), an area of the brain that Shallice (1982) suggests is associated with the supervisory attentional system.

In conclusion, while our existing results do not provide a direct test of the Norman and Shallice model, they fit into the model sufficiently well to suggest that it does provide a promising account of the central executive component of working memory. As such, it would certainly seem to justify further exploration. The acid test of the model will come in its ability to generate new research findings; in the meantime, an interim method of evaluating the approach is to attempt to apply it to existing data in a novel area. The next two sections will be concerned with the application of the model to neuropsychological data from patients with frontal lobe damage, and to the effects of normal ageing and senile dementia on cognitive performance.

The frontal lobes and the dysexecutive syndrome

Shallice (1982) suggests that the supervisory attentional system proposed by Norman and himself might offer a suitable explanation for the intriguing but puzzling pattern of deficits sometimes associated with damage to the frontal lobes (Luria 1969). Before going on to discuss the application of the model, it is necessary to say a little about the frontal lobe syndrome.

In a chapter entitled 'The riddle of frontal lobe function in man', Teuber (1964) gives an intriguing historical overview of work on the frontal lobes. As he points out, there have been extreme differences in the functional importance assigned to the frontal lobes, ranging from the views of authors such as Goldstein (1936) who regarded them as the source of all abstract behaviour, and Burdoch (1819; cited by Shallice 1982) who described them as 'the special workshop of the thinking processes', to Hebb (1949, pp. 286–9) and Teuber himself (1959) who observed no evidence for a disruption of function following frontal lobe damage.

As Teuber points out, at least one source of difficulty in this area probably stems from the contrast between striking results from individual cases, coupled with much weaker and more variable findings when groups of patients are studied. Why should this be? I think there are two reasons, first the complexity of the functions probably subserved by the frontal lobes and secondly the probable absence of a simple mapping of function on to location within this large area of the brain.

The functions subserved by the frontal lobes probably involve quite complex relationships with other brain systems. One can contrast this with the more specific and limited functions served by other areas of the brain such as the sensory projection areas, or areas involved in motor output which show clearer localization of function. This is likely to lead to a more complex pattern of disruption in frontal patients, with performance depending on the involvement of other components of the system. Furthermore, adequately measuring, or even identifying these functions is likely to depend upon an adequate conceptualization of such functions. As Shallice (1982) points out, theoretical development in this area is at a very elementary level. All too frequently, the only guiding framework in this area has been that based on localization within the brain. While there is certainly evidence that different parts of the frontal lobe do have somewhat different functions (see for example Milner 1982) localization *per se* offers a totally inadequate model for understanding even relatively simple cognitive functions let alone those which are typically attributed to the frontal lobes.

Clearly localization of function is extremely important to the neurosurgeon about to perform a brain operation. It is likely to be helpful to the therapist treating a stroke patient. For the cognitive psychologist however its contribution is much more dubious. Information on localization of function is worth bearing in mind as an incidental source of information, but its ability to function as a theoretical framework is extremely limited, for at least three reasons. First, the type of function that cognitive psychology attempts to explain depends crucially on the functional specification of processes; explanations that rely purely on anatomical localization are unlikely ever to be able to do justice to such functions; specifying the position of a piece of neural hardware will not provide an adequate explanation of how it works.

A second reason why localizational models are unlikely to prove profitable stems from the problem of accurately localizing the damage suffered by a particular patient. Although the technology for achieving this has advanced substantially and is continuing to develop, we still virtually never have detailed anatomical data and good psychological data from the same patients. That is not to say that such information is not important and relevant to neuropsychology, but merely that the quantity and quality of available information is such that it seems unwise to use it as a principal basis for theoretical development. The third point is related, and concerns the question of the extent to which localization of function will be identical across individuals. Unless we can make this assumption, we are clearly unwise to draw firm conclusions from data based on the small sample of subjects on whom we do have good information.

In the area of amnesia, which is the aspect of neuropsychology with which I myself am most familiar, I would argue that attempts to localize the deficit associated with global amnesia have been much less successful than attempts to provide a functional account of the deficit. I would furthermore argue that those aspects of long-term memory deficit that have proved most amenable to interpretation through localization have shown the least theoretical development. A prime example of this is the association between hemisphere and visual/verbal processing. There is no doubt that hemispheric differences do occur and can produce striking differences in carefully selected patient samples (Milner 1971). The ratio of theoretical progress to pages published in this area however must be among the lowest in cognitive psychology or neuropsychology. However, having by now no doubt offended most of my neuropsychological colleagues, perhaps I should return to the frontal lobes.

A logical extension of my dissatisfaction with localization as an underlying framework is a dissatisfaction with the whole concept of a frontal lobe syndrome. If, as seems likely, the frontal lobes are complex and far from homogeneous, it seems unwise to use the term *frontal* to describe the many possible deficits that may be observed. Even within neuro-psychology, classifying dysfunctions on a purely localizational basis is the exception. We talk of amnesia, aphasia, dyslexia, dyscalculia, and so forth, describing the dysfunction, and leaving open the question of its possible localization. I would like to suggest that a similar approach be taken in the case of possible dysfunctions of the central executive. Unfortunately no term exists for this, and I for one cannot think of an obvious neat descriptive label (no doubt because I lack the classical education of the inventors of the standard neuropsychological vocabulary). As a stop-gap I suggest the term *dysexecutive syndrome (DES)*.

To what extent then does there appear to be a deficit resembling the inadequate functioning of our hypothetical central executive system? It is certainly not the case that any patient with damage anywhere in the frontal lobes will behave as if he were dramatically impaired. It is how-ever the case that certain characteristics of behaviour do show up in groups of frontal patients, and show up in an extremely striking way in certain individual cases.

Teuber discusses an extensive study by Feuchtwanger (1923) of 200 cases who had suffered gunshot wounds to the frontal lobes during the First World War, and who were compared with 200 cases with wounds elsewhere in the brain. Feuchtwanger's theoretical background was intro-spectionist, and he concluded that the principal change in his frontal cases was in the sphere of voluntary action and in the ability to evaluate situations, dysfunctions that he pointed out could not be accounted for in 'associationistic' or 'sensationalistic' psychological terms. Discussing this some 20 years ago, Teuber has the following interesting comment on Feuchtwanger. 'If he were with us, and unreformed, he might say that the objective behaviorist can note the changes after frontal lobe lesions but can not understand them since he has lost the 'problems of will' and 'values'—as being outside the realm of the scientific study of behaviour. Yet it is precisely this problem of finding an objective approach to such dimensions of behaviour that makes the study of frontal syndromes a particular challenge for experimental psychology' (Teuber 1964, p. 416).

Teuber's own account has a slightly schizophrenic character to it, with the clinician on the one hand emphasizing the richness of the frontal syndrome, while the theorist is still clearly limited by the concepts of stimulus and response. He rejects stimulus-bound interpretations of the frontal syndrome, but advocates instead something which he regards as an extrapolation of 'Kleist's interesting attempt to interpret all frontal changes as 'psychomotor' symptoms' (Teuber 1964, p. 416). With the benefit of hindsight, the idea that phenomena should be related either to stimulus input or motor output seems excessively simplistic. It was inter-esting to reflect that my own attempt to explain the data from my random generating experiments carried out at about the same time also asserted the importance of response factors in opposition to the emphasis on stimulus discrimination that was the dominant view at the time, despite the fact that the concept of response production seemed far too simple to account for the available data.

At a clinical level however there did seem to be a good deal of agreement about what characterized the classic frontal syndrome. Shallice quotes the following description from Rylander (1939), that the characteristic dysfunction involves 'disturbed attention, increased distractability, a difficulty in grasping the whole of a complicated state of affairs ... well able to work along old routine lines ... (but) ... cannot learn to master new types of task, in new situations ... (the patient is) ... at a loss' (Rylander 1939, p. 20).

While milder cases will often show some of these symptoms, the classic pattern is based on relatively rare cases who show the pattern in its extreme form, typically with substantial bilateral frontal damage. Luria (1969) discussed a number of such patients who tend to be deficient in initiative and judgment, finding great difficulty in tackling novel problems that would be relatively easily soluble by most patients. For example Luria and Homskaya (1964) attempted to teach a patient with a massive frontal tumour to respond to a green light with the left hand and a red light with the right. The patient was quite unsuccessful, despite being able to repeat the instructions accurately and to demonstrate which was the left and which the right hand.

Before going on to discuss the theoretical interpretation of the syndrome, it might perhaps be worth describing in rather more detail a particular case that I myself happened to have encountered while carrying out collaborative work on amnesia (Baddeley and Wilson, in press). The patient, R.J., had suffered bilateral damage to the frontal lobes when his car ran into the back of a horsebox. He was unconscious for several weeks, but gradually recovered physically. He was a trained engineer with a managerial post at the time of the accident, and an estimated premorbid IQ in the region of 120. When tested, several months after his accident, his verbal IQ was in the region of 100, while his performance IQ had dropped to 76. While his digit span was within the normal range, his long-term learning ability was very substantially impaired. His semantic memory was also abnormal. Although his vocabulary score was not grossly impaired, he responded slowly and tended to omit items. His performance on a semantic sentence-processing test was also slow and inaccurate. Many of his errors were perseverations, cases in which he made the same response as he had made to the previous item.

The most bizarre aspect of R.J.'s memory however was his autobiographical 'recall' (Baddeley and Wilson in press). This was tested by giving him certain cue words and asking him if they reminded him of a particular incident that he himself had experienced (Galton 1883). This produced a number of rather colourful incidents which were delivered with the appearance of complete conviction, with full environmental detail. For example the cue word 'river' evoked an 'incident' where he had taken his niece rowing on the river, had subsequently got out of the boat, called to her and when she turned thrown a stone that hit her eye. This was followed by an elaborate description of taking her to hospital, a word-by-word account of his conversation with the doctor and so forth. When subsequently given the same cue he produced a completely different recall and denied any knowledge of the previous incident, an incident which his wife confirmed had not occurred. When asked about his accident he would always volunteer a detailed description. On each occasion the description was different, the only common feature being that he was involved in a car crash and that he remained conscious throughout. In actual fact he was unconscious for several weeks following the accident.

In addition to confabulating incidents that had not occurred he also denied all knowledge of events that had. He returned home from the Rehabilitation Centre each weekend, and one Saturday night he sat up in bed and turned to his wife and asked 'Why do you keep telling people we are married?'. His wife replied that they were married, had been for several years and pointed to their children as evidence. This he correctly pointed out did not necessarily imply that they were married. She then took out the wedding photographs and showed them to him, to which his response was 'Yes, that chap does look just like me but it isn't me'.

A characteristic of the syndrome is a lack of flexibility and a tendency to perseverate. This shows up particularly clearly on sorting tasks such as the Wisconsin card sorting test. This involves giving the subject a pack of cards, the cards contain varying numbers of symbols of various types printed in various colours. They subject is instructed to sort according to one of these dimensions and is told whether he is correct or not after each response. Having successfully sorted on the basis of one dimension, he is then required to switch to a second dimension and so forth. Frontal patients find this extremely difficult (Milner 1964), and R.J. was no exception, failing to break away from his first sorting strategy. This tendency to perseveration was also apparent in his behaviour. Instructed to measure out a piece of string in order to cut it later, he immediately started to cut and when told not to replied 'Yes I know I'm not to cut it' meanwhile continuing the cutting action.

Such patients often find difficulty in initiating activity, a deficit that shows up in the fluency or category generation task. When first tested, and asked to produce as many animal names as possible in 60 seconds, R.J. produced only four whereas a normal person would be expected to produce at least a dozen. The problem was not that the information had been lost from semantic memory since given cues such as 'an animal beginning with K', he almost invariably responded accurately and quickly. It is often said of such patients that provided someone else can serve as their frontal lobes by initiating behaviour, they can often perform surprisingly well.

In learning novel tasks, his lack of flexibility and tendency to stereotyped behaviour was a major problem. When asked to assemble a simple 12-piece child's jigsaw puzzle, his performance was slow, and showed little sign of improving with practice. Observing his behaviour suggested that he did speed up on some of the more straightforward pieces, but continued to stick at one or two more difficult points. He would for example take a piece and try to fit it in a location that was clearly inconsistent with the picture, systematically varying the orientation in an attempt to fit the shape. He appeared to be incapable of processing picture and shape information simultaneously.

I have described one patient in some detail just to give a flavour of one aspect of a rather extreme case of damage to the frontal lobes. It is important to bear in mind however that such patients vary enormously, most fortunately having much less extreme symptoms, while others have equally drastic symptoms but of a somewhat different nature. For example a more recent frontal patient in the same rehabilitation centre appeared to be completely different. Whereas R.J. was often talkative and expansive, this patient was initially virtually mute. The difficulty stemmed not from a specific linguistic deficit but from an inability to initiate speech, so-called *dynamic aphasia*. His problem of initiation extended far beyond speech and made him of course very difficult to investigate in detail. He did however show the standard impaired performance and perseveration on the Wisconsin card sorting task and appeared to be amnesic when tested using a two-alternative forced-choice verbal recognition procedure.

To what extent then can the classic frontal syndrome be associated with a defective functioning of the central executive? Shallice (1982) suggests that the frontal lobes may be involved in the operation of the supervisory attentional system, the system involved in monitoring and controlling behaviour and in the planning of future activities. He argues that routine activities can carry on relatively normally on the basis of the contention scheduling procedure which relies on schemata that are not dependent on the frontal lobes. Problems occur however when the subject is required to initiate new behaviour or to discontinue or modify ongoing activity. Hence the Wisconsin card sorting task is one in which the frontal patient can acquire the first concept, but is unable to break away from that concept and sort on the basis of a new one.

An apparent paradox in the case of such patients is that they are on the one hand highly distractable, and on the other inclined to perseverate.

Shallice explains this as follows: Since the SAS system is not functioning properly, the patient is at the mercy of the currently active schemata. If a situation exists in which one schema is clearly dominant, then it will continue to dominate, leading to perseveration. If on the other hand there are a number of competing schemata of approximately equal strength, then with no direction from the SAS, there will be a tendency for control to switch from one schema to another on the basis of relatively minimal changes in the environmental context.

A similar process could explain the confabulation shown by R.J. in his autobiographical memory. He does appear to be densely amnesic, but of course most amnesics do not confabulate in this way. It is as if R.J. is distracted by associations generated by the story he is telling and allows the story to 'tell itself' with no overall constraint by the teller (Baddeley and Wilson in press).

The difficulty that such patients have in category generation presumably stems from the fact that this is a task in which the subject must plan and initiate. It is interesting in this context that our previous study of WM and retrieval indicated that the effect of a concurrent digit load was much more pronounced on this task than on any of the other measures of retrieval (see Chapter 4, p. 63).

Shallice (1982) attempted to devise a task that would maximize the planning demand, on the assumption that this would prove to be particularly sensitive to frontal deficits. The task he chose was based on the Tower of Hanoi puzzle, but was simplified so that it could readily be used with patients. The new task, called the Tower of London is shown in Fig. 10.5; it comprises three sticks of different length and three beads of different colours. The starting point is that shown on the left, and the subject is given a range of end points which he must achieve with a specified number of moves. Examples are given in Fig. 10.5. In order to perform the task, the subject needs to think through the problem and plan ahead. The task proved very difficult for patients with lesions in the left frontal area, a result that is consistent with Shallice's prediction that such patients should have planning problems. One would expect a more

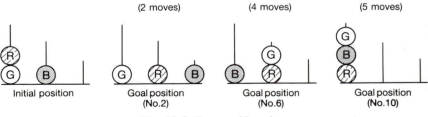

Fig. 10.5. Tower of London.

severe bilateral case such as R.J. to perform extremely badly on this test; while we have not tested him on the Tower of London, he was tested using the Tower of Hanoi, which he proved completely incapable of tackling.

It would be interesting to test frontal patients on the random generation task. We have not yet done this systematically, but preliminary data from the few cases we have so far tested suggest that they find the task either very difficult or impossible. Milner (1982) reports the performance of frontal patients on a task that has certain features in common with random generation. It involves presenting the subject with a stack of cards, each of which has 6, 8, 10, or 12 stimuli displayed in a regular array. The same set of stimuli occur on each card in the pack, but in a different location. The subject's task is to go through the pack pointing to a different item on each card, avoiding repetitions of either item or location. For the frontal patients, the difficulty of the task increases with set size, with left frontals being significantly impaired with set sizes of 8 and above, while right frontals are significantly impaired only at set size 12. In one sense this task is analogous to random generation, with subjects required to choose a different response on each trial. However, whether it is this element of selection or the memory component that is crucial remains to be seen.

In conclusion, although the Norman and Shallice model is new, and the problem of the functioning of the frontal lobes a difficult and frustrating one, I would agree with Shallice in concluding that the model does offer a very promising theoretical framework for tackling this intriguing problem. Since frontal components almost certainly occur as one factor in many other syndromes including the dementias, there should be considerable scope for exploring its generality and power over the next few years.

Working memory and ageing

The section that follows examines the evidence for a defect of working memory in the elderly. In concentrating on working memory, I do not of course wish to suggest that this is the only process that deteriorates with age. Long-term or secondary memory shows clear impairment, while speed of reaction, muscular strength and the efficiency of the senses also declines. However, if working memory does play the important controlling role in human information processing that has often been suggested, any decline in its efficiency may well have particularly far-reaching consequences, since it would contribute to impaired performance across a wide range of skills and situations. The brief review that follows will concentrate on three questions. First, what STM tasks if any are comparatively spared in ageing, secondly what memory tasks show particularly striking impairment, and thirdly what more general information processing tasks show a decrement that could reasonably be attributed to a working memory deficit.

What is spared in ageing?

While long-term learning appears to be quite substantially impaired in the elderly, there is good evidence to suggest that the recency effect in free recall is relatively unimpaired (Craik 1968*b*; Raymond 1971; Spinnler *et al.* submitted).

The standard memory span procedure is another task in which the elderly perform relatively well, although there is a slight decline with age (Craik 1977; Spinnler *et al.* submitted); in contrast, the backward span procedure appears to be more susceptible to ageing effects (Bromley 1958).

In conclusion, the elderly seem to be relatively unimpaired on standard tests of STM, including recency, which as we saw earlier probably reflects the most passive form of storage. One might argue that these are tasks that place the least demands on the central executive, in contrast to the memory tasks to be described in the next section. It is perhaps worth pointing out that the tasks that are spared in the elderly are not necessarily spared simply because they are the least sensitive or least demanding. It will be recalled that both children with specific reading disabilities, and STM patients show an impairment in span, while being unimpaired on long-term learning. Hence, while accepting that ageing probably produces a wide range of impairments, the section that follows will explore the possibility that a decline in the capacity of the central executive is a particularly important feature of ageing.

Working memory and ageing: what is impaired?

In his classic work on ageing, Welford (1958) suggested that some aspects of short-term memory might be particularly sensitive to the effects of age. As we have seen above, some STM tasks are relatively unimpaired, but it has been known for many years that other aspects of STM might show a clear decrement. Inglis and Caird (1963) used Broadbent's dichotic listening test, presenting three items to each of the subjects' ears. They observed that recall of items from the ear that was tested first was unimpaired by age, whereas recall of the second group of three digits was quite sensitive to the age of the subject. Such a result is not attributable to acoustic masking, since comparable differences between first and second set recalled are found when one set of items is presented visually and the other auditorily.

Evidence that the need for active organisation of the material is critical comes from a study by Broadbent and Gregory (1965). They presented a mixture of letters and digits to each ear, but required the subject to recall

all the digits then all the letters or vice versa. This requirement to reorganize the material increased the sensitivity of the task to the effects of age.

Further evidence of the difficulty the elderly find in simultaneously storing and manipulating material comes from an ingenious study by Talland (1965). This task involved presenting the subject with a sequence of words of which every word in the first half of the sequence was repeated in a different order in the second, with the exception of one word that was not repeated. The subject's task was to repeat back the sequence, but to ensure that the single word is spoken last. This means that the subject not only has to listen and retain the incoming words, but in addition has to classify words as repeated or not repeated, and subsequently to reorganise recall accordingly. This proved to be much more sensitive to the effects of ageing than the standard span procedure. It would seem to have many of the characteristics desirable for a working memory span test (Daneman and Carpenter 1980), and as such could prove a useful measure of the capacity of the central executive. It has the further advantage over Daneman and Carpenter's measure that it does not have to be based on words; it could for example be run using numbers or shapes, thereby separating out the language component of the Daneman and Carpenter measure.

The tasks we have studied so far have all involved purely memory tasks, albeit memory tasks that require considerable manipulation of the material. Broadbent and Heron (1962) have shown that memory performance in the elderly is also particularly susceptible to distraction from a secondary nonmemory task, in this case visual search. Their study involved two separate tasks, one requiring the crossing out of certain target digits, while the second involved listening to sequences of ten letters and responding whenever a sequence was repeated. The elderly proved quite capable of performing the two tasks separately, but when the two were combined, their memory performance declined much more than did that of the young.

There is no doubt that the elderly do appear to have difficulty when memory tasks involve either complex manipulations of the material, or time-sharing between information from two sources. In reviewing the literature on memory and ageing Craik concludes "To the extent that the experimental (or real life) situation involves manipulation and reorganization of the input, Welford's (1958) suggestion that 'short-term memory' deficits underlie the poorer performance of older subjects on a variety of tasks has been borne out by the subsequent data" (Craik 1977, pp. 399–400).

What are the implications of these results for a model such as that of working memory? The memory tasks that show the clearest impairment are those which would be most likely to make demands on the central executive; the dichotic listening task requires concurrent storage, selection and output. Tasks using visual presentation may be particularly demanding since the relatively effective .but passive auditory store can not then be used except via subvocal recoding. The need to reorganize the input is something that would be expected to demand the intervention of the supervisor rather than a simple regurgitation of the material presented, and hence to show clear age effects. Talland's task is a particularly good example of one in which the subject is required to combine storage with the active manipulation of the material to be recalled, Indeed, Welford himself has subsequently revised his view, suggesting that working memory rather than primary memory is particularly vulnerable to the effects of ageing (Welford 1980), a conclusion that is also emphasised by Rabbitt (1981) in a later review of ageing and human performance.

Ageing, working memory and information processing

The essence of the concept of working memory lies in its implication that memory processes play an important role in nonmemory tasks. It ought therefore to follow that the effects of defective working memory should be revealed quite widely. I shall discuss a range of tasks suggesting that this is the case, relying heavily but not exclusively on the previously mentioned review by Rabbitt (1981).

In an ingenious series of experiments, Rabbitt and his colleagues investigated the often reported finding that the elderly show very slow performance on reaction time tasks. By combining information from both speed and accuracy, Rabbitt is able to show that all subjects tend to monitor their performance, gradually speeding up their responses until an error occurs, causing them to re-adjust their response criterion so as to minimize subsequent errors. In short, errors form a crucial feedback mechanism to tell the subject whether he is going fast enough; a subject who never makes errors is not going as fast as he could, just as a bridge player who always makes whatever contract he bids is bidding too conservatively. Rabbitt shows that the elderly are capable of responding just as rapidly as the young, but that their response to error feedback is much less finely tuned, leading to more errors and more extremely long reaction times. One could describe this phenomenon within a working memory model by saying that the supervisory system is performing less adequately in the elderly than in the young. Further evidence for poorer supervisory control of reaction time comes from another of Rabbitt's studies involving a serial reaction time task in which successive stimuli were nonrandom. Both young and old subjects were able to take advantage of cueing from a prior stimulus, however the elderly, unlike the young, were unable to take advantage of constraints extending across two or three successive responses.

Studies of visual search tell a similar story. Sanford and Maule (1973) studied the performance of young and old subjects on a task simulating industrial inspection. The subject was required to monitor three sources of possible signals, pressing one of three buttons in order to obtain information on the current state of that source. Probability of a signal appearing at the three sources differed markedly, and both young and old were able to report the differences in signal probability across sources relatively accurately. However, while the young used this information to improve their performance, detecting the signals on the more probable source more rapidly, the elderly made no use of this information. It appears to be the case then that the supervisory system is capable of registering information, a process that appears to be largely automatic, at least according to the work of Hasher and Zacks (1979), but no use is made of this by the elderly in controlling behaviour. It is as if the elderly supervisor can observe but not act.

The last result suggests that the elderly do not spontaneously control their behaviour on the basis of the best available information; it could of course either mean that they are incapable of doing so, or simply that they do not adopt the optimal strategy. Another of Rabbitt's (1981) studies bears on this issue by contrasting two visual search tasks, one requiring control on the basis of a relatively static memory load, while the second involves a more dynamic memory control. In both cases subjects were searching for the letters *A B C D E F G* and *H*. In the first condition, subjects scan a list of letters looking for any of these. In the second condition, the subject must first look for *A*, then for *B*, then for *C* and so forth. Speed and accuracy of performance of young and old subjects is shown on Table 10.1. Both young and old are able to perform the task very accurately when searching simultaneously for 8 letters, but in the successive scanning task when they are required to keep track of which letter they are seeking, the performance of the elderly deteriorates dramatically, with errors increasing from 1.6 per cent to 26.8 per cent.

TABLE 10.1

Twenty young people (aged 18 to 30 years) and twenty elderly people (aged 70 to 76 years) matched for verbal IQ scores searched displays of eight letters to locate any one of eight targets or eight different targets in turn (Rabbitt 1981)

	Searching for eight targets at once	Searching in turn for each of eight targets
Young: errors	1.4 per cent	6.3 per cent
Old: errors	1.6 per cent	26.8 per cent
Young: mean time per display	790 msec ($\sigma=84$)	630 msec ($\sigma=6\%$)
Old: mean time per display	972 msec ($\sigma=138$)	896 msec ($\sigma=152$)

Since there is no evidence of a strategy difference between young and old, it seems likely that the decrement is due to the decline in the capacity of the central executive with age.

One task which we have consistently suggested relies heavily on working memory is comprehension. This has been studied in the elderly by Cohen and Faulkner (1984) who ran one experiment in which subjects heard brief passages on a given theme and were then asked to answer questions. These could either be answered directly in terms of the information overtly given, or could depend on drawing plausible inferences from the material presented. Cohen and Faulkner looked at two samples of subjects, a group of highly educated subjects, of whom half were young and half were elderly, and a rather less carefully matched group of young and old subjects of lower educational achievement. The most confident conclusions were based on the more highly educated groups since they were matched for educational background and were more nearly similar in general life experience. The elderly proved to be not significantly impaired in recalling literal detail, but were much less likely to give correct answers to questions requiring inference. These effects occurred even more clearly in the less educated group.

A second study required subjects to listen to a series of statements and detect anomalies. These comprised statements which were inconsistent either with what had gone before or with general world knowledge. The elderly proved less good than the young at detecting both types of anomaly, a deficit that Cohen and Faulkner attribute to their difficulty in concurrently processing the spoken message and relating it to prior information either from the same passage or semantic memory.

A third and final study examined the capacity of young and old subjects to recall stories. Overall recall was poorer in the elderly, particularly in the poorly educated group. More importantly however, whereas the young subjects showed the standard tendency for recall to be much higher for important features of the story than for incidental details, this was not shown by the elderly subjects. It is interesting to compare this result with the comparable experiment carried out by Torgesen on learning disabled children that was described in the previous chapter. Unlike the elderly, the LD children showed a normal pattern of gist recall. This is of course what would be expected if the children with reading disability were suffering from impaired capacity of the articulatory loop, whereas the elderly are suffering from a central executive deficit.

In discussing the possibility that Norman and Shallice's supervisory attentional system might provide a good model for the central executive, I made the further suggestion that random generation might be an indication of the capacity of this system. If so, and if the elderly do indeed show impairment in functioning of the SAS, then random generation should be a task that is sensitive to the effects of age. Recalling that I had carried out such a study some 23 years ago I located it in a dusty and leperous looking box labelled 'Random Generation'. It was an experiment in which I had taken advantage of returning home for Christmas to test numerous aunts and uncles, using cousins as their controls. In each case the task was introduced and a short practice run was followed by the requirement to generate a hundred random letters at a rate of 1 per second.

The results were analysed using a Wilcoxon matched-pairs test in which each young subject was matched with an old subject from the same family, or on one or two occasions from a family of equivalent socio-economic status. There was a clear age effect, with some of the more elderly generating an extremely high proportion of stereotyped responses. As in all studies of ageing, substantially greater variance occurred among the elderly than among the young suggesting that some of my relatives were rather better preserved than others. It would be nice to do a retest, thereby turning it into a longitudinal study, but unfortunately only one of the elderly has survived (she was incidentally one of the best performers on the task of either group).

What conclusions can we draw from these nonmemory tasks? Reaction time and visual search, comprehension and random generation all have in common a need for performance to be closely controlled by something analogous to a central executive or attentional supervisor. In all cases, the aspect of performance that is most clearly impaired was that making most demands on such a supervisor. As far as it goes then the evidence is once again consistent with the hypothesis that the impaired capacity of the central executive places important constraints on the information processing of the elderly.

Working memory and dementia

'Dementia is a global impairment of higher cortical functions, including memory, the capacity to solve the problems of everyday living, the performance of learned perceptual-motor skills and the correct use of social skills and control of emotional reactions, in the absence of gross clouding of consciousness' (Anon. 1981). The condition is characteristically irreversible and progressive and affects between 5 and 15 per cent of the population over the age of 65. Bearing in mind its prevalence and the enormous strain it places on relatives and hospital services, it is a problem of major practical significance.

There is considerable evidence for neurochemical changes in the brains of demented patients, and intense activity is currently being directed towards identifying drugs that might arrest, or even reverse this neurochemical deficit. In addition however, there is a need to understand the psychological and behavioural consequences of dementia, both to provide a means of monitoring the success of any treatment, and also to allow early diagnosis. Memory deficit is one of the earliest and most significant signs of dementia, and it is probable that memory testing will play an important role in any test battery designed to detect dementia at an early stage. If any of the searches for suitable drugs are successful, then it will become extremely important to be able to produce tests that can be used to screen very large numbers of the elderly since it is probable that the earlier the disease is detected, the better the probability of successful treatment.

There are a number of different types of dementia, probably having somewhat different patterns of symptoms, so accurate diagnosis of patients studied is an important though difficult component of work in this area. The most common and most widely studied form of dementia however is senile dementia of the Alzheimer's type (SDAT).

I myself became indirectly involved in work in this area both through discussions with Robin Morris, a research student at the Applied Psychology Unit working on dementia, and through collaborative work with a group of neurologists and neuropsychologists at the University of Milan. Both Morris and the Italian group were interested in the possibility that the concept of working memory might be applicable in this area. One hypothesis that suggests itself is that senile dementia may be an exaggerated form of the deficit shown in normal ageing, which I have speculated might be attributable to a deficit of the central executive.

Morris began by exploring the articulatory loop system in demented (SDAT) patients, comparing their performance with normal elderly subjects. Working with demented patients is difficult since they tend to have shorter attention spans, to be easily distractable and often to have difficulty in comprehending instructions. An unselected sample of demented patients is likely to contain some who are so deteriorated as to perform badly on virtually any test given to them, and this will clearly militate against the attempt to separate out subcomponents of their deficit. An experiment that merely shows that demented patients are worse than controls is unlikely to be very enlightening. For this reason, Morris selected mild dements at an early stage of the disease.

In his first study Morris (1984) concentrated on exploring their utilization of the articulatory loop system. In general demented patients are less flexible and less adept at using strategies, and it seemed possible that utilization of the subvocal rehearsal process involved in the articulatory loop might be beyond their capacities (Miller 1971). Morris studied the effects of phonological similarity and word length coupled with auditory and visual presentation and articulatory suppression.

Given the difficulty of working with this sample of patients, the data are remarkably clean and clear-cut (Morris 1984). Although the overall memory span of the demented group was substantially less than that of the controls, they showed just as much evidence of the utilization of subvocal rehearsal. Both demented patients and normal elderly showed clear evidence of phonological similarity and word-length effects with both auditory and visual presentation. Articulatory suppression abolished both effects when presentation was visual, but abolished only the word-length effect when auditory presentation was used, as is the case with young normal subjects (Baddeley, Lewis, and Vallar 1984). In short, Morris' data indicate that mildly demented patients do have an impaired memory span, but that this is not due to their failure to use the articulatory loop subsystem.

In a further series of experiments, Morris (1986) studied the short-term retention of items using the Peterson paradigm. In the standard procedure whereby an item is presented and tested after a delay filled by some attention-demanding activity, Morris observed that the performance of his demented patients was consistently poorer than that of his elderly controls. Even more striking however was the observation that merely requiring the subject to suppress articulation during the delay caused forgetting in the case of the demented patients, while little or no forgetting occurred for the normal elderly controls, whose pattern of results was equivalent to that observed in young normal subjects by Vallar and Baddeley (1982). When the interval was unfilled, both demented patients and normals performed virtually perfectly.

Is this performance deficit due to the excessive reliance of demented patients on articulatory rehearsal, or is it due to the attentional demands of performing two tasks simultaneously? It seems likely that both of these factors are important. An additional condition was included in which subjects were required to tap on a table rather than suppress articulation. This manipulation had no effect on the performance of the controls, but produced a decrement in the performance of the dements that was clear, but less dramatic than that produced by articulatory suppression.

The memory deficit of SDAT patients is being explored further in a series of experiments carried out jointly by Spinnler and Della Sala, neuropsychologists from the University of Milan and myself. In one study (Spinnler *et al.* submitted) the performance of patients suffering from senile dementia of the Alzheimer type, elderly controls and young subjects was studied on verbal free recall, verbal span and spatial span, measured by the block-tapping task devised by Corsi (Milner 1971). The results showed that the SDAT patients were clearly impaired on memory span whether verbal or spatial, and showed a considerable decrement in the LTM component of the free recall curve. Their recency effect however was relatively unimpaired, indicating that this rather passive component of working memory was still operating effectively. Other studies have produced broadly similar results, with recency showing a comparatively slight impairment in performance in mild to moderate cases of dementia (Wilson, Baker, Fox, and Kazniak 1983). Miller (1975) reported a substantial decrement in recency in an earlier study, but this probably reflects his use of a more severely deteriorated group.

Evidence so far then suggests that although patients suffering from senile dementia exhibit a clear memory impairment, this is not due to a decrement in every aspect of memory, at least in mild cases. Morris's work shows that demented patients are quite capable of using the articulatory loop system, showing clear evidence of subvocal rehearsal. Despite this, overall level of performance on memory span is impaired. Similarly the results of Spinnler *et al.* indicate that the recency effect in SDAT patients is well preserved, in contrast to performance on the earlier part of the free recall curve or to their performance on a verbal or spatial memory span. One possibility is that such patients are suffering from a deficit in the operation of the central executive component of working memory.

We are at present conducting a series of experiments to explore the central executive deficit hypothesis further. One of the assumed functions of the central executive is to perform the scheduling and time sharing operations necessary if a subject is required to perform more than one task at the same time. Spinnler, Della Sala, Logie and myself are currently carrying out a series of experiments that examine the capacity of mild to moderate SDAT patients to time-share the performance of two concurrent tasks. We selected tasks that were either expected to be minimally interfering, for example a visuo-spatial tracking task and articulatory suppression, or tasks where we expected some interference due to both tasks involving the central executive. For example we combined tracking with concurrent digit span, adjusting the level of tracking difficulty so as to match the SDAT patients and their elderly controls, and in both cases selecting a digit sequence length that was just within span. Despite the fact that the two constituent tasks were made equally difficult for the two groups, combining them created particular difficulties for the SDAT patients, as a central executive interpretation would predict. Hence, although this line of research is still at an early stage, it seems promising, both theoretically in terms of its possible implications for the nature of the central executive, and practically, since it is likely to help in suggesting tests for detecting dementia at an early stage.

Normal ageing and dementia

While one may be justified in arguing for an involvement of the Central Executive in normal ageing, dementia and indeed the dysexecutive frontal lobe syndrome, this would at first sight appear to have a further implication, namely that these three groups of subjects should all behave in a similar manner. I would not wish to claim that this is the case. For example, preliminary work by my colleagues in Milan comparing the performance of SDAT patients with the very elderly indicates that performance is not equivalent. Nor is it the case that old people behave like dysexecutive frontal lobe cases. However, while this may imply that I am simply over-generalizing the Central Executive hypothesis, this need not be so. One might for example argue for a distinction between two aspects of the Central Executive, its total processing capacity, and its flexibility. Looked at from this viewpoint, the dysexecutive syndrome might be regarded as primarily a defect of the control processes, whereas normal ageing could be regarded as principally reflecting a drop in overall processing capacity. Looked at from this viewpoint, senile dementia could be seen as involving both of these deficits. Clearly, if such a distinction is to be any more than a *post hoc* means of defending the Central Executive hypothesis, we shall need to develop ways of independently measuring these proposed aspects of performance. Whether or not we are successful in doing so, it seems unlikely that the Central Executive will prove to be a simple unitary system. We clearly have a long way to go in understanding the processes that control working memory.

Conclusion

The central executive remains the most important but least understood component of working memory. I believe however that the Norman and Shallice model does offer a way of tackling this problem. Understanding the function of the frontal lobes, and the processes of normal ageing and of senile dementia seem likely to offer some stimulating and fruitful challenges of the potential applicability to the concept of working memory.

Epilogue

I began this book some two and a half years ago, as the preface indicates, with considerable hesitation. I find that I am ending it with a similar degree of reluctance. By now, the reluctance is not about whether or not I should write the book at all, that decision was taken, or took itself some time ago. It is clear that I should finish it and do so reasonably quickly, and yet the last stages appear to have been shot through with a feeling of incompleteness. There are so many points at which I feel that it could be improved by delaying until the next experiment has been run or until I have had time to survey some additional part of the literature, or to think through a particular problem. I have reached a point where I must finish the book now or leave it for a year, and it is very tempting to leave it. However, I know perfectly well that if I leave it, then next year there will be other experiments that are almost ready to be included, other problems I have almost thought through and another year's worth of literature of more or less direct relevance to what has already been written. I have decided therefore to accept that what I produce will literally be work in progress with all the shortcomings that that implies.

What are these shortcomings? The most obvious limitations are those of incompleteness. This is particularly clear in the case of the central executive, a component of the system that plays a crucial and central role and yet one which has received very little direct investigation and where theoretical development is minimal and at present largely speculative. We do not have good techniques for exploring the central executive, for example tasks that can reliably be assumed to place a heavy load on the executive without impairing performance on other subsystems. Furthermore, while one can speculate on the crucial role of the central executive in understanding the processes of ageing, dementia, the role of the frontal lobes, or indeed about its role in intelligence, exploring any of these is likely to prove difficult. Unlike the articulatory loop, where one can make relatively specific predictions, disruption of the operation of the central executive is likely to have general and far-reaching consequences. Consequently, a sceptic might argue that a pattern of dysfunction claimed to be characteristic of an impairment of the central executive merely represents a general overall deterioration in performance, with those aspects of performance that are most disrupted not being those that are most dependent on the central executive, but merely those that are the most difficult and hence most sensitive to general disruption.

Such arguments are not easy to counter, and should always be considered, at least as a null hypothesis against which any more complex model must be compared. The weakness of such a general cognitive impairment approach however stems from its reliance on some concept such as difficulty, which is typically specified only in a *post hoc* way. Hence such an interpretation becomes circular and ultimately unproductive. A concept such as the central executive should in the long run have an advantage over such an approach in that it does attempt to specify in more detail exactly what decrements are to be anticipated. While initially, such specification may be little more complex than that offered by the general impairment hypothesis, as the system is explored further, it should prove possible to characterize the central executive deficit more precisely. I believe that at this point it will begin to become clear that a general deficit hypothesis is too simple to account for the complexity of observed dysfunction. At present this is an act of faith, though I would claim that a comparable act of faith has proved justified in the case of the articulatory loop.

A somewhat more tractable problem is offered by the question of visual working memory. I believe that we have made real progress here in analysing at least some components of the system responsible for manipulating visual images, the visuo-spatial sketchpad. I am sure however that this is by no means the whole story. It seems likely that we are capable of manipulating and utilising non-spatial visual information such as colour and brightness; whether these are manipulated within the VSSP, or rely on some separate system remains an open question.

It also seems probable that a specialized subsystem occurs that is capable of storing visually presented lexical information such as sequences of letters. It seems likely that this relies on processes developed during the acquisition of reading. Is this system also part of the VSSP? I suspect not, since my assumption is that the sketchpad is specialized for storing visual information and is designed to hold spatially distributed information in parallel, being relatively poor at storing temporally ordered sequences. In contrast, the system involved in retaining letters appears to be quite capable of holding strings of successively presented items such as letters. In evolutionary terms, it seems very unlikely that man has been reading for long enough to allow his brain to have adapted to the specific demands of text, and hence such a system is presumably based on older systems, possibly initially developed in connection with the evolution of language.

There is then a great deal that we do not understand about visual working memory, but I think the problems are relatively tractable, and that progress will continue to be made over the coming years. One might reasonably argue however that the research carried out on the VSSP could have gone on independent of a working memory framework. The concept of a central executive is crucial to working memory, but little progress has been made, while recency, another aspect of the current model has a long history of being studied outside a working memory concept. What is the evidence that a working memory approach is in fact useful? The subcomponent which has been examined most vigorously within this framework is the articulatory loop, and it is to this that I think one should turn for evidence as to the general viability of a working memory approach to cognition.

The essence of the articulatory loop concept is that it appears to provide a simple coherent interpretation of a large body of well-established data. It is able to handle the phonological similarity effect, the word-length effect, articulatory suppression, the unattended speech effect and neuropsychological evidence, all within a system that assumes only two components, a phonological store and an articulatory control process. Individually, each of these phenomena can be explained in other ways, but I know of no coherent explanation that can handle all of this evidence with the possible exception of Barnard's (1985) much more complex interacting cognitive subsystem model.

The articulatory loop model is relatively imprecise, compared for example with STM models of the late 1960s, such as those presented in the volume *Models of Human Memory* edited by Norman in 1970. It is possible that a more precise mathematical formulation, or possibly a computer simulation would be fruitful. I myself lack the necessary technical skills to model the articulatory loop in detail, and am uncertain as to the value at this stage of more precise modelling. One advantage might be that a mathematical model or computer simulation could provide a stronger test of the model. For my own part I have relied on the more qualitative approach, attempting to fit patterns of well-established data, exploring apparent anomalies in greater depth. An example here is the question of the effects of articulatory suppression on the word-length and phonological similarity effects as a function of material presented visually or auditorily (Baddeley, Lewis, and Vallar 1984). The particular pattern of results obtained was crucial to separating the two components of the articulatory loop, the phonological store and the articulatory control process. Had the results not worked out in this way, it would have been necessary to modify the model quite seriously. It seems likely that the puzzle of why articulatory suppression appears to remove phono-logical coding when tested by memory, but does not prevent judgements of homophony or rhyme will present a similarly fruitful puzzle, that should tell us more about the underlying structure of the articulatory loop.

Suppose however that one provisionally at least accepts the articulatory loop as a useful means of summarizing the available data from a range of STM studies, does the system have any importance outside the laboratory? Or to quote my friend Jim Reason, 'Is the articulatory loop any more than a pimple on the face of cognition?'. It is certainly the case that patients such as P.V., discussed in Chapter 5 do seem to be able to cope with life relatively easily. Indeed more recently Campbell, Butterworth, and Howard (1985) have identified someone who appears to have been born with a very defective articulatory loop, and yet who speaks normally, lives a normal life and was able to obtain a very reasonable psychology degree.

However, although this subject was able to perform adequately on most comprehension tasks (Campbell, Butterworth, and Howard 1985), she nevertheless had experienced difficulty in learning to read, having little or no success when taught by a phonic method, but subsequently succeeding when taught by a look-say procedure that minimizes the reliance on phonological coding. Moreover, having learnt to read she is still by no means a normal reader, resembling a phonological dyslexic in being unable to read non-words such as *plic*, unless they are very similar to words with which she is familiar (Campbell and Butterworth 1985). It seems likely then that the articulatory loop is extremely useful in learning to read, although of less critical importance once reading has been acquired. It is perhaps also worth pointing out that although this subject's span was short, she could still process and hold 3 to 4 items which is of course very different from being totally without the aid of an articulatory loop. Indeed it is interesting to speculate whether someone who was completely devoid of phonological input store would be able to comprehend even single words.

Other evidence suggests that although the articulatory loop may not be by any means the most important component of working memory, nevertheless it does play a role in certain types of fluent reading (Baddeley, Eldridge, and Lewis 1981), and in learning to read, with dyslexia typically being associated with impaired memory span (see Chapter 9). There is furthermore evidence that working memory plays an important role in mental arithmetic (Hitch 1978) and in counting, where Logie and Baddeley (in preparation) have shown that articulatory suppression impairs accuracy substantially in that the majority of responses are incorrect, though not catastrophically so, in that erroneous responses are typically reasonably close to the correct total. A much more dramatic disruption appears to occur in the case of children, for whom the counting skill is much less overlearned (Hitch personal communication).

Finally, the articulatory loop has proved a very useful model for studying the effects of unattended speech, where in contrast to the very small effects of noise on performance, speech proves to have a very clear disrupting effect on memory for visually presented items (Salame and Baddeley 1982, 1983). It is perhaps worth noting that in addition to its implications for the practical question of how noise might influence behaviour, this phenomenon also has implications for the understanding of speech perception. Since unattended speech appears to have access to the phonological store, while white noise does not, this implies some form of filtering. Such a filter could be extremely useful in assisting the perception of speech against the background of non-speech noise. The unattended speech effect would seem to offer a very useful tool for exploring the characteristics of this filter, a task which Salame and I have already begun. In one study for example we have examined the effects of unattended vocal and orchestral music on memory for visually presented digits. We observed clear disruption from vocal music together with a small but significant disruption from orchestral music. Since orchestral music has a relatively small effect, it allows us to rule out many acoustic features which might appear to be likely to be important for the assumed noise filter.

In conclusion then I would like to suggest that in that area where the working memory approach has been explored most vigorously, namely the articulatory loop, the approach has proved fruitful, not only in producing a simple model accounting for a wide range of laboratory phenomena, but also in its implications outside the original focus of interest, implications that are of both practical and theoretical significance. Hence, while it is important not to exaggerate what has been achieved, I believe that the concept of working memory has served us well. For a decade it has provided a coherent framework for exploring the role of human memory in many aspects of cognition both within the laboratory and in the world outside. Both the general concept and the specific model of working memory show every sign of continuing to be fruitful.

References

Adams, J. A. and Dijkstra, S. (1966). Short-term memory for motor responses. *Journal of Experimental Psychology* **71**, 2.

Allport, D. A. (1980). Patterns and actions: Cognitive mechanisms are content-specific. In *Cognitive psychology: new directions* (G. Claxton, ed.) pp. 26–64. Routledge and Kegan Paul, London.

Allport, D. A. (1984). Auditory-verbal short-term memory and conduction aphasia. In *Attention and performance X* (H. Bouma and D. G. Bouwhuis, eds.) pp. 313–26. Erlbaum, London.

Allport, D. A., Antonis, B. and Reynolds, P. (1972). On the division of attention: A disproof of the single channel hypothesis. *Quarterly Journal of Experimental Psychology* **24**, 225–35.

Anderson, J. and Hinton, G. (1981). Models of information processing. In *Parallel models of associative memory* (G. Hinton and J. Anderson, eds.) pp. 9–48. Erlbaum, Hillsdale, N.J.

Anon. (1981). Organic mental impairment of the elderly. *Journal of the Royal College of Physicians of London* **15**, 142, 167.

Antrobus, J. S., Antrobus, J. S. and Singer, J. L. (1964). Eye movements accompanying day dreaming, visual imagery and thought suppression. *Journal of Abnormal and Social Psychology* **69**, 244–52.

Atkinson, R. C. and Shiffrin, R. M. (1968). Human memory: A proposed system and its control processes. In *The psychology of learning and motivation: advances in research and theory Vol. 2* (K. W. Spence, ed.) pp. 89–195. Academic Press, New York.

Atkinson, R. C. and Shiffrin, R. M. (1971). The control of short-term memory. *Scientific American* **225**, 82–90.

Atwood, G. E. (1971). An experimental study of visual imagination and memory. *Cognitive Psycholgoy* **2**, 290–9.

Baddeley, A. D. (1963). A Zeigarnik-like effect in the recall of anagram solutions. *Quarterly Journal of Experimental Psychology* **15**, 63–4.

Baddeley, A. D. (1966*a*). Short-term memory for word sequences as a function of acoustic, semantic and formal similarity. *Quarterly Journal of Experimental Psychology* **18**, 362–5.

Baddeley, A. D. (1966*b*). The influence of acoustic and semantic similarity on long-term memory for word sequences. *Quarterly Journal of Experimental Psychology* **18**, 302–9.

Baddeley, A. D. (1966*c*). The capacity for generating information by randomization. *Quarterly Journal of Experimental Psychology* **18**, 119–29.

Baddeley, A. D. (1968*a*). Delay and the digit probe. *Psychonomic Science* **12**, 147–8.

Baddeley, A. D. (1968*b*). A three-minute reasoning test based on grammatical transformation. *Psychonomic Science* **10**, 341–2.

Baddeley, A. D. (1970*a*). Effects of acoustic and semantic similarity on short-term paired-associate learning. *British Journal of Psychology* **61**, 335–43.

Baddeley, A. D. (1970*b*). Estimating the short-term component in free recall. *Brit-*

ish Journal of Psychology **61**, 13–15.

Baddeley, A. D. (1972). Retrieval rules and semantic coding in short-term memory. *Psychological Bulletin* **78**, 379–85.

Baddeley, A. D. (1976). *The psychology of memory.* Basic Books, New York.

Baddeley, A. D. (1979). Working memory and reading. In *Processing of visible language* (P. A. Kolers, M. E. Wrolstad, and H. Bouma, eds.) pp. 355–70. Plenum Publishing Corporation, New York.

Baddeley, A. D. (1981). The cognitive psychology of everyday life. *British Journal of Psychology* **72**, 257–69.

Baddeley, A. D. (1982*a*). Amnesia: A minimal model and an interpretation. In *Human memory and amnesia* (L. S. Cermak, ed.) pp. 305–36. Erlbaum, Hillsdale, N.J.

Baddeley, A. D. (1982*b*). Domains of recollection. *Psychological Review* **89**, 708–29.

Baddeley, A. D. (1982*c*). Implications of neuropsychological evidence for theories of normal memory. *Philosophical Transactions of the Royal Society London* B **298**, 59–72.

Baddeley, A. D. and Dale, H. C. A. (1966). The effect of semantic similarity on retroactive interference in long- and short-term memory. *Journal of Verbal Learning and Verbal Behavior* **5**, 417–20.

Baddeley, A. D., Eldridge, M. and Lewis, V. J. (1981). The role of subvocalization in reading. *Quarterly Journal of Experimental Psychology* **33**, 439–54.

Baddeley, A. D., Eldridge, M., Lewis, V., and Thomson, N. (1984). Attention and retrieval from long-term memory. *Journal of Experimental Psychology: General* **113**, 518–40.

Baddeley, A. D., Grant, W., Wight, E., and Thomson, N. (1975). Imagery and visual working memory. In *Attention and performance V* (P. M. A. Rabbitt and S. Dornic, eds.) pp. 205–17. Academic Press, London.

Baddeley, A. D. and Hitch, G. J. (1974). Working memory. In *Recent advances in learning and motivation Vol. VIII* (G. Bower, ed.) pp. 47–90. Academic Press, New York.

Baddeley, A. D. and Hitch, G. J. (1977). Recency re-examined. In *Attention and performance VI* (S. Dornic, ed.) pp. 647–67. Erlbaum, Hillsdale, N.J.

Baddeley, A. D. and Hull, A. (1979). Prefix and suffix effects: Do they have a common basis? *Journal of Verbal Learning and Verbal Behavior* **18**, 129–40.

Baddeley, A. D. and Levy, B. A. (1971). Semantic coding and short-term memory. *Journal of Experimental Psychology* **89**, 132–6.

Baddeley, A. D. and Lewis, V. J. (1981). Inner active processes in reading: The inner voice, the inner ear and the inner eye. In *Interactive processes in reading* (A. M. Lesgold and C. A. Perfetti, eds.) pp. 107–29. Erlbaum, Hillsdale, N.J.

Baddeley, A. D. and Lewis, V. J. (1984). When does rapid presentation enhance digit span? *Bulletin of the Psychonomic Society* **22**, 403–5.

Baddeley, A. D., Lewis, V. J., and Vallar, G. (1984). Exploring the articulatory loop. *Quarterly Journal of Experimental Psychology* **36**, 233–52.

Baddeley, A. D. and Lieberman, K. (1980). Spatial working memory. In *Attention and performance VIII* (R. Nickerson, ed.) pp. 521–39. Erlbaum, Hillsdale, N.J.

Baddeley, A. D., Logie, R. H., and Ellis, N. C. Characteristics of developmental dyslexia. Manuscript in preparation.

Baddeley, A. D., Logie, R. H., Nimmo-Smith, M. I. and Brereton, N. (1985). Components of fluent reading, *Journal of Memory and Language* **24**, 119–31.

Baddeley, A. D. and Scott, D. (1971). Short-term forgetting in the absence of proactive inhibition. *Quarterly Journal of Experimental Psychology* **23**, 275–83.

Baddeley, A. D., Scott, D., Drynan, R., and Smith, J. C. (1969). Short-term memory and the limited capacity hypothesis. *British Journal of Psychology* **60**, 51–5.

Baddeley, A. D., Thomson, N., and Buchanan, M. (1975). Word length and the structure of short-term memory. *Journal of Verbal Learning and Verbal Behavior* **14**, 575–89.

Baddeley, A. D. and Warrington, E. K. (1970). Amnesia and the distinction between long- and short-term memory. *Journal of Verbal Learning and Verbal Behavior* **9**, 176–89.

Baddeley, A. D. and Wilson, B. (1985). Phonological coding and short-term memory in patients without speech. *Journal of Memory and Language* **24**, 490–502.

Baddeley, A. D. and Wilson, B. Amnesia, autobiographical memory and confabulation. To appear in *Autobiographical Memory* (D. Rubin, ed.). In press. Cambridge University Press, New York.

Baddeley, A. D. and Woodhead, M. M. (1982). Depth of processing, context, and face recognition. *Canadian Journal of Psychology* **36**, 148–64.

Barnard, P. (1985). Interacting cognitive subsystems: A psycholinguistic approach to short-term memory. In *Progress in the psychology of language Vol. 2* (A. Ellis, ed.) pp. 197–258. Lawrence Erlbaum, London.

Baron, J. (1973). Phonemic stage not necessary for reading. *Quarterly Journal of Experimental Psychology* **25**, 241–6.

Basso, A., Spinnler, H., Vallar, G., and Zanobio, E. (1982). Left hemisphere damage and selective impairment of auditory verbal short-term memory: A case study. *Neuropsychologia* **20**, 263–74.

Battig, W. F. and Montague, W. E. (1969). A replication and extension of the Connecticut Category Norms. *Journal of Experimental Psychology* **80**, No 3, Pt. 2.

Bekerian, D. A. and Baddeley, A. D. (1980). Saturation advertising and the repetition effect. *Journal of Verbal Learning and Verbal Behavior* **19**, 17–25.

Belbin, E. (1950). The influence of interpolated recall on recognition. *Quarterly Journal of Experimental Psychology* **2**, 163–9.

Besner, D. and Davelaar, E. (1982). Basic processes in reading: two phonological codes. *Canadian Journal of Psychology* **36**, 701–11.

Besner, D., Davies, J., and Daniels, S. (1981). Phonological processes in reading: the effects of concurrent articulation. *Quarterly Journal of Experimental Psychology* **33**, 415–38.

Bjork, R. A. and Whitten, W. B. (1974). Recency-sensitive retrieval processes. *Cognitive Psychology* **6**, 173–89.

Boder, E. (1971). Developmental dyslexia: Prevailing diagnostic concepts and a new diagnostic approach. In *Progress in learning disabilities Vol. 2* (H. R. Myklebust, ed.). Grune and Stratton, New York.

Boder, E. (1973). Developmental dyslexia: a diagnostic approach based on three atypical reading–spelling patterns. *Developmental Medicine and Child Neurology* **15**, 663–87.

Bower, G. H. and Karlin, M. B. (1974). Depth of processing pictures of faces and recognition memory. *Journal of Experimental Psychology* **103**, 751–7.

Bradley, L. and Bryant, P. E. (1983). Categorising sounds and learning to read: A causal connection. *Nature* **301**, 419–21.

Bradley, M. H., Glenberg, A. M., and Kraus, T. A. (Personal Communication). Very long-term recency. Unpublished manuscript.

Broadbent, D. E. (1957). A mechanical model for human attention and immediate memory. *Psychological Review* **64**, 205–15.

Broadbent, D. E. (1958). *Perception and communication*. Pergamon Press, London.

Broadbent, D. E. (1979). Human performance and noise. In *Handbook of noise control* (C. M. Harris, ed.). McGraw Hill, New York.

Broadbent, D. E. (1982). Task combination and selective intake of information. *Acta Psychologica* **50**, 253–90.

Broadbent, D. E. (1984). The Maltese Cross: A new simplistic model for memory. *Behavioral and Brain Sciences* **7**, 55–94.

Broadbent, D. E. and Gregory, M. (1965). Some confirmatory results on age differences in memory for simultaneous stimulation. *British Journal of Psychology* **56**, 77–80.

Broadbent, D. E. and Heron, A. (1962). Effects of a subsidiary task on performance involving immediate memory in younger and older men. *British Journal of Psychology* **53**, 189–98.

Broadbent, D. E., Vines, R., and Broadbent, M. (1978). Recency effects in memory as a function of modality of intervening events. *Psychological Research* **40**, 5–13.

Bromley, D. B. (1958). Some effects of age on short-term learning and memory. *Journal of Gerontology* **13**, 398–406.

Brooks, D. N. (1975). Long- and short-term memory in head-injured patients. *Cortex* **11**, 329–40.

Brooks, L. R. (1967). The suppression of visualization by reading. *Quarterly Journal of Experimental Psychology* **19**, 289–99.

Brooks, L. R. (1968). Spatial and verbal components in the act of recall. *Canadian Journal of Psychology* **22**, 349–68.

Brown, J. (1958). Some tests of the decay theory of immediate memory. *Quarterly Journal of Experimental Psychology* **10**, 12–21.

Bugelski, B. R. (1962). Presentation time, total time, and mediation in paired-associate learning. *Journal of Experimental Psychology* **63**, 409–12.

Byrne, B. (1974). Item concreteness vs. spatial organization as predictors of visual imagery. *Memory and Cognition* **2**, 53–9.

Byrne, B. and Shea, P. (1979). Semantic and phonemic memory in beginning readers. *Memory and Cognition* **7**, 333–41.

Campbell, R. and Butterworth, B. (1985). Phonological dyslexia and dysgraphia in a highly literate subject: a developmental case with associated deficits of phonemic processing and awareness. *Quarterly Journal of Experimental Psychology* **37A**, 435–76.

Campbell, R., Butterworth, B., and Howard, D. (1985). The uses of immediate memory. Paper presented at Experimental Psychology Society Meeting, London, January 3rd, 1985.

Campbell, R. and Dodd, B. (1980). Hearing by eye. *Quarterly Journal of Experimental Psychology* **32**, 85–99.

Carpenter, P. A. and Just, M. A. (1977). Reading comprehension as the eye sees it. In *Cognitive processes in comprehension* (M. A. Just and P. Carpenter, eds.) pp. 109–39. Erlbaum, Hillsdale, N.J.

Carter, R. C., Kennedy, R. S., and Bittner, A. S. (1981). Grammatical reasoning: A stable performance yard stick. *Human Factors* **23**, 587–92.

Case, R. D., Kurland, D. M., and Goldberg, J. (1982). Operational efficiency and the growth of short-term memory span. *Journal of Experimental Child Psychology* **33**, 386–404.

Cavanagh, P. (1977). Locus of rotation effects in recognition. *Bulletin of the Psychonomic Society* **10**, 152–4.

Cermak, L. S. (1982). The long and short of it in amnesia. In *Human memory and amnesia* (L. S. Cermak, ed.) pp. 43–60. Erlbaum, Hillsdale, N.J.

Cermak, L. S., Butters, N., and Moreines, J. (1974). Some analyses of the verbal encoding deficit of alcoholic Korsakoff patients. *Brain and Language* **1**, 141–50.

Chi, M. T. H. (1978). Knowledge structures and memory development. In *Children's thinking: what develops?* (R. S. Siegler, ed.). Erlbaum, Hillsdale, N.J.

Cohen, N. J. and Squire, L. R. (1980). Preserved learning and retention of pattern-analysing skills in amnesia: Dissociation of knowing and knowing that. *Science* **210**, 207–10.

Cohen, G. and Faulkner, D. (1984). Memory for text. Some age differences in the nature of the information that is retained after listening to texts. In *Attention and performance X: control of language processes* (H. Bouma and D. G. Bouwhuis, eds.). Erlbaum, London.

Colle, H. A. (1980). Auditory encoding in visual short-term recall: Effects of noise intensity and spatial location. *Journal of Verbal Learning and Verbal Behavior* **19**, 722–35.

Colle, H. A. and Welsh, A. (1976). Acoustic masking in primary memory. *Journal of Verbal Learning and Verbal Behavior* **15**, 17–32.

Collins, A. M. and Loftus, E. F. (1975). A spreading-activation theory of semantic processing. *Psychological Review* **82**, 407–28.

Collins, A. M. and Quillian, M. R. (1969). Retrieval time from semantic memory. *Journal of Verbal Learning and Verbal Behavior* **8**, 240–7.

Coltheart, M. (1983). Iconic memory. *Philosophical Transactions of the Royal Society London* B **302**, 283–94.

Coltheart, M., Davelaar, E., Jonasson, J. T., and Besner, D. (1977). Phonological coding and lexical access. In *Attention and performance VI* (S. Dornic, ed.) pp. 535–55. Erlbaum, Hillsdale, N.J.

Coltheart, M. and Patterson, K. The assessment of acquired disorders of reading. Manuscript in preparation.

Coltheart, M., Patterson, K. E., and Marshall, J. C. (eds.) (1980). *Deep dyslexia*. Routledge and Kegan Paul, London.

Conrad, C. (1972). Cognitive economy in semantic memory. *Journal of Experimental Psychology* **92**, 149–54.

Conrad, R. (1958). Accuracy of recall using keyset and telephone dial, and the effect of a prefix digit. *Journal of Applied Psychology* **42**, 285–8.

Conrad, R. (1960a). Very brief delay of immediate recall. *Quarterly Journal of Experimental Psychology* **12**, 45–7.

Conrad, R. (1960b). Letter sorting machines: paced, "lagged" or unpaced? *Ergonomics* **3**, 149–53.

Conrad, R. (1964). Acoustic confusion in immediate memory. *British Journal of*

Psychology **55**, 75–84.

Conrad, R. (1967). Interference or decay over short retention intervals? *Journal of Verbal Learning and Verbal Behavior* **6**, 49–54.

Conrad, R. (1970). Short-term memory processes in the deaf. *British Journal of Psychology* **61**, 179–95.

Conrad, R. (1971). The chronology of the development of covert speech in children. *Developmental Psychology* **5**, 398–405.

Conrad, R. (1972). Speech and reading. In *Language by ear and by eye* (J. F. Kavanagh and I. G. Mattingley, eds.) pp. 205–40. M.I.T. Press, Cambridge, Mass.

Conrad, R. and Hull, A. J. (1964). Information, acoustic confusion and memory span. *British Journal of Psychology* **55**, 429–32.

Conrad, R. and Hull, A. J. (1968). Input modality and the serial position curve in short-term memory. *Psychonomic Science* **10**, 135–6.

Cooper, E. C. and Pantle, A. J. (1967). The total time hypothesis in verbal learning. *Psychological Bulletin* **68**, 221–34.

Cooper, L. A. (1976). Demonstration of a mental analog of an external rotation. *Perception and Psychophysics* **19**, 296–302.

Cooper, L. A. and Podgorny, P. (1976). Mental transformations and visual comparison processes: Effects of complexity and similarity. *Journal of Experimental Psychology: Human Perception and Performance* **2**, 503–14.

Corcoran, D. W. J. (1967). Acoustic factor in proof reading. *Nature* **214**, 851–2.

Craik, F. I. M. (1968a). Types of error in free recall. *Psychonomic Science* **10**, 353–4.

Craik, F. I. M. (1968b). Two components in free recall. *Journal of Verbal Learning and Verbal Behavior* **7**, 996–1004.

Craik, F. I. M. (1970). The fate of primary memory items in free recall. *Journal of Verbal Learning and Verbal behavior* **9**, 143–8.

Craik, F. I. M. (1971). Primary memory. *British Medical Bulletin* **27**, 232–6.

Craik, F. I. M. (1977). Age differences in human memory. In *Handbook of the psychology of ageing* (J. E. Birren and K. W. Schaie, eds.). von Nostrand Reinhold, New York.

Craik, F. I. M. and Levy, B. A. (1970). Semantic and acoustic information in primary memory. *Journal of Experimental Psychology* **86**, 77–82.

Craik, F. I. M. and Levy, B. A. (1977). The concept of primary memory. In *Handbook of learning and cognitive processes Vol. IV* (W. K. Estes, ed.).

Craik, F. I. M. and Lockhart, R. S. (1972). Levels of processing: A framework for memory research. *Journal of Verbal Learning and Verbal Behavior* **11**, 671–84.

Craik, F. I. M. and Tulving, E. (1975). Depth of processing and the retention of words in episodic memory. *Journal of Experimental Psychology: General* **104**, 268–94.

Craik, F. I. M. and Watkins, M. J. (1973). The role of rehearsal in short-term memory. *Journal of Verbal Learning and Verbal Behavior* **12**, 599–607.

Crowder, R. G. (1976). *Principles of learning and memory.* Erlbaum, Hillsdale, N.J.

Crowder, R. G. (1982a). The demise of short-term memory. *Acta Psychologica* **50**, 291–323.

Crowder, R. G. (1982*b*). Disinhibition of masking in auditory sensory memory. *Memory and Cognition* **10**, 424–83.

Crowder, R. G. (1983). The purity of auditory memory. *Philosophical Transactions of the Royal Society London* B **302**, 251–65.

Crowder, R. G. and Morton, J. (1969). Precategorical acoustic storage (PAS). *Perception and Psychophysics* **5**, 365–73.

Dale, H. C. A. (1973). Short-term memory for visual information. *British Journal of Psychology* **64**, 1–8.

Dale, H. C. A. and Baddeley, A. D. (1969). Acoustic similarity in long-term paired-associate learning. *Psychonomic Science* **16**, 209–11.

Dalezman, J. J. (1976). Effects of output order on immediate, delayed and final recall performance. *Journal of Experimental Psychology: Human Learning and Memory* **2**, 597–608.

Daneman, M. and Carpenter, P. A. (1980). Individual differences in working memory and reading. *Journal of Verbal Learning and Verbal Behavior* **19**, 450–66.

Daneman, M. and Carpenter, P. A. (1983). Individual differences in integrating information between and within sentences. *Journal of Experimental Psychology: Learning, Memory and Cognition* **9**, 561–84.

Davies, F. (1973). *Teaching reading in early England*. Pitman, London.

Davis, R., Moray, N., and Treisman, A. (1961). Imitative responses and rate of gain of information. *Quarterly Journal of Experimental Psychology* **13**, 78–90.

Dempster, F. N. (1981). Memory span: Sources of individual and developmental differences. *Psychological Bulletin* **89**, 63–100.

De Renzi, E. (1982). Memory disorders following focal cortical damage. *Philosophical Transactions of the Royal Society London* B **298**, 73–83.

Eddy, J. K. and Glass, A. L. (1981). Reading and listening to high and low imagery sentences. *Journal of Verbal Learning and Verbal Behavior* **20**, 333–45.

Ellis, N. C. and Hennelley, R. A. (1980). A bilingual word-length effect: Implications for intelligence testing and the relative ease of mental calculation in Welsh and English. *British Journal of Psychology* **71**, 43–52.

Ellis, N. C. and Miles, T. R. (1978). Visual information processing in dyslexic children. In *Practical aspects of memory* (M. M. Gruneberg, P. E. Morris, and R. N. Sykes, eds.). Academic Press, London.

Ellis, N. C. and Miles, T. R. (1981). A lexical encoding deficiency I: Experimental evidence. In *Dyslexia research and its applications to education* (G. Th. Pavlidis and T. R. Miles, eds.) pp. 177–216. John Wiley, Chichester.

Ericsson, K. A., Chase, W. G., and Falloon, S. (1980). Acquisition of a memory skill. *Science* **208**, 1181–2.

Estes, W. K. (1973). Phonemic coding and rehearsal in short-term memory. *Journal of Verbal Learning and Verbal Behavior* **12**, 360–72.

Feuchtwanger, E. (1923). Die Funktionen des Stirnhirns: Ihre Pathologie und Psychologie. *Monogr. Gesmtgeb. Neurol. Psychiatr. (Berlin)* **38**, 4–194.

Fox, B. and Routh, D. A. (1983). Reading disability, phonemic analysis, and a disphonetic spelling: A follow-up study. *Journal of Clinical and Child Psychology* **12**, 28–32.

Frankish, C. (1985). Modality-specific grouping effects in short-term memory. *Journal of Memory and Language* **24**, 200–9.

Galton, F. (1883). *Enquiries into human faculty and its development*. Macmillan,

London.

Gardiner, J. M. (1983). On recency and echoic memory. *Philosophical Transactions of the Royal Society London* B **302**, 267–82.

Glanzer, M. (1972). Storage mechanisms in recall. In *The psychology of learning and motivation: advances in research and theory, Vol. V* (G. H. Bower, ed.). Academic Press, New York.

Glanzer, M. and Cunitz, A. R. (1966). Two storage mechanisms in free recall. *Journal of Verbal Learning and Verbal Behavior* **5**, 351–60.

Glanzer, M., Dorfman, D., and Kaplan, B. (1981). Short-term storage in the processing of text. *Journal of Verbal Learning and Verbal behavior* **20**, 656–70.

Glanzer, M., Gianutsos, R., and Dubin, S. (1969). The removal of items from short-term storage. *Journal of Verbal Learning and Verbal Behavior* **8**, 435–47.

Glanzer, M., Koppenaal, L., and Nelson, R. (1972). Effects of relations between words on short-term storage and long-term storage. *Journal of Verbal Learning and Verbal Behavior* **11**, 403–16.

Glass, A. L., Eddy, J. K., and Schwanenflugel, J. (1980). The verification of high and low imagery sentences. *Journal of Experimental Psychology: Human Learning and Memory* **6**, 692–704.

Glenberg, A. M., Bradley, M. M., Stevenson, J. A., Kraus, T. A., Tkachuk, M. J., Gretz, A. L., Fish, J. H., and Turpin, B. A. M. (1980). A two-process account of long-term serial position effects. *Journal of Experimental Psychology: Human Learning and Memory* **6**, 355–69.

Glenberg, A., Smith, S. M., and Green, C. (1977). Type I rehearsal: Maintenance and more. *Journal of Verbal Learning and Verbal Behavior* **16**, 339–52.

Goldstein, K. (1936). The significance of the frontal lobes for mental performance. *Journal of Neurology and Psychopathology* **17**, 27–40.

Graf, P. and Mandler, G. (1984). Activation makes words more accessible, but not necessarily more retrievable. *Journal of Verbal Learning and Verbal Behavior* **23**, 553–68.

Halford, G. S. and Wilson, W. H. (1980). A category theory approach to cognitive development. *Cognitive Psychology* **12**, 356–411.

Hall, J. W., Wilson, K. P., Humphreys, M. S., Tinzmann, M. B., and Bowyer, P. M. (1983). Phonemic similarity effects in good vs poor readers. *Memory and Cognition* **11**, 520–7.

Hardyk, C. D. and Petrinovitch, L. R. (1970). Subvocal speech and comprehension level as a function of the difficulty level of reading material. *Journal of Verbal Learning and Verbal Behavior* **9**, 647–52.

Hasher, L. and Zacks, R. T. (1979). Automatic and effortful processes in memory. *Journal of Experimental Psychology: General* **108**, 356–88.

Hatano, G. and Osawa, K. (1983). Digit memory of grand experts in abacus-derived mental calculation. *Cognition* **15**, 95–110.

Hebb, D. O. (1949). *Organization of behavior.* Wiley, New York.

Hebb, D. O. (1968). Concerning imagery. *Psychological Review* **75**, 466–77.

Hick, W. E. (1952). On the rate of gain of information. *Quarterly Journal of Experimental Psychology* **4**, 11–26.

Hinton, G. (1979). Some demonstrations of the effects of structural descriptions in mental imagery. *Cognitive Science* **3**, 231–50.

Hinton, G. E. (1981). Implementing semantic networks in parallel hardware. In *Parallel models of associative memory* (G. E. Hinton and J. A. Anderson, eds.)

pp. 168–87. Erlbaum, Hillsdale, N.J.

Hinton, G. and Anderson, J. (1981). *Parallel models of associative memory.* Erlbaum, Hillsdale, N.J.

Hinton, G. and Parsons, L. M. (1981). Frames of reference and mental imagery. In *Attention and performance IX.* (J. Long and A. D. Baddeley, eds.). Erlbaum, Hillsdale, N.J.

Hintzman, D. L. (1967). Articulatory coding in short-term memory. *Journal of Verbal Learning and Verbal Behavior* **6**, 312–16.

Hitch, G. J. (1978). The role of short-term working memory in mental arithmetic. *Cognitive Psychology* **10**, 302–23.

Hitch, G. J. (1984). Short-term memory processes in humans and animals. In *Memory in humans and animals* (A. R. Mayes, ed.). van Nostrand, London.

Hitch, G. J. and Baddeley, A. D. (1976). Verbal reasoning and working memory. *Quarterly Journal of Experimental Psychology* **28**, 603–21.

Hitch, G. J. and Halliday, M. S. (1983). Working memory in children. *Philosophical Transactions of the Royal Society London* B **302**, 325–40.

Hitch, G. J., Halliday, M. S., and Littler, J. (1984). Memory span and the speed of mental operations. Paper presented at the joint Experimental Psychology Society/Netherlands Psychonomic Foundation Meeting, Amsterdam.

Hitch, G. J., Rejman, M. J., and Turner, N. C. (1980). A new perspective on the recency effect. Paper presented at the Experimental Psychology Society July Meeting, Cambridge.

Hockey, G. R. J. (1973). Rate of presentation in running memory and direct manipulation of input processing strategies. *Quarterly Journal of Experimental Psychology* **25**, 104–11.

Horowitz, L. M. and Prytulak, L. S. (1969). Redintegrative memory. *Psychological Review* **76**, 519–31.

Huey, E. B. (1908). *The psychology and pedagogy of reading.* Macmillan, New York.

Hulme, C. (1981). *Reading retardation and multi-sensory teaching.* Routledge and Kegan Paul, London.

Hulme, C., Thomson, N., Muir, C., and Lawrence, A. (1984). Speech rate and the development of short-term memory span. *Journal of Experimental Child Psychology* **38**, 241–53.

Hunt, E., Frost, N., and Lunneborg, C. (1973). Individual differences in cognition: A new approach to intelligence. In *The psychology of learning and motivation Vol. 7* (G. Bower, ed.) pp. 87–123. Academic Press, New York.

Hyde, T. S. and Jenkins, J. J. (1969). Differential effects of incidental tasks on the organization of recall of a list of highly associated words. *Journal of Experimental Psychology* **83**, 472–81.

Indow, T. and Togano, K. (1970). On retrieving sequence from long-term memory. *Psychological Review* **77**, 317–31.

Inglis, J. and Caird, W. K. (1963). Age differences in successive responses to simultaneous stimulation. *Canadian Journal of Psychology* **17**, 98–105.

Jackson, M. D. and McClelland, J. L. (1979). Processing determinants of reading speed. *Journal of Experimental Psychology: General* **108**, 151–81.

Jacoby, L. L. and Witherspoon, D. (1982). Remembering without awareness. *Canadian Journal of Psychology* **36**, 300–24.

James, W. (1890). *The principles of psychology.* Holt, Rinehart and Winston, New York.

Janssen, W. H. (1976). Selective interference during the retrieval of visual images. *Quarterly Journal of Experimental Psychology* **28**, 535–9.

Jarvella, R. J. (1971). Syntactic processing of connected speech. *Journal of Verbal Learning and Verbal Behavior* **10**, 409–16.

Johnston, C. D. and Jenkins, J. J. (1971). Two more incidental tasks that differentially affect associative clustering in recall. *Journal of Experimental Psychology* **89**, 92–5.

Johnston, R. (1982). Phonological coding in dyslexic readers. *British Journal of Psychology* **73**, 455–60.

Just, M. A. and Carpenter, P. A. (1980). A theory of reading: From eye fixations to comprehension. *Psychological Review* **87**, 329–54.

Kay, H. (1955). Learning and retaining verbal material. *British Journal of Psychology* **46**, 81–100.

Keevil-Rogers, P. and Schnore, M. (1969). Short-term memory as a function of age in persons of above-average intelligence. *Journal of Gerontology* **24**, 184–8.

Kennedy, A. (1983). On looking into space. In *Eye movements in reading: perceptual and language processes* (K. Rayner, ed.). Academic Press.

Keppel, G. and Underwood, B. J. (1962). Proactive inhibition in short-term retention of single items. *Journal of Verbal Learning and Verbal Behavior* **1**, 153–61.

Kinsbourne, M. (1970). The cerebral basis of lateral asymmetries in attention. *Acta Psychologica* **33**, 193–201.

Kinsbourne, M. (1974). Mechanisms of hemispheric interaction in man. In *Hemispheric disconnection and cerebral function* (M. Kinsbourne and W. L. Smith, eds.) pp. 260–85. Thomas, Springfield, Illinois.

Kinsbourne, M. (1981). Single channel theory. In *Human skills* (D. Holding, ed.). John Wiley, Chichester.

Kintsch, W. and Buschke, H. (1969). Homophones and synonyms in short-term memory. *Journal of Experimental Psychology* **80**, 403–7.

Kintsch, W. and van Dijk, T. A. (1978). Toward a model of text comprehension and production. *Psychological Review* **85**, 363–94.

Kintsch, W. and Vipond, D. (1979). Reading comprehension and readability in educational practice. In *Perspectives on memory research* (L.-G. Nilsson, ed.) pp. 329–65. Erlbaum, Hillsdale, N.J.

Kleiman, G. M. (1975). Speech recoding in reading. *Journal of Verbal Learning and Verbal Behavior* **24**, 323–39.

Kolers, P. A. (1976). Reading a year later. *Journal of Experimental Psychology: Human Learning and Memory* **2**, 554–65.

Kosslyn, S. M. (1975). Information representation in visual images. *Cognitive Psychology* **7**, 341–70.

Kosslyn, S. M. (1978). Measuring the visual angle of the minds' eye. *Cognitive Psychology* **10**, 356–89.

Kosslyn, S. M. (1980). *Image and mind*. Harvard University Press, Cambridge, Mass.

Kosslyn, S. M. and Schwartz, S. P. (1981). Empirical constraints on theories of visual mental imagery. In *Attention and performance IX*. (J. Long and A. D. Baddeley, eds.) pp. 241–60. Erlbaum, Hillsdale, N.J.

Kroll, N. E. A. (1975). Visual short-term memory. In *Short-term memory* (D. Deutsch and J. A. Deutsch, eds.). Academic Press, New York.

Kroll, N. E. A. and Parks, T. E. (1978). Interference with short-term visual memory produced by central processing. *Journal of Experimental Psychology: Human Learning and Memory* **4**, 111–20.

Kroll, N. E., Parks, T., Parkinson, S. R., Bieber, S. L. and Johnson, A. L. (1970). Short-term memory while shadowing: Recall of visually and aurally presented letters. *Journal of Experimental Psychology* **85**, 220–4.

Landauer, T. K. (1962). Rate of implicit speech. *Perceptual and Motor Skills* **15**, 646.

Landauer, T. K. and Bjork, R. A. (1978). Optimum rehearsal patterns and name learning. In *Practical aspects of memory* (M. M. Gruneberg, P. E. Morris and R. N. Sykes, eds.) pp. 625–32. Academic Press, London.

Latham, D. S. (1983). Memory span and the use of context cues in young children's reading. Unpublished MA dissertation. University of Kent at Canterbury.

Levy, B. A. (1971). The role of articulation in auditory and visual short-term memory. *Journal of Verbal Learning and Verbal Behavior* **10**, 123–32.

Levy, B. A. (1977). Reading: Speech and meaning processes. *Journal of Verbal Learning and Verval Behavior* **16**, 623–638.

Levy, B. A. (1978). Speech analysis during sentence processing. Reading and listening. *Visible Language* **12**, 81–101.

Levy, B. A. (1981). Interactive processing during reading. In *Interactive processes in reading* (A. M. Lesgold and C. Perfetti, eds.). Erlbaum, Hillsdale, N.J.

Liberman, I. Y. A language-oriented view of reading and its disabilities. To appear in *Progress in Learning Disabilities Vol. 5* (H. Myklebust, ed.). In press. Grune and Stratton, New York.

Liberman, I. Y., Mann, V. A., Shankweiler, D., and Werfelman, M. (1982). Childrens' memory for recurring linguistic and nonlinguistic material in relation to reading ability. *Cortext* **18**, 367–75.

Liberman, I. Y., Shankweiler, D., Liberman, A. M., Fowler, C., and Fischer, F. W. (1977). Phonetic segmentation and recoding in the beginning reader. In *Toward a psychology of reading: the proceedings of the C.U.N.Y. conference* (A. S. Reber and D. Scarborough, eds.). Erlbaum, Hillsdale, N.J.

Loess, H. (1968). Short-term memory and item similarity. *Journal of Verbal Learning and Verbal Behavior* **7**, 87–92.

Logie, R. H. (in press). Visuo-spatial processing in working memory. *Quarterly Journal of Experimental Psychology A*.

Logie, R. H. and Baddeley, A. D. (1983). A trimix saturation dive to 660 m: Studies of cognitive performance, mood and sleep quality. *Ergonomics* **26**, 359–74.

Logie, R. H. and Baddeley, A. D. (in preparation). Cognitive processes in counting.

Luria, A. R. (1969). Frontal lobe syndromes. In *Handbook of clinical neurology Vol. 2* (Vinke and Bruyn, eds.). North Holland Publishing Company, Amsterdam.

Luria, A. R. and Homskaya, E. D. (1964). Disturbance in the regulative role of speech with frontal lobe lesions. In *The frontal granular cortex and behavior* (J. M. Warren and K. Akert, eds.) pp. 353–71. McGraw Hill, New York.

McClelland, J. L. (1979). On the time relations of mental processes: An examination of systems of processes in cascade. *Psychological Review* **86**, 287–330.

McConkie, G. and Zola, D. (1981). Language constraints and the functional stimulus in reading. In *Interactive processes in reading* (A. M. Lesgold and C. A. Perfetti, eds.). Erlbaum, Hillsdale, N.J.

McGaugh, J. L. and Gold, P. E. (1974). Conceptual and neurobiological issues in studies of treatments affecting memory storage. In *The psychology of learning and motivation, 8.* (G. H. Bower, ed.). Academic Press, New York.

McKoon, G. and Ratcliffe, R. (1980*a*). Priming in item recognition: The organisation of propositions in memory for text. *Journal of Verbal Learning and Verbal Behavior* **19**, 369–86.

McKoon, G. and Ratcliffe, R. (1980*b*). The comprehension processes and memory structures involved in anaphoric reference. *Journal of Verbal Learning and Verbal Behavior* **19**, 668–82.

McLeod, P. and Posner, M. I. (1984). Privileged loops from percept to act. In *Attention and performance X.* (H. Bouma and D. G. Bouwhuis, eds.) pp. 55–66. Erlbaum, London.

Mandler, G. (1980). Recognizing: The judgment of previous occurrence. *Psychological Review* **87**, 252–71.

Mann, V. A. and Liberman, I. Y. Phonological awareness and verbal short-term memory: Can they presage early reading problems? *Journal of Learning Disabilities,* in press.

Mann, V. A., Liberman, I. Y., and Shankweiler, D. (1980). Childrens' memory for sentences and word strings in relation to reading ability. *Memory and Cognition* **8**, 329–35.

Marcel, A. J. (1983). Conscious and unconscious perception: Experiments on visual masking and word recognition. *Cognitive Psychology* **15**, 197–237.

Mark, L. S., Shankweiler, D., and Liberman, I. Y. (1977). Phonetic recoding and reading difficulty in beginning readers. *Memory and Cognition* **5**, 623–9.

Marks, D. F. (1973). Visual imagery differences and eye movements in the recall of pictures. *Perception and psychophysics* **14**, 407–12.

Marshall, J. C. and Newcombe, F. (1966). Syntactic and semantic errors in paralexia. *Neuropsychologia* **4**, 169–76.

Marshall, J. C. and Newcombe, F. (1973). Patterns of paralexia: A psycholinguistic approach. *Journal of Psycholinguistic Research* **2**, 175–99.

Marslen-Wilson, W. D. and Tyler, L. K. (1981). Central processes in speech understanding. *Philosophical Transactions of the Royal Society London* B **295**, 317–32.

Martin, D. W. (1970). Residual processing capacity during verbal organization in memory. *Journal of Verbal Learning and Verbal Behavior* **9**, 391–7.

Martin, M. and Jones, G. V. (1979). Modality dependency of loss of recency in free recall. *Psychological Research* **40**, 273–89.

Mayes, A., Meudell, P., and Neary, D. (1980). Do amnesics adopt inefficient encoding strategies with faces and random shapes. *Neuropsychologia* **18**, 527–40.

Mechanic, A. (1964). The responses involved in the rote learning of verbal materials. *Journal of Verbal Learning and Verbal Behavior* **3**, 30–6.

Melton, A. W. (1963). Implications of short-term memory for a general theory of memory. *Journal of Verbal Learning and Verbal Behavior* **2**, 1–21.

Miller, E. (1971). On the nature of the memory disorder in presenile dementia. *Neuropsychologia* **9**, 75–8.

Miller, E. (1975). Impaired recall and the memory disturbance in presenile dementia. *British Journal of Social and Clinical Psychology* **14**, 73–9.

Miller, G. A. (1956). The magical number seven, plus or minus two: Some limits on our capacity for processing information. *Psychological Review* **63**, 81–97.

Milner, B. (1964). Some effects of frontal leucotomy in man. In *The frontal granular cortex and behavior* (J. M. Warren and K. Akert, eds.). McGraw Hill, New York.

Milner, B. (1966). Amnesia following operation on the temporal lobes. In *Amnesia* (C. W. M. Whitty and O. L. Zangwill, eds.) pp. 109–33. Butterworths.

Milner, B. (1971). Interhemispheric differences in the localization of psychological processes in man. *British Medical Bulletin* 3 (Cognitive Psychology), 272–7.

Milner, B. (1982). Some cognitive effects of frontal-lobe lesions in man. *Philosophical Transactions of the Royal Society London* B **298**, 211–26.

Monsell, S. (1984). Components of working memory underlying verbal skills: A 'distributed capacities' view—A tutorial review. In *Attention and performance X*. (H. Bouma and D. G. Bouwhuis, eds.) pp. 327–50. Erlbaum, London.

Morris, C. D., Bransford, J. D., and Franks, J. J. (1977). Levels of processing versus transfer appropriate processing. *Journal of Verbal Learning and Verbal Behavior* **16**, 519–33.

Morris, R. G. (1984). Dementia and the functioning of the articulatory loop system. *Cognitive Neuropsychology* **1**, 143–58.

Morris, R. G. (1986). Short term memory in senile dementia of the Alzheimer's type. *Cognitive Neuropsychology* **3**, 77–97.

Morton, J. (1967). A singular lack of incidental learning. *Nature* **215**, 203–4.

Morton, J. (1969). Interaction of information in word recognition. *Psychological Review* **76**, 165–78.

Morton, J. (1979). Facilitation in word recognition: Experiments causing change in the logogen model. In *Processing of visible language, Vol. 1*. (P. A. Kolers, M. E. Wrolstad, and H. Bouma, eds.). Plenum Press, New York.

Murdock, B. B. Jr. (1961). The retention of individual items. *Journal of Experimental Psychology* **62**, 618–25.

Murdock, B. B. Jr. (1965). Effects of a subsidiary task on short-term memory. *British Journal of Psychology* **56**, 413–19.

Murdock, B. B. Jr. (1974). *Human memory: theory and data*. Erlbaum, Hillsdale, N.J.

Murray, D. J. (1965). Vocalization-at-presentation, with varying presentation rates. *Quarterly Journal of Experimental Psychology* **17**, 47–56.

Murray, D. J. (1967). The role of speech responses in short-term memory. *Canadian Journal of Psychology* **21**, 263–76.

Murray, D. J. (1968). Articulation and acoustic confusability in short-term memory. *Journal of Experimental Psychology* **78**, 679–84.

Navon, D. and Gopher, D. (1980). Task difficulty, resources, and dual-task performance. In *Attention and performance VIII*. (R. S. Nickerson, ed.) pp. 297–315. Erlbaum, Hillsdale, N.J.

Nebes, R. N. (1975). The nature of internal speech in a patient with aphemia. *Brain and Language* **2**, 489–97.

Neisser, U. (1976). *Cognition and reality*. W. H. Freeman, San Francisco.

Neisser, U. (1978). Memory: What are the important questions? In *Practical aspects of memory* (M. M. Gruneberg, P. E. Morris, and R. N. Sykes, eds.). Academic Press, London.

Nelson, T. O. (1977). Repetition and depth of processing. *Journal of Verbal Learning and Verbal Behavior* **16**, 151–72.

Newell, A. (1974). You can't play 20 questions with nature and win. In *Visual information processing* (W. G. Chase, ed.). Academic Press, New York.

Newell, A. and Simon, H. A. (1972). *Human problem solving*. Prentice Hall, Englewood Cliffs, N.J.

Nickerson, R. S. (1980). Motivated retrieval from archival memory. In *Proceedings of the Nebraska Symposium on Motivation Vol. 28,* pp. 73–119.

Nickerson, R. S. and Adams, M. J. (1979). Long-term memory for a common object. *Cognitive Psychology* **11**, 287–307.

Nicolson, R. (1981). The relationship between memory span and processing speed. In *Intelligence and Learning* (M. Friedman, J. P. Das, and N. O'Connor, eds.) pp. 179–84. Plenum Press.

Norman, D. A. (1970). *Models of human memory.* Academic Press, New York.

Norman, D. A. and Bobrow, D. G. (1975). On data-limited and resource-limited processes. *Cognitive Psychology* **7**, 44–64.

Norman, D. A. and Shallice, T. (1980). Attention to action. Willed and automatic control of behavior. *University of California San Diego CHIP Report 99.*

Ostergaard, A. L. and Meudell, P. R. (1984). Immediate memory span: Recognition memory for subspan series of words, and serial position effects in recognition memory for supraspan series of verbal and nonverbal items in Broca's and Wernicke's aphasia. *Brain and Language* **22**, 1–13.

Paivio, A. (1971). *Imagery and verbal processes.* Holt, Rinehart and Winston, New York.

Paivio, A. (1975). Perceptual comparisons through the mind's eye. *Memory and Cognition* **3**, 635–47.

Paivio, A. and Csapo, K. (1969). Concrete image and verbal memory codes. *Journal of Experimental Psychology* **80**, 279–85.

Parkinson, S. R., Parks, T. E., and Kroll, N. E. A. (1971). Visual and auditory short-term memory: Effects of phonemically similar auditory shadow material during the retention interval. *Journal of Experimental Psychology* **87**, 274–80.

Parks, T. E., Kroll, N. E. A., Salzberg, P. M., and Parkinson, S. R. (1972). Persistence of visual memory as indicated by decision time in a matching task. *Journal of Experimental Psychology* **92**, 437–8.

Pascual-Leone, J. A. (1970). A mathematical model for the transition rule in Piaget's developmental stages. *Acta Psychologica* **32**, 301–45.

Patterson, K. E. and Baddeley, A. D. (1977). When face recognition fails. *Journal of Experimental Psychology: Human Learning and Memory* **3**, 406–17.

Perfetti, C. A. and Goldman, S. R. (1976). Discourse memory and reading comprehension skill. *Journal of Verbal Learning and Verbal Behavior* **14**, 33–42.

Perfetti, C. A. and Lesgold, A. N. (1977). Discourse comprehension and sources of individual differences. In *Cognitive processes in comprehension* (M. Just and P. Carpenter, eds.). Erlbaum, Hillsdale, N.J.

Peterson, L. R. (1966). Short-term verbal memory and learning. *Psychological Review* **73**, 193–207.

Peterson, L. R. and Gentile, A. (1963). Proactive interference as a function of time between tests. *Journal of Experimental Psychology* **70**, 473–8.

Peterson, L. R. and Johnson, S. T. (1971). Some effects of minimizing articulation on short-term retention. *Journal of Verbal Learning and Verbal Bahavior* **10**, 346–54.

Peterson, L. R. and Peterson, M. J. (1959). Short-term retention of individual verbal items. *Journal of Experimental Psychology* **58**, 193–8.

Phillips, W. A. (1974). On the distinction between sensory storage and short-term visual memory. *Perception and Psychophysics* **16**, 283–90.

Phillips, W. A. and Baddeley, A. D. (1971). Reaction time and short-term visual memory. *Psychonomic Science* **22**, 73–4.

Phillips, W. A. and Christie, D. F. M. (1977*a*). Components of visual memory. *Quarterly Journal of Experimental psychology* **29**, 117–33.

Phillips, W. A. and Christie, D. F. M. (1977*b*). Interference with visualization. *Quarterly Journal of Experimental psychology* **29**, 637–50.

Pillsbury, W. B. and Sylvester, A. (1940). Retroactive and proactive inhibition in immediate memory. *Journal of Experimental Psychology* **27**, 532–45.

Pinto, A.-Da C. and Baddeley, A. D. Where did you park your car? Analysis of a naturalistic long-term recency effect. Manuscript submitted for publication.

Posner, M. I., Boies, S. J., Eichelman, W. H., and Taylor, R. L. (1969). Retention of visual and name codes of single letters. *Journal of Experimental Psychology* **79**, 1–16.

Posner, M. I., Cohen, Y., and Raffal, R. D. (1982). Neural systems control of spatial orienting. *Philosophical Transactions of the Royal Society London* B **298**, 187–98.

Posner, M. I. and Keele, S. W. (1967). Decay of visual information from a single letter. *Science* **158**, 137–9.

Postman, L. (1975). Verbal learning and memory. *Annual Review of Psychology* **26**, 291–335.

Postman, L. and Phillips, L. W. (1965). Short-term temporal changes in free recall. *Quarterly Journal of Experimental Psychology* **17**, 132–8.

Poulton, E. C. (1979). Composite model for human performance in continuous noise. *Psychological Review* **86**, 361–75.

Rabbitt, P. (1981). Cognitive psychology needs models for changes in performance with old age. In *Attention and performance X*. (J. B. Long and A. D. Baddeley, eds.). Erlbaum, Hillsdale, N.J.

Raymond, B. J. (1971). Free recall among the aged. *Psychological Reports* **29**, 1179–82.

Reason, J. T. (1979). Actions not as planned: The price of automatisation. In *Aspects of consciousness Volume 1: Psychological issues* (G. Underwood and R. Stevens, eds.). Academic Press, London.

Reitman, J. S. (1974). Without surreptitious rehearsal, information in short-term memory decays. *Journal of Verbal Learning and Verbal Behavior* **13**, 365–77.

Richardson, J. T. E. (1980). *Mental imagery and human memory*. Macmillan, London.

Richardson, J. T. E. and Baddeley, A. D. (1975). The effect of articulatory suppression in free recall. *Journal of Verbal Learning and Verbal Behavior* **14**, 623–9.

Rubenstein, H., Lewis, S. S., and Rubenstein, M. A. (1971). Homographic entries in the internal lexicon: effects of systemacity and relative frequency of meanings. *Journal of Verbal Learning and Verbal Behavior* **10**, 57–62.

Rumelhart, D. E., Lindsay, P. J., and Norman, D. A. (1972). A process model for long-term memory. In *Organization and memory* (E. Tulving and W. Donaldson, eds.). Academic Press, New York.

Rundus, D. (1971). Analysis of rehearsal processes in free recall. *Journal of Experimental Psychology* **89**, 63–77.

Rylander, G. (1939). Personality changes after operations on the frontal lobes. *Acta Psychiatrica Neurologica,* Supplement No. 30.

Sachs, J. S. (1967). Recognition memory for syntactic and semantic aspects of connected discourse. *Perception and Psychophysics* **2**, 437–42.

Saffran, E. M. and Marin, O. S. M. (1975). Immediate memory for word lists and sentences in a patient with deficient auditory short-term memory. *Brain and Language* **2**, 420–33.

Salame, P. and Baddeley, A. D. (1982). Disruption of short-term memory by unattended speech: Implications for the structure of working memory. *Journal of Verbal Learning and Verbal Behavior* **21**, 150–64.

Salame, P. and Baddeley, A. D. (1983). Differential effects of noise and speech on short-term memory. In *The Proceedings of the Fourth International Congress on Noise as a Public Health Problem,* Turin, Italy, pp. 751–8. Edizioni Tecniche a cura del Centro Ricerche e Studi Amplifon.

Salame, P. and Wittersheim, G. (1978). Selective noise disturbance of the information input stage in short-term memory. *Quarterly Journal of Experimental Psychology* **30**, 693–704.

Sanford, A. J. and Garrod, S. C. (1981). *Understanding written language: explorations in comprehension beyond the sentence.* Wiley, Chichester.

Sanford, A. J. and Maule, A. J. (1973). The allocation of attention in multi-source monitoring behaviour: Adult age differences. *Perception* **2**, 91–100.

Schaeffer, B. and Wallace, R. (1969). Semantic similarity and the comparison of word meanings. *Journal of Experimental Psychology* **82**, 343–6.

Schiano, D. J. and Watkins, M. J. (1981). Speech-like coding of pictures in short-term memory. *Memory and Cognition* **9**, 110–14.

Schmidtke, H. (1961). Zur Frage der informations theorischer Analyse von Wohlreaktionsexperimenter. *Psychologisch Forschung* **26**, 157–78.

Schonfield, D. (1969). Learning and retention. In *Contemporary gerontology: issues and concepts* (J. E. Birren, ed.). University of Southern California Press, Los Angeles.

Schulman, A. I. (1971). Recognition memory for targets from a scanned word list. *British Journal of Psychology* **62**, 335–46.

Schulman, A. I. (1974). Memory for words recently classified. *Memory and Cognition* **2**, 47–52.

Scripture, E. W. (1905). *The new psychology.* Scott, London.

Seibel, R. (1963). Discrimination reaction time for a 1023-alternative task. *Journal of Experimental Psychology* **66**, 215–26.

Shaffer, W. O. and Shiffrin, R. M. (1972). Rehearsal and storage of visual information. *Journal of Experimental Psychology* **92**, 292–6.

Shallice, T. (1975). On the contents of primary memory. In *Attention and performance V.* (P. M. A. Rabbitt and S. Dornic, eds.) pp. 269–80. Academic Press, London.

Shallice, T. (1982). Specific impairments of planning. *Philosophical Transactions of the Royal Society London* B **298**, 199–209.

Shallice, T. and Butterworth, B. (1977). Short-term memory impairment and spontaneous speech. *Neuropsychologia* **15**, 729–35.

Shallice, T. and Warrington, E. K. (1970). Independent functioning of verbal memory stores: A neuropsychological study. *Quarterly Journal of Experimental Psychology* **22**, 261–73.

Shallice, T. and Warrington, E. K. (1974). The dissociation between long-term retention of meaningful sounds and verbal material. *Neuropsychologia* **12**, 553–5.

Shallice, T. and Warrington, E. K. (1977). Auditory-verbal short-term memory impairment and conduction aphasia. *Brain and Language* **4**, 479–91.

Shand, M. A. and Klima, E. S. (1981). Nonauditory suffix effects in congenitally deaf signers of American sign language. *Journal of Experimental Psychology:*

Human Learning and Memory 7, 464–74.

Shankweiler, D. and Liberman, I. Y. (1976). Exploring the relations between reading and speech. In *The neuropsychology of learning disorders: theoretical approaches* (R. M. Knights and D. K. Bakker, eds.). University Park Press, Baltimore.

Shepard, R. N. (1980). *Internal representations: studies in perception imagery and cognition.* Bradford Books, Montgomery, Vermont.

Shepard, R. N. and Metzler, J. (1971). Mental rotation of three-dimensional objects. *Science* 171, 701–3.

Shiffrin, R. M. (1970). Forgetting: Trace erosion or retrieval failure? *Science* 168, 1601–3.

Siegel, L. S. and Linder, B. A. (1984). Short-term memory processes in children with reading and arithmetic learning disabilities. *Developmental Psychology* 20, 200–7.

Silverstein, C. and Glanzer, M. (1971). Difficulty of a concurrent task in free recall: Differential effects of LTS and STS. *Psychonomic Science* 22, 367–8.

Slowiaczek, M. L. and Clifton, C. (1980). Subvocalization and reading for meaning. *Journal of Verbal Learning and Verbal Behavior* 19, 573–82.

Smith, S. M., Glenberg, A., and Bjork, R. A. (1978). Environmental context and human memory. *Memory and Cognition* 6, 342–53.

Sokolov, E. N. (1963). *Perception and the conditional reflex.* Translated by S. W. Waydenfold. Pergamon Press, Oxford.

Spinnler, H., Della Sala, S., Bandera, R., and Baddeley, A. Dementia, ageing and the structure of human memory (submitted).

Spring, C. and Capps, C. (1974). Encoding speed, rehearsal, and probed recall of dyslexic boys. *Journal of Educational Psychology* 66, 780–6.

Spring, C. and Perry, L. Naming speed, articulation speed, and serial recall in poor and adequate readers. (Personal communication).

Sunderland, A., Harris, J. E. and Baddeley, A. D. (1983). Do laboratory tests predict everyday memory? A neuropsychological study. *Journal of Verbal Learning and Verbal Behavior* 22, 341–57.

Talland, G. (1965). Three estimates of the word span and their stability over the adult years. *Quarterly Journal of Experimental Psychology* 17, 301–7.

Taylor, W. L. (1953). "Cloze Procedure" a new tool for measuring readability. *Journalism Quarterly* 30, 415–33.

Temple, C. M. and Marshall, J. C. (1983). A case study of developmental phonological dyslexia. *British Journal of Psychology* 74, 517–33.

Teuber, H.-L. (1959). Some alterations in behaviour after cerebral lesions in man. In *Evolution of nervous control from primitive organisms to man* (A. D. Bass, ed.). American Association for the Advancement of Science, Washington.

Teuber, H.-L. (1964). The riddle of frontal lobe function in man. In *The frontal granular cortex and behavior* (J. M. Warren and K. Akert, eds.). McGraw Hill, New York.

Torgesen, J. K. and Goldman, T. (1977). Rehearsal and short-term memory in reading disabled children. *Child Development* 48, 58–60.

Torgeson, J. K., Greenstein, J. J., Houck, A. G. and Portes, P. (1985). Further examinations of information processing difficulties of learning disabled children with memory span difficulties. Unpublished manuscript, Florida State University (Experiments 1, 2, 3, and 4).

Torgeson, J. K. and Houck, D. G. (1980). Processing deficiencies of learning-disabled children who perform poorly on the digit span test. *Journal of Educational Psychology* **72**, 141–60.

Torgeson, J. K. and Houck, D. G. Learning disabled children with extreme performance difficulties on memory span tasks. In *Memory and Learning Disabilities* (H. L. Swanson, ed.). (In press). JAÌ Press, Inc., New York.

Torgeson, J. K., Rashotte, C. A., and Greenstein, J. J. (1985). Listening comprehension in learning disabled children who perform poorly on memory span tasks. Unpublished manuscript, Florida State University (Experiments 5, 6, and 7).

Trumbo, D. and Milone, F. (1971). Primary task performance as a function of encoding, retention and recall on a secondary task. *Journal of Experimental Psychology* **91**, 273–9.

Tulving, E. (1966). Subjective organization and effects of repetition in multi-trial free-recall learning. *Journal of Verbal Learning and Verbal Behavior* **5**, 193–7.

Tulving, E. (1968). Theoretical issues in free recall. In *Verbal behavior and general behavior theory* (T. R. Dixon and D. L. Horton, eds.). Prentice Hall, New Jersey.

Tulving, E. (1983). *Elements of episodic memory.* Oxford University Press, Oxford.

Tune, G. S. (1964). A brief survey of variables that influence random generation. *Perceptual and Motor Skills* **18**, 705–10.

Tzeng, O. J. L. (1973). Positive recency effect in delayed free recall. *Journal of Verbal Learning and Verbal Behavior* **12**, 436–9.

Underwood, B. J. and Postman, L. (1960). Extra experimental sources of interference in forgetting. *Psychological Review* **67**, 73–95.

Vallar, G. and Baddeley, A. D. (1982). Short-term forgetting and the articulatory loop. *Quarterly Journal of Experimental Psychology* **34**, 53–60.

Vallar, G. and Baddeley, A. D. (1984*a*). Fractionation of working memory: Neuropsychological evidence for a phonological short-term store. *Journal of Verbal Learning and Verbal Behavior* **23**, 151–61.

Vallar, G. and Baddeley, A. D. (1984*b*). Phonological short-term store, phonological processing and sentence comprehension: A neuropsychological case study. *Cognitive Neuropsychology* **1**, 121–41.

Vellutino, F. R. (1979). *Dyslexia: theory and research.* M.I.T. Press, Cambridge, Mass.

Wagner, D. (1978). Memories of Morocco: The influence of age, schooling and environment on memory. *Cognitive Psychology* **10**, 1–28.

Walker, P. and Marshall, E. (1982). Visual memory and stimulus repetition effects. *Journal of Experimental Psychology: General* **111**, 348–68.

Warrington, E. K. (1982). The double dissociation of short- and long-term memory deficits. In *Human memory and amnesia* (L. S. Cermak, ed.) pp. 61–76. Erlbaum, Hillsdale, N.J.

Warrington, E. K. and Shallice, T. (1972). Neuropsychological evidence of visual storage in short-term memory tasks. *Quarterly Journal of Experimental Psychology* **24**, 30–40.

Wason, P. C. and Johnson-Laird, P. N. (1972). *Psychology of reasoning: structure and content.* Batsford, London.

Watkins, M. J. and Graefe, T. M. (1981). Delayed rehearsal of pictures. *Journal of Verbal Learning and Verbal Behavior* **20**, 276–88.

Watkins, M. J. and Peynircioglu, Z. F. (1983). Three recency effects at the same time. *Journal of Verbal Learning and Verbal Behavior* **22**, 375–84.

Waugh, N. C. (1970). Retrieval time in short-term memory. *British Journal of Psychology* **61**, 1–12.

Waugh, N. C. and Norman, D. A. (1965). Primary memory. *Psychological Review* **72**, 89–104.

Welford, A. T. (1958). *Ageing and human skill.* Oxford University Press, London.

Welford, A. T. (1967). *Fundamentals of skill.* Methuen, London.

Welford, A. T. (1980). Memory and age: A perspective view. In *New directions in memory and ageing* (L.-W. Poon, J. L. Fozard, L. Cermak, D. Arenberg, and L. W. Thompson, eds.) pp. 1–17. Erlbaum, Hillsdale, N.J.

Wickelgren, W. A. (1965). Short-term memory for phonemically similar lists. *American Journal of Psychology* **78**, 567–74.

Wickelgren, W. A. (1969). Auditory or articulatory coding in verbal short-term memory. *Psychological Review* **76**, 232–5.

Wickelgren, W. A. (1977). Speed–accuracy trade-off and information processing dynamics. *Acta Psychologica* **41**, 67–85.

Wickens, D. D. (1970). Encoding categories of words: An empirical approach to meaning. *Psychological Review* **77**, 1–15.

Wickens, D. D., Born, D. G., and Allen, C. K. (1963). Proactive inhibition and item similarity in short-term memory. *Journal of Verbal Learning and Verbal Behavior* **2**, 440–5.

Wilding, J. and Mohindra, N. (1980). Effects of subvocal suppression, articulating aloud and noise on sequence recall. *British Journal of Psychology* **71**, 247–62.

Wilkins, A. J. (1971). Conjoint frequency, category size, and categorization time. *Journal of Verbal Learning and Verbal Behavior* **10**, 382–5.

Wilson, R. S., Baker, L. D., Fox, J. H. and Kazniak, A. (1983). Primary memory and secondary memory in senile dementia of the Alzheimer type. *Journal of Clinical Neuropsychology* **37**, 8–19.

Winograd, E. (1976). Recognition memory for faces following nine different judgments. *Bulletin of the Psychonomic Society* **8**, 419–21.

Wright, P., Holloway, C. M. and Aldrich, A. R. (1974). Attending to visual or auditory information while performing other concurrent tasks. *Quarterly Journal of Experimental Psychology* **26**, 454–63.

Zangwill, O. L. (1946). Some qualitative observations on verbal memory in cases of cerebral lesion. *British Journal of Psychology* **37**, 8–19.

Author index

Subject index